how to
show your own dog

by virginia tuck nichols

t.f.h.

Frontispiece:
Ch. Puttencove Playboy, Standard Poodle owned by Puttencove Kennels.
Photo by Evelyn M. Shafer.

ISBN 0-87666-661-6

Distributed in the U.S.A. by T.F.H. Publications, Inc., 211 West Sylvania Avenue, P.O. Box 27, Neptune City, N.J. 07753; in England by T.F.H. (Gt. Britain) Ltd., 13 Nutley Lane, Reigate, Surrey; in Canada to the book store and library trade by Clarke, Irwin & Company, Clarwin House, 791 St. Clair Avenue West, Toronto 10, Ontario; in Canada to the pet trade by Rolf C. Hagen Ltd., 3225 Sartelon Street, Montreal 382, Quebec; in Southeast Asia by Y.W. Ong, 9 Lorong 36 Geylang, Singapore 14; in Australia and the south Pacific by Pet Imports Pty. Ltd., P.O. Box 149, Brookvale 2100, N.S.W., Australia. Published by T.F.H. Publications, Inc. Ltd., The British Crown Colony of Hong Kong.

THIS BOOK IS WRITTEN SOLELY FOR THE NOVICE

Photo Credits

CONTENTS

Characters in this book are not fictitious,
and any similarity to persons
living or dead is purely
intentional.

HOW TO SHOW YOUR OWN DOG

The English Cocker Spaniel, Champion Silvermine Dauntless shown to his championship along with many kennelmates by his amateur breeder-owner, the author Virginia Tuck Nichols.

CHAPTER 1

THE DOG SHOW

Very few people realize just what a LARGE dog show is like. Perhaps they have seen a local pet show or a small show in the neighborhood, but few have any conception of a really big show. Let me tell you something about a large show. As an example let us use the largest outdoor show ever held in the United States: the last Morris and Essex Kennel Club show in Madison, New Jersey, in May of 1957, at Giralda, the beautiful estate of Mrs. Geraldine R. Dodge. The lovely grounds were not used for any other event except this one dog show one day each year.

On the grounds there was a permanent first-aid building, staffed for the day with nurses; a permanent press reporters' building; and two large permanent storage buildings to hold equipment during the year. Permanent ladies' rooms and men's rooms were freshly painted each year, and even telephones were brought into the grounds for the big day. The parking lots accommodated 10,000 cars. There were 16 drinking-water fountains all piped underground. The great event was held on a polo field, and the lawn there was manicured to within an inch of its life. Caterers were on the grounds with hot lunches as well as sandwiches and soft drinks. Flags flew from the tops of tents and buildings, and little pennants in the club colors of purple and orange ran up and down the tent ropes. Electric lights were strung under the tents for the people and dogs who arrived the night before the show, and a dog-food company supplied food for the dogs.

One hundred very polite policemen were hired for the day to act as guards and to help direct traffic on the grounds as well as through the town of Madison. Incidentally, there were so many cars driving into the show that even five entrances into the show grounds were not really adequate to keep traffic moving completely smoothly. If you were an exhibitor, you were notified in advance which one of the entrances would be closest to where your dog would be shown and where his bench would be located. I will explain all the terms I have used later, such as bench, exhibitor, et cetera, but right now I am trying to give you a mental picture of this one show.

The dog-show catalogue of approximately 375 pages, with a cover in club colors, was sold at each of the entrances as well as on the show field. Each of the four exercise pens was approximately 3,700 square feet, and each had electric lights strung for night use. These pens circled groups of trees so that if it was a hot day, there was shade for the dogs. In the exact center of the grounds there was a permanent building for the show superintendent and the show secretary from where they directed the many activities. There were 100 young men hired for the day to act as runners and messengers. There were 42 large show rings roped off and all 42 were used at one time, each with its judge, stewards (who help the judge), runners (who help locate the dogs), and the many exhibitors and spectators interested in each breed. Each ring had an umbrella under which the judge sat to get relief from the sun while waiting for the classes to start. On his table was a carafe of water in case he got thirsty, and there also were many sterling-silver trophies as well as crisp new one-, five-, and ten-dollar bills used as prize money. There were also lots of satin ribbons to be given the lucky winners in the sought-after two colors of purple and gold, red and white, purple and white, blue and white, as well as the single colored ribbons of blue, red, yellow and white. Around each ring was a row of chairs for the spectators and for the exhibitors when they were not in the ring.

I have given you an idea of what there was on the polo field at the start of the day. Had it been a rainy day, this whole setup could have been moved under tents. There were enough tents available to have all the 42 judging rings under cover at a moment's notice. In addition to the judging tents there were the benching tents. This show was an unbenched show, which term I shall explain in detail later, but for our purposes now I will say only that the dogs at this show need not have been placed in stalls. In spite of the fact that the dogs *did not need to be* benched, there was available for each dog entered in this show a stall with his number on it for his use alone, raised off the ground and partitioned off from the next dog, all under tents to keep the sun or rain off the dog, whichever the day may have brought. There were also enormous tents for the use of the exhibitors and handlers under which they kept their crates (in which many dogs travel to and from shows); or their collapsible tables (on which they clean up the dogs); or their lunch baskets, show equipment kits, or duffel bags. All of this may not sound very enormous to you until I tell you that this show had an entry of 4,456 dogs! Each dog was very often accompanied by two or more members of its owner's family! Of course you might find a brave man or woman who brought three or four dogs there without any assistance; however, the show was somewhat of a spectacle and almost all the "doggy" folks who could do so, got there somehow. Now, *let's imagine ourselves there.*

There is a gay, almost too gay, attitude here in the early hours of the show day. Everyone arriving is wearing a smile, even if a bit forced and tense, everyone is wearing his or her best manners as well as best clothes. They are waving hello to friends they haven't seen for almost a year as well as to those they saw just last night. Most are hurrying to find a spot to place their equipment so that they can rush to get their car parked, rush to get a ringside seat, so that they can place an article on it, and rush back to prepare their dogs for the big entrance into the ring where all of a sudden no one is rushing and they will have to wait patiently until all dogs are in the ring and the judge begins his painstaking task of selecting the best in the class.

Meanwhile, under the handler's tent the job of cleaning up the dogs after their journey goes on with a last-minute check on trimming, a last-minute check of the show lead, a bit more combing and brushing, with many fingers crossed and silent prayers being said. Thermos bottles of steaming hot coffee are very much in evidence, so much so that a crate top or table top will be completely covered with plastic or paper cups, some full of coffee, some emptied. On one table a dog is being sprayed with something that smells like perfume but which is actually just giving a shine to the coat. Another dog will be getting a rubdown with something that smells like alcohol. It is being used to wipe away the dust which has been attracted to the dark sleek coat. Nearby someone is furiously throwing medicinally scented talcum powder on the snow-white coat of his charge who either is still wet from a bath or who did not get a bath and whose owner is now trying to whiten him with the powder. (This powder

A wonderful panoramic view of a Morris and Essex dog show by the dog photographer, William Brown. This picture shows only part of the huge

tents—each umbrella you see is in a separate judging ring! Morris and Essex was really a big and important show.

must be completely removed before the dog is shown.) Of course the powder blows over on the black dog next to him, and many a dagger look passes between the owners. Almost every crate or table has a bucket or pan of water setting on it or under it or next to it, and frequently a nervous person will drop some piece of equipment into it or stumble over it and get his new suit all splashed. Every so often a dog will look longingly at a bucket of water and get tired of waiting until it is offered to him, jump down from his crate, and help himself until the owner is able to reach him and place him on the table again, where he must then be all dried off with a towel for sure as shootin' he has managed to dribble it all down the front of his chest.

Occasionally you will hear the shouts of congratulations from a happy group gathering to look over a dog who has just made a nice win, and occasionally you will hear a warning cry go up from someone who did not carefully lock the exercise pen and from which one or two or more dogs are making their escape, or from someone whose dog has decided to take a piece out of another dog and who needs help in separating the quarreling dogs. You will hear high-pitched barks, deep, low barks, yelps, howls, growls, and all the other types of canine noises. If you look over your shoulder you are bound to see a young woman crying, either because her dog has just won or because her dog has not won—either one can bring on the tears.

About this time many people are walking to the enormous parking lots to sit quietly in their cars and have a bite of lunch which they stayed up late the night before to fix. Or they will bring the basket back either under the tent or just outside it and join another group who are about to have lunch. Groups of four and five will be heading for the huge caterer's tent to buy a meal or just a cup of coffee to tide them over until they have time for more. Oftentimes this will mean they will have nothing but coffee until dinnertime, when the show is finished, the cars have left, and the once immaculate show grounds are completely littered with scraps of paper, used arm bands, empty paper cups and other debris.

This, then, is a large outdoor show. Picture all this, if you can, at an indoor show! Yes, the same thing goes on in the wintertime in large buildings all over the United States. Once again, to keep it to shows that no longer exist, let's use as an example the Westminster Kennel Club show as it was held at the *old* Madison Square Garden

A Westminster Kennel Club show held at the old Madison Square Garden in New York City. For the Best In Show judging in which only six dogs compete, this entire arena was one big show ring.

Ch. Elfinbrook Simon, West Highland White Terrier owned by Barbara Sayres, is shown winning Best in Show at the Westminster Kennel Club Show. Pictured from left to right are William A. Rockefeller, President of the club, George Ward, handler of Simon, and judge Heywood Hartley.

in New York City in mid-February. (Westminster still holds shows but not at the *old* Madison Square Garden.) Because the building was not really big enough, the club limited the number of entries they accepted to 2,500 dogs. The mail that brought the 2,500th entry closed the entries, although the actual final total often ran about 2,550 dogs.

At this show there were problems which you would never realize existed. The unloading of a station wagon with five or ten or more dogs in it is difficult at any time, but here in the heart of New York City it was extremely trying. The old Garden had but one ramp into its depths, and only a few cars were allowed to go down at one time and the rest waited until the first cars came out before they could enter. On a freezing cold day I have seen ten or twelve cars lined up with their motors running, waiting almost an hour to gain entry into the building. This, however, concerned only those who arrived the day before the show started, usually those who had driven great distances. By five or six o'clock the day before the show no

Ch. Jo Jac's Pouring It On, Skye Terrier, shown here receiving Best of Winners at the Westminster Kennel Club Show; owned and handled by Jacqueline MacDonald. Photo by William P. Gilbert.

more cars were allowed to go down the ramp and all dogs arriving after that time had to be walked down the ramp or their crates placed on trolleys and taken down by the owners or attendants. The morning of the show day you would see hundreds of dogs being walked along the street to the Forty-ninth Street entrance, the exhibitors' entrance. Now, *let's imagine ourselves there! This is how it was.*

At Madison Square Garden there is an entirely different setup from the one described on the polo field at Madison, New Jersey. This show is a benched show; all dogs at all times, except when they are being exercised, being judged, or being prepared for judging must be on their benches. The benching takes up almost all the space on the basement floor with just the handlers' crates, the exercise pens, and a few concessions using the balance of the space.

On the main floor the arena is used entirely for the twelve judg-

Ch. Shirkhan of Grandeur, Afghan Hound owned by Mrs. Sunny Shay, posed among just a few of his impressive awards and trophies. Shirkhan won the coveted Best in Show at Westminster in 1957. Photo by George Pickow, Three Lions, Inc.

This photograph depicts a Westminster Kennel Club Show in 1959. In the foreground is Ch. Honey Hollow Stormi Rudio, Great Dane, being led by his owner. Stormi won the Working Group and was a runner-up for Best in Show.

ing rings, and in the lobby there are a few concessions such as Macy's Dog Department, Abercrombie and Fitch's Dog Department, a bookseller or two, and perhaps a charitable organization. In each of the judging rings there are telephones used to call downstairs for the dogs wanted in the ring. As part of its show, the Westminster Kennel Club used to present, twice on the final day of judging, a special exhibition of dogs of various breeds in demonstrations of their specialized areas of work. Sometimes there were Border Collies herding sheep; other times you would see several breeds of sporting dogs performing as they would in the field. Today there is no more of this. Instead the finals of the Junior Showmanship competition is offered. The child that wins the Junior Showmanship class at Westminster is considered the Champion Junior Handler for the year.

This is a two-day show, and all dogs must be present both days. An exhibitor may remove his dog from the building at night but he must post $5.00, which he gets back the next morning when he returns with the dog. This is to insure that the spectator who pays his way into the show on the second day will see all the dogs who have been entered.

The large indoor show presents much the same picture in and around the handler's crate section except that here all the smells and noises are magnified by the closeness—there's the perfume, the alcohol, the dog food, the soiled crate; and as far as the noises are concerned, you can feel as well as hear the barks of the dogs. A crate being shifted sounds as if you were moving Grand Central Station and everyone raises his voice to be heard over the next fellow who has raised his to be heard over the other noises.

Many dogs will travel completely across country to be at these very large shows; the very cream of the crop is present. As a result the competition is extremely keen, and you will find most exhibitors

Ch. Candy the Kerry Blue Miss, Kerry Blue Terrier, owned by George B. Rodda. Candy's sire was Ch. Topman's Blue Dinny; her dam was Peg O' My Heart. Photo by Evelyn Shafer.

A Doberman, Ferry v. Rauhfelsen, judged Best in Show at the Westminster Kennel Club Show several decades ago.

wearing their nerves very close to the skin around the big shows. Most exhibitors are very tense prior to the judging of their dogs, and with the tenseness you very often get a sort of gaiety that, while not exactly forced, is usually *very* gay and noisy. You will find exhibitors who cannot eat because they are nervous, and you will find exhibitors who must eat constantly for the same reason. It is not at all unusual to find an exhibitor holding on to a dog's leash with one hand and pushing a sandwich into his mouth with the other while the wife or the husband or a kind friend gives the dog the final combing out before the dog is called for the judging.

Charley horses and sore feet are the order of the day here, as very few of the exhibitors are accustomed to running up and down stairs all day long, and they are not used to the concrete floors. Those who go every year always bring an extra pair of shoes to change into when the day is partly over. Almost everyone wishes he had an extra pair of feet, for those he came with get very tired before it is all over. At the International Kennel Club show, which is held in the International Amphitheater in Chicago, either late in March or early in April, you do not have the stairs to contend with, but the building is so large that there are times when you wish you had a pair of roller skates to help you get from one place to another. At Chicago the entry is not limited to numbers, and it is expected that someday this might become the largest of indoor shows.

Incidentally, Morris and Essex was referred to as a limited-breed show because only certain breeds were shown there. Only breeds that ordinarily drew big entries had classes provided for them at that show; breeds such as Sussex Spaniels, Harriers or Komondorok were not included. At Westminster at the old Madison Square Garden the show was limited not only to numbers, the 2,500 dogs I spoke of earlier, but to dogs who had previously won a blue ribbon. This insured that those dogs which were entered there would be at least fairly representative of their breeds. But because of the great surge of the popularity of dog shows in recent years Westminster has been forced to restrict their entries even further than the blue ribbon requirement. To be eligible to compete at this show dogs must either be Champions or must have won major points. (This term is explained in Chapter 3.)

At Westminster you are apt to see just one dog of a breed which is known as a rare breed, such as the Kuvasz or the English Foxhound. However, at Morris and Essex you saw only the fairly popular breeds, but you could be sure that each breed had a large entry.

Although there are many others, there is one man whose organization was, is, and probably will be for a long time to come, responsible for the smooth running of these huge shows and many others of all sizes. He is George Foley, president of the Foley Dog Show Organization, Inc., 2009 Ranstead Street, Philadelphia, Pennsylvania 19103. His men erect the large tents, put up the benching, lay out the rings, help get dogs into the show ring, and give out arm bands which each exhibitor wears in the ring so that the spectators know which dog is being shown. George Foley's huge organization owns and manufactures its own benching. It owns more tenting than is owned by Ringling Brothers, Barnum and Bailey Circus. It owns large amounts of wire fencing used at outdoor shows, as well as solid wood fencing that is used at indoor shows for the exercise pens; it owns wood partitions which make up the show rings at many indoor shows. It also owns rubber matting, which is used as a runway on slippery floors at indoor shows. All of this is transported to the shows in Foley's own trailer trucks.

The Foley organization prints the show catalogue, an enormous job which must be accomplished in less than two weeks; it prints up the ribbons given for each award; it supplies the books in which the judges write their decisions; it arranges for the supply of new bills to be used for prize money and for which it is reimbursed by the show-giving clubs.

These and many more tasks fall to the dog-show superintendent, of which the Foley organization is one of approximately twelve authorized by the American Kennel Club to function at shows held under its jurisdiction. It also falls to the dog-show superintendent to see that all of the American Kennel Club rules pertaining to shows are obeyed during the show hours. It is also his responsibility to see that the show goes along according to the printed schedule known as the judging program.

This is a faint idea of what it is like at a big show. The smaller shows? Well, very much the same except that it is all on a smaller basis, and for the most part the exhibitors are not quite so nervous and tense. Here large groups will get together and have pleasant chats concerning their newest dogs or their puppies. Usually there are fewer rings going at a time, with fewer judges doing the whole show. There is more time to kill, there is not so much noise. Groups will go out to lunch or dinner together and tempers do not flare so easily with the exhibitors or with the dogs. A small outdoor show may have only one small tent which will be used only if it rains. After all, you cannot expect the judge to stand out in the rain all day while he is judging the dogs. At a small outdoor show very often the dogs are kept in cars until they are required for the judging and they will be cleaned up on the tailgate of a station wagon or on a table set up next to the car. Here the groups are inclined to gather in the parking lots, close to the dogs and to the food in the picnic baskets. You will see someone heading for the car with five or six soda bottles in one hand and the dog on the end of a lead held with the other hand. They stop to visit other dogs and other people and either say, "My, isn't it hot today," or, "My, I'm glad I brought my overcoat." You will see groups sitting on the ground next to a car with the dog or dogs tied to the bumper of the car. The dog of his own accord will stay in the shade of the car on a hot day, or lie in the sun on a cool day, one eye on the lunch basket. Yes, he will get his share of whatever it contains. These are happy groups!

At a small indoor show I have found that the exhibitors watch the judging a great deal more closely than at any other show. There is not much else to do, and the chairs around the ringside look inviting. Unless the building boasts a lunchroom or the neighborhood a good eating place, the picnic basket is as much in evidence here as at all the other shows.

Talking of small shows leads us quite naturally to the discussion of the Sanctioned Match, or Puppy Match. These I will explain in detail later, but right now I would like to say that they are similar to the small shows but are rightly thought of as "practice" shows. Practice for the dogs and, more important, practice for the one who will do the showing. A poor placing of a dog at a Sanctioned Match (sanctioned by the American Kennel Club) does not go against his show record, nor do any of the wins made at a match count toward making the dog a Champion.

People who have any knowledge of cattle shows often think of a dog as "The Grand Champion" if he has won an award similar to Best of Breed at a dog show. I have heard novices at a dog show refer to the winner of Best in Show as *The* Champion. This is not so. In the dog game the making of a Champion is done by the accumulation of points and cannot be done in less than three shows. This, too, is explained in detail later under the discussion of points, but it will help you to understand the language employed in this book if this little detail is cleared up now. Incidentally, it is possible to have as many as 200 or more Champion dogs entered in one show with a total entry of approximately 500 dogs.

How and when did all this get started? From old books on the subject and from much older field-trial records we gather that sportsmen were the first to compare their dogs for beauty's sake when they got together for field trials. The very first bench show (and here we mean bench as compared with field, not referring to benched meaning dogs on benches) for which records have ever been found was held at Chicago on June 4, 1874, by the Illinois State Sportsmen's Association. On June 6 a report in *Field and Stream* (afterward *Chicago Field and American Field*) says of the show, "An exhibition of dogs without any attempt at testing their hunting ability, 21 entries." The exhibition was held in conjunction with a field trial.

Encore Silver Showman, Toy Poodle, owned by Mrs. Jane Fitts of Palmetto, Georgia. This dog won the Great Lakes Poodle Specialty at the age of six months.

The first show catalogue in the possession of the American Kennel Club is dated November 26, 27, 28, 29, and 30, 1877, seven years before that organization was born. The American Kennel Club was founded in 1884 and dog shows were already popular. The early shows were held mostly in large cities, such as New York, Boston, Chicago, and Philadelphia, completely independent of each other particularly as far as time and dates were concerned. In 1885 a special meeting was called by the American Kennel Club which largely decided the future of dog shows. A record of this meeting,

which is the very foundation of present-day shows, reads in part, "Proposed that clubs give shows during the next season in a circuit and committee of three for each breed of dogs to report a Standard for the judging of these respective breeds in shows given under the jurisdiction of the club." These were wise men who saw ahead and made arrangements for judging according to Standards for each breed and who also saw the necessity of approving dates for dog shows.

From those early days of shows held in big cities, completely unrelated to each other, the shows did finally run in circuits. By 1925 a circuit went something like this: New York, New York; Newark, New Jersey; New Haven, Connecticut; Boston, Massachusetts; Buffalo, New York; Cleveland, Ohio; Dayton, Ohio; Columbus, Ohio; and then to Cincinnati, Ohio. New York was a three-day show; Boston, Buffalo, Cleveland, and Cincinnati were two-day shows; and the rest were one-day shows. Handlers, either private or professional, traveled with the dogs by train. The handlers were away from home quite a long time to make such a circuit and they spent a great deal of their time in baggage cars with the dogs. One handler went so far as to hire an orchestra to accompany him on a trip, and I can just imagine the faces of people who happened to be close to the railroad tracks as the musical baggage car went by.

There are circuits today: New England in July, Carolinas in March, Deep South in the fall, the Montana circuit, Florida in winter, etc. Practically no dogs, handlers, or owners travel by train today. Instead, you see quite a procession of station wagons making their way from one show town to the next. Many more owners go on circuits today than did those in the past, the main reason being the time element—you can take in the major part of a circuit during a two-week vacation.

The first of the uninterrupted series of annual dog shows sponsored by the Westminster Kennel Club was held at New York's Hippodrome in 1877.

CHAPTER 2

YOU DON'T NEED A PROFESSIONAL HANDLER

Who are the people who show dogs? Are they lunatics or fanatics? The dog people have a favorite joke about themselves. They say you don't have to be crazy to enjoy shows, but it certainly helps! This is because they actually go through many hardships and disappointments but still enjoy it and call it fun. It is one of the fascinating peculiarities of the dog game that the people who are thrown together in the pursuit of this sport are from so many different walks of life: dentists, carpenters, teachers, bankers, housewives, farmers, musicians, engineers, artists, industrialists, young and old, rich and poor. All have the same desire—to take home a blue ribbon.

Perhaps you wonder why they show dogs. I take it you are interested in showing or you wouldn't be reading this book. I warn you, however, that the day may come when you will wonder why you ever decided to go in for something involving so much hard work and heartaches but so much sheer enjoyment! Well, why *do* they show dogs? There are many reasons, and here are a few. First, we have the serious dog breeder. He makes a promise to himself to improve the breed in which he is interested, and he is anxious to compare his dogs with good competition, for it lets him know if he is on the right track in his breeding program. This is important. Many dogs look very good at home and only when they are compared with other good dogs can you see if they are better. Comparison is the material of which dog shows are made. Every dog looks good in the back yard, but how does he look in the ring? To the serious breeder showing is important for another reason. It gives him a chance to let other breeders and fanciers see what he has accomplished. He may own an excellent specimen of the breed, one which would be very

Ch. Sharevalpad Pandora, Staffordshire Terrier, winner of Best in Show under judge Anton B. Korbel. This magnificent dog is owned by Mr. and Mrs. Albert Williams.

Ch. Toby of Iradell, Skye Terrier, is seen here winning at the Huntington Valley Kennel Club Show in 1957; owned by Iradell Kennels, Ridgefield, Connecticut. Photo by Evelyn M. Shafer.

valuable particularly for his ability to sire exceptional puppies—but no one would know about him if he were not shown.

Then we have a group of people who look at the dog shows as a competitive and active sport. The dog game affords plenty of action but is not so strenuous as, let us say, skiing or tennis. As a matter of fact, there are a great many physically handicapped persons who show dogs successfully.

We have another group. A man buys as a pet or receives as a gift a puppy which turns out exceptionally well, and he is advised to show it. He does so—makes some nice wins, and the dog becomes a Champion. (I'll explain Champion a bit later on.) Very frequently this man is "bitten by the bug," he succumbs, he dreams about *breeding* his own Champion—he stays around and often becomes an important member of the first group, the serious breeder.

If show training is started at home with a young puppy and continued until the show career starts, the handler and the dog will enjoy the shows a great deal more. Once you are in the show ring only a slight touch under the muzzle, or perhaps a gentle stroke or two, will be necessary to keep the dog in position resulting in a more relaxed dog and handler and usually a higher placing from the judge.

The Brussels Griffon (a toy breed), Champion Barnumtown Penneywise Gala shown to her championship by her amateur breeders and owners, Edgar and Ruby W. Klein.

Ch. Prince Albert of Palos Verdes, Basset Hound, winning points at an outdoor dog show at Santa Maria, California. Owner: Virginia Merrimer; handler, Rex Kane.

Then we have the person looking for a hobby or perhaps a weekend activity. What better hobby than one which offers you some traveling, some outdoor activity, and a great deal of pleasure and good fellowship while also keeping you fairly active and very much interested? I remember being at an outdoor show rather early one very beautiful Sunday morning talking to Mr. Percy Roberts. Percy was then a top professional handler—one who shows other people's dogs for pay; he is now a well-known professional all-round judge—one who is eligible to judge all breeds of dogs. Percy told me that one of his relatives had chided him earlier that morning for being in a profession which occupied all his weekends. He looked around the beautiful show grounds, at Long Island Sound sparkling in the background and dotted with a few sailboats, at the clear blue sky overhead, and as he lovingly patted his dog he began to laugh,

35

and he said to me, "And to think I get paid for this!" Yes, there is much enjoyment to be had in the dog game.

Finally on our list of those who exhibit dogs we have the "show-off," the exhibitionist. If you like to be in the public eye, here is your chance. Go ahead, show a *good* dog, you'll really enjoy it! But I'll tell you something. One of two things will happen: either you'll fall in love with the sport and become serious about it and a part of it, giving you an interest which will lessen your need for the spotlight; or you'll look elsewhere for that spotlight, for without a genuine love for and interest in dogs and the dog game you can't last, you will become bored, you'll be forced to find a new spotlight.

If you have thought that you might like to get into dogs, but have not yet purchased your first one, let me give you a word of advice. There are so many wonderful breeds, each with its own particular charm, that I'm sure you can find just the right breed for you. However, decide on one whose size and temperament fit into your

Regular and careful grooming is required by longhaired dogs like this Shih Tzu to keep them from looking disheveled. If you are not ready to devote your attention to such chores, longhairs are not for you.

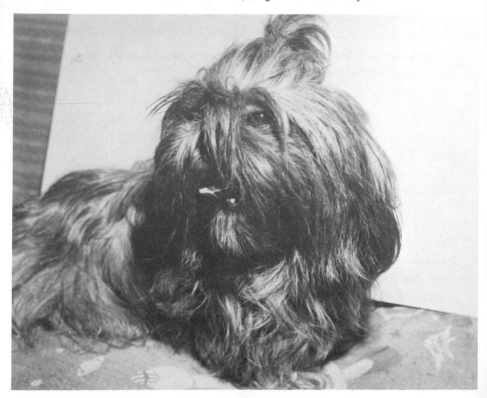

Umpachene Sir Van v. Edelberz, Great Dane, winner at the Great Dane Club of America Specialty Show. It can be inadvisable to confine large dogs in limited quarters such as an apartment or small house. Photo by Evelyn M. Shafer.

This photo of the Boxer International Ch. Bangles N' Beads of Blossomlea was taken when she went Winner's Bitch, Best of Winners, and Best of Opposite Sex for a five-point major to complete her United States championship in 1963 at the St. Louis Boxer Club Specialty. She belonged to Daniel John and Margaret Ann Macateer.

life. Don't get a Great Dane if you live in a tiny apartment, and don't get a tiny dog if a high-pitched bark grates on your nerves. Once you have decided which breed you want, *please* do some studying about what is right and what is wrong for a dog of that particular breed. Read a book on your chosen breed, go to shows, watch the judging, talk to the breeders. Be sure you don't buy a dog which has a disqualification for his breed and, too, you will be ever so much happier in the show game if you at least start out with a dog which has no serious faults. I cannot tell you here what the disqualifications or faults are, as there are more than one hundred breeds for you to choose from and each breed has its own particular faults.

When you are ready to buy, go to a reliable breeder and tell him that you intend to show. A sincere breeder would not sell you an inferior animal if he knows it is to be shown. Many people when they are buying a dog ask for "just a pet," thinking they will get the animal cheaper. A good breeder wants his stock shown and does not want to be embarrassed by having a dog of his breeding with a serious fault show up at a show, and by the same token he does not want to sell a top dog to someone who will never show it, as for all practical purposes the dog would be lost to the show and breeding world. He would rather sell you a good dog for less money if you promised it would be shown. If he is a big breeder, he cannot possibly get all the dogs he raises to the shows under his own name, and he is always looking for someone to come along who is interested in showing. He will not give the dog away, because experience has taught him that the dog receives better care if he has been purchased and he has a much better chance of actually getting into the show ring when the new owner has paid something for the dog.

Owner handlers have been successful in every breed, even where artful grooming procedures are called for. One such example is the Miniature Poodle Ch. Hermscrest Jamal. This lovely silver is shown being handled by her owner to a win of Best of Opposite Sex under judge Majorie Siebern at the Southern Adirondack Dog Club. Jamal is owned by Mrs. Frances Herms.

It would be hard for me to tell you exactly what you ought to pay for a dog good enough to show and have some fun with. In addition to the fact that prices vary a great deal in the various breeds, and not taking into consideration the actual worth of a dog because of his good or bad points, there are many other things that enter into the price you must pay for a good dog. Here are a few:

1. How many other good dogs has the seller in his kennel? By selling you the only good one, he may be left without anything to show himself, and if he wants to show, the price may go up.

2. How crowded are the seller's facilities? If he is overcrowded, he may be willing to sell at a lower price than usual.

3. Can the owner afford to show? If not, he may sell for less in order to give the dog the opportunity to be shown more frequently.

4. How many other persons are interested? Naturally, if several persons express the desire to buy the same dog, the price of that dog might go up.

I've known of show dogs which were sold for $50 and I've known of some which sold at about $7,500. But if you know your breed

The Smooth Dachshund, Champion Hardway Welcome Stranger shown to his championship and to five Best In Shows by his amateur breeder-owner Mrs. Jeannette W. Cross. Photo by Tauskey.

40

A lovely photograph of a lovely animal. She is Champion Silvermine Swift, one of three champions in a litter, bred, owned and shown to their championships by the author.

before you start out to buy, you at least will know *what* you are getting —and remember, the price paid for a dog is not the most important consideration. I once knew a man who thought his dog should win over another simply because he paid more for his dog than did the owner of the other dog.

The advice and helpful hints you will find in this book will help you to understand the rules, will help you to get your dog entered at a show, to the show, and into the ring. We will attempt to tell you how to show it to its best advantage, but remember, the quality of the dog itself is up to you. We will not cover in this book obedience trials or field trials except to tell you what they are, as they are activities completely unto themselves and you will find them fully covered in other books.

Now let me bring up another point. There is one thing you are going to hear frequently, and if you take my advice you won't pay any attention to it. You'll hear that in order to win at shows you must be rich or at least employ a professional handler. This talk usually comes from the disgruntled or bad loser. It is not true! I have known owners, sincere about their dogs, who could not afford the entry fees at shows and as a result attended very few shows. Yet when they did, their dogs won many times over dogs handled by professionals. I do not mean to insinuate that these people were exceedingly poor—no—but they were not rich, and they won. Indeed, their dogs won over dogs who were owned by really rich people.

The professional handlers? Yes, they win, and very frequently. But just consider it a moment. They work at their jobs all day, every day, not just at weekend shows, as do most of the people who complain about how much winning is done by the professionals. Why, I've known more than one professional handler who has gone from early-morning breakfast until nine or ten at night without any food because he or she was too busy to stop. By nine or ten at night in some towns there is no decent place to get a meal, and the handler winds up at some "greasy spoon" with a dinner of ham and eggs, the same thing he had for breakfast that day and the same thing he will have for breakfast the next day. Yes, they really work at their jobs. I make you a prediction: given an equally good dog on which you spend as much time as do the professionals, and when you learn how to show a dog as well, you will win just as often as they do. Many a time you will see the top professional handlers placed last in a good class, with an amateur in first place. So let's not complain when professionals beat us, but let's watch them, learn their secrets, equal their knowledge and ability, and you'll come out on top.

Aside from costing you a lot less, I believe you will have a great deal more fun if you show your own dog and you will learn about dogs a lot faster. A good professional handler, one licensed by the American Kennel Club and one who is a member of the Professional Handlers Association, will usually charge $20 to $30 to show your dog at a show. This does not include the entry fee—it might include the trimming charge, or the transportation charge, but it might not! If the dog wins a Group, an additional charge is made, but this charge is usually agreed upon in advance. The owner gets the trophies but it is customary for the handler to keep all the prize money won by the dog. This in part explains why the professional handlers will always try to take into the show ring only good dogs who are really ready for competition. Naturally, they want prize money. The amount of prize money a dog wins is offered by and determined by the show-giving club, and usually varies according to the number of dogs entered in any given class. In a way, it is unfortunate that there are too many owners who are so anxious to show their dog that they cannot wait until a dog is mature or in the proper coat or weight before they start to show. The professional is in a much better position in this regard. He can wait until a dog is ready to be shown because, if he is a good handler, his services are much in demand— he may even have a waiting list. He can choose from many dogs which one he thinks is really ready to go.

When a person employs a professional handler to show his dog, he is inclined to come to the show only if it is convenient, because he knows the dog will be properly cared for and handled. When he is going to handle his dog himself, he must be there at the appointed hour and he must stay until the time when the dogs are released. However, it is during this time, begrudged by many, that you learn so much about dogs and about shows. It is during this time that you meet other interested people, that you have time to see other dogs in your breed, and see where yours is better or where it is not. When you begin to know these things, you really begin to have fun—with a capital F—at dog shows.

I have told you a little bit about dog shows, about the history of shows, and the people interested in the sport of showing their dogs. Now I want to make you a promise. Once you become interested in what we call "the dog game," aside from giving you a hobby which will keep you busy and happy, you'll meet some of the nicest folks in the world; some will become your lifelong and closest friends.

CHAPTER 3

HOW A CHAMPION IS MADE

The first question most people ask is how one "makes" a Champion. This is done on a point system. The American Kennel Club, upon whose rules the main part of this book is based and which is the principal organization governing dog shows, registrations, pedigrees, dog-club activities, judging, et cetera, issues a Schedule of Points to be awarded, based on the number of dogs entered in one sex at any given show. The United States is divided into four sections: East and North as Division 1; West and South as Division 2; State of California as Division 3; and Pacific Northwest as Division 4 (Hawaii, Puerto Rico and Alaska are special divisions); and the points are different in each section. The Schedule of Points pertaining to each section must be printed in every show catalogue for that particular section. In certain annual issues of *Pure Bred DOGS —American Kennel Gazette*, the official organ of the American Kennel Club, you will find the complete Schedule of Points for the entire country brought up to date. The Schedule of Points becoming effective on May 15, 1968, is given here primarily with the thought that even when it becomes outdated, you might be interested in seeing how the number of dogs necessary to acquire points changes in the different sections of the country and in the different breeds.

You will notice that the number of dogs necessary to make a point varies in the different breeds according to the breed's show popularity. For instance, in the Eastern division of the United States, where German Shepherds are very popular at the moment, it takes 33 to 37 competing in one sex for a three-point show, but only 5 to 7 Black Cocker Spaniels, only 13 to 14 St. Bernards, or 13 Afghan Hounds. That is, it will take 33 *male* German Shepherds to make three points for the winning *male* Shepherd. It will take 37 Shepherd

44

Ch. Agony Acres Devotee of Zeno, Doberman Pinscher, owned by Mr. and Mrs. James Woods and handled by Mrs. Woods, has made many heads turn in the Doberman fancy. This stylish male has a number of good wins to his credit. In this photo he is seen winning the breed at the Wachusett Kennel Club under Mrs. Connie Bosold.

bitches to make three points for the Winners Bitch. In some breeds it takes more bitches than dogs, in some more dogs than bitches. The American Kennel Club keeps very close watch, and these ratings change periodically. If it becomes too easy to find a three-point show in your breed, the rating will change; if it is very difficult to find a three-point show, this will also change. Incidentally, the maximum number of points awarded at any show, regardless of the number of entries, is five.

To "make a Champion," or, more correctly, become a Champion of Record, a dog must win a total of fifteen points. These fifteen points must include two major shows and be won under at least three different judges. A major show is a three-, four-, or five-point show, and since the maximum number that can be won is five, it must take even a top winning dog at least three shows to finish his championship. Insisting that a dog win *two* major shows convinces us that the

Ch. Shillalah Napper Tandy, C.D., Irish Water Spaniel, owned by Erwin Hutzmann, made a stunning record for so rare a breed. He was a group winner, and is shown here winning Best of Breed at the Irish Water Spaniel Club of America in 1959. This was the largest entry of Irish Water Spaniels ever. The judge here was Joseph C. Quirk.

SCHEDULE OF POINTS FOR DIVISION 1 - EFFECTIVE MAY 15, 1968

Division 1 is comprised of: Maine, New Hampshire, Vermont, Massachusetts, Rhode Island, Connecticut, New York, Pennsylvania, New Jersey, Delaware, Maryland, District of Columbia, Virginia, AND Ohio, Michigan, Indiana, Illinois, Wisconsin.

	1 POINT		2 POINTS		3 POINTS		4 POINTS		5 POINTS	
	Dogs	Bitches	Dogs	Bitches	Dogs	Bitches	Dogs	Bitches	Dogs	Bitches
Pointers	2	2	3	3	4	4	5	5	7	7
Pointers (German Shorthaired)	2	2	6	6	10	11	15	15	20	20
Pointers (German Wirehaired)	2	2	3	3	4	4	5	5	7	6
Retrievers (Chesapeake Bay)	2	2	3	3	4	4	6	7	8	9
Retrievers (Golden)	2	2	5	5	11	11	14	14	21	19
Retrievers (Labrador)	2	2	5	4	8	8	10	11	14	13
Setters (English)	2	2	3	4	5	6	8	10	18	20
Setters (Gordon)	2	2	3	3	4	4	6	6	10	12
Setters (Irish)	3	3	7	9	13	16	18	21	42	51
Spaniels (Brittany)	2	2	3	3	5	5	7	9	11	13
Spaniels (Cocker, Solid Color, Black)	2	2	3	4	5	7	8	12	12	18
Spaniels (Cocker), Any Solid Color other than Black, including Black and Tan	2	2	4	4	6	7	10	11	18	15
Spaniels (Cocker), Parti-Color	2	2	3	4	5	6	8	10	14	16
Spaniels (English Cocker)	2	2	3	4	5	6	8	8	12	12
Spaniels (English Springer)	2	2	5	4	9	8	16	12	24	28
Vizslas	2	2	3	3	4	4	6	6	9	9
Weimaraners	2	2	5	5	9	9	15	14	24	25
Afghan Hounds	3	3	8	8	13	13	21	19	39	40
Basenjis	2	2	4	6	8	11	12	15	16	18
Basset Hounds	2	2	5	6	10	10	16	15	24	24
Beagles (13 inches)	2	2	3	3	4	4	5	6	6	9
Beagles (15 inches)	2	2	3	3	4	4	6	5	8	8
Bloodhounds	2	2	3	3	4	4	6	7	7	9
Borzois	2	2	3	3	5	5	7	7	12	13
Dachshunds (Longhaired)	2	2	4	3	5	5	8	9	17	21
Dachshunds (Smooth)	2	2	5	6	9	12	13	19	27	32
Dachshunds (Wirehaired)	2	2	3	3	4	5	6	6	8	15
Irish Wolfhounds	2	2	3	3	4	4	6	6	9	11
Norwegian Elkhounds	2	2	3	3	5	5	7	7	9	11
Rhodesian Ridgebacks	2	2	3	3	4	4	5	5	8	7
Salukis	2	2	3	3	4	4	6	6	9	8
Whippets	2	2	3	4	5	7	7	11	12	22
Alaskan Malamutes	2	2	4	4	7	7	10	11	14	16
Belgian Sheepdogs	2	2	3	3	4	4	6	5	8	6
Belgian Tervuren	2	2	3	3	4	4	5	6	6	8
Bouviers des Flandres	2	2	3	3	4	4	5	6	6	8
Boxers	3	4	8	10	15	17	23	26	32	37
Bullmastiffs	2	2	3	3	4	4	5	6	6	8
Collies (Rough)	3	3	8	9	15	19	28	34	43	51
Doberman Pinschers	4	4	9	10	15	17	19	21	29	31
German Shepherd Dogs	7	7	18	19	33	37	46	56	70	80
Great Danes	3	4	9	10	17	18	23	25	38	39
Great Pyrenees	2	2	3	3	4	4	6	6	8	11
Mastiffs	2	2	3	3	4	4	5	5	7	6
Newfoundlands	2	2	3	4	5	6	7	8	11	10
Old English Sheepdogs	2	2	3	3	4	4	5	5	12	12
Pulik	2	2	3	3	4	4	6	6	8	8
Rottweilers	2	2	3	3	4	4	5	5	12	10
Samoyeds	2	2	3	3	4	5	6	7	9	10
Schnauzers (Standard)	2	3	6	8	12	14	18	21	28	39
Shetland Sheepdogs	2	2	5	5	9	9	14	13	21	21
Siberian Huskies	2	2	7	7	13	14	20	19	38	47
St. Bernards	2	2	4	4	6	7	10	11	15	22
Welsh Corgis (Pembroke)	2	2	3	4	5	6	7	9	11	17
Airedale Terriers	2	2	3	3	4	4	6	6	9	9
Australian Terriers	2	2	3	3	4	5	7	7	11	13
Bedlington Terriers	2	2	3	3	4	4	5	6	6	7
Bull Terriers (White)	2	2	3	4	5	5	7	10	10	14
Cairn Terriers	2	2	3	4	4	4	6	6	7	9
Fox Terriers (Smooth)	2	2	3	3	5	5	7	7	14	16
Fox Terriers (Wire)	2	2	3	3	4	4	6	6	8	9
Kerry Blue Terriers	2	2	3	3	4	5	6	9	12	20
Norwich Terriers	2	2	3	3	4	4	6	6	7	11
Schnauzers (Miniature)	2	2	6	6	10	11	14	16	22	24
Scottish Terriers	2	2	4	4	7	7	10	10	16	21
Sealyham Terriers	2	2	3	3	4	4	5	5	6	8
Welsh Terriers	2	2	3	3	4	4	5	6	6	10
West Highland White Terriers	2	2	4	4	4	4	8	10	19	16
Affenpinschers	2	2	3	3	4	4	5	5	6	6
Chihuahuas (Long Coat)	2	2	3	3	4	4	6	7	8	10
Chihuahuas (Smooth Coat)	2	2	3	3	4	6	7	9	10	13
Italian Greyhounds	2	2	3	3	4	4	5	6	6	9
Maltese	2	2	3	3	4	4	5	5	6	7
Manchester Terriers (Toy)	2	2	3	3	4	4	5	5	7	8
Papillons	2	2	3	4	4	4	5	6	7	8
Pekingese	2	2	5	4	9	7	12	9	14	11
Pinschers (Miniature)	2	2	3	3	4	4	6	7	8	12
Pomeranians	2	2	4	4	6	6	7	9	9	14
Poodles (Toy)	2	3	6	8	12	14	18	21	26	25
Pugs	2	2	3	3	4	7	8	8	13	14
Silky Terriers	2	2	3	3	4	5	5	6	6	8
Yorkshire Terriers	2	2	4	5	6	8	9	11	12	17
Boston Terriers	2	2	3	4	5	6	8	11	15	19
Bulldogs	2	2	4	5	7	9	13	14	20	36
Chow Chow	2	2	3	3	4	4	5	6	6	8
Dalmatians	2	2	4	4	7	9	10	14	15	21
Keeshonden	2	2	4	4	6	6	8	8	14	14
Lhasa Apsos	2	2	3	3	5	5	6	7	8	9
Poodles (Miniature)	3	3	8	9	13	15	19	21	29	30
Poodles (Standard)	2	2	5	5	8	10	12	14	15	18
Schipperkes	2	2	3	3	4	4	5	5	7	7
ALL OTHER BREEDS OR VARIETIES	2	2	3	3	4	4	5	5	6	6

Division 2 is comprised of: West Virginia, Kentucky, Tennessee, North Carolina, South Carolina, Georgia, Florida, Alabama, Mississippi, Louisiana, Arkansas, Oklahoma, Texas, New Mexico, Arizona AND Minnesota, Iowa, Missouri, Kansas, Nebraska, Colorado.

	1 POINT		2 POINTS		3 POINTS		4 POINTS		5 POINTS	
	Dogs	Bitches	Dogs	Bitches	Dogs	Bitches	Dogs	Bitches	Dogs	Bitches
Pointers	2	2	3	3	4	4	5	5	7	6
Pointers (German Shorthaired)	2	2	4	4	6	7	9	9	13	11
Retrievers (Golden)	2	2	4	4	5	5	8	7	12	10
Retrievers (Labrador)	2	2	4	3	5	5	7	7	9	8
Setters (English)	2	2	3	3	4	4	5	6	7	10
Setters (Gordon)	2	2	3	3	4	4	6	5	7	6
Setters (Irish)	2	2	5	5	9	9	13	15	19	22
Spaniels (Brittany)	2	2	3	3	4	4	7	6	12	8
Spaniels (Cocker), Solid Color, Black	2	2	4	4	6	7	8	10	10	14
Spaniels (Cocker), Any Solid Color other than Black, including Black and Tan	2	2	4	4	7	7	10	11	13	14
Spaniels (Cocker), Parti-Color	2	2	4	4	7	8	9	10	11	13
Spaniels (English Springer)	2	2	3	4	5	7	7	8	11	11
Weimaraners	2	2	4	4	8	8	12	11	17	16
Afghan Hounds	2	2	5	5	10	10	12	13	15	16
Basenjis	2	2	5	6	9	10	12	13	16	18
Basset Hounds	2	2	6	6	11	11	15	14	18	18
Beagles (13 inches)	2	2	3	3	4	5	5	6	6	8
Beagles (15 inches)	2	2	3	3	5	4	7	7	10	10
Borzois	2	2	3	3	4	4	6	6	7	8
Dachshunds (Longhaired)	2	2	3	3	5	5	8	8	11	12
Dachshunds (Smooth)	2	2	6	6	10	11	13	16	15	22
Dachshunds (Wirehaired)	2	2	3	4	4	5	6	7	7	9
Norwegian Elkhounds	2	2	3	3	4	4	6	7	9	8
Whippets	2	2	3	3	4	5	5	7	7	9
Alaskan Malamutes	2	2	3	3	4	4	6	7	10	10
Belgian Tervuren	2	2	3	3	4	4	5	6	6	7
Boxers	3	3	7	9	14	18	20	25	26	33
Collies (Rough)	3	3	8	8	16	17	23	26	34	39
Doberman Pinschers	3	4	10	10	16	17	19	21	22	27
German Shepherd Dogs	7	7	22	22	39	40	50	51	67	68
Great Danes	3	3	7	9	13	17	18	21	25	26
Old English Sheepdogs	2	2	3	4	4	5	5	8	6	11
Pulik	2	2	3	3	4	4	5	5	6	7
Samoyeds	2	2	3	3	6	5	9	7	11	9
Schnauzers (Standard)	2	2	3	3	4	4	6	5	7	6
Shetland Sheepdogs	3	3	7	8	12	16	15	20	21	27
Siberian Huskies	3	2	3	3	4	4	11	8	14	10
St. Bernards	2	2	5	4	8	7	13	11	16	15
Welsh Corgis (Pembroke)	2	2	4	4	6	7	8	9	9	12
Airedale Terriers	2	2	3	3	4	4	5	6	6	7
Cairn Terriers	2	2	3	4	5	6	7	8	8	10
Fox Terriers (Smooth)	2	2	3	3	4	4	6	5	7	6
Fox Terriers (Wire)	2	2	3	4	5	4	7	8	9	12
Kerry Blue Terriers	2	2	3	3	4	4	6	6	8	8
Schnauzers (Miniature)	2	2	5	6	9	10	11	15	12	20
Scottish Terriers	2	2	4	4	6	7	9	10	12	15
Skye Terriers	2	2	3	3	4	4	5	5	7	8
West Highland White Terriers	2	2	3	4	4	5	5	7	7	8
Chihuahuas (Long Coat)	2	2	3	3	4	4	5	6	6	8
Chihuahuas (Smooth Coat)	2	2	4	4	6	7	7	9	8	13
Italian Greyhounds	2	2	3	4	4	6	6	7	7	8
Japanese Spaniels	2	2	3	3	4	4	5	6	6	7
Maltese	2	2	3	4	4	4	5	8	7	9
Papillons	2	2	3	3	4	4	5	6	6	7
Pekingese	2	2	5	4	9	8	12	10	16	12
Pinschers (Miniature)	2	2	4	4	5	6	6	8	8	10
Pomeranians	2	2	4	4	8	7	10	9	12	11
Poodles (Toy)	4	4	11	11	18	17	24	22	29	26
Pugs	2	2	4	4	8	6	10	9	15	14
Silky Terriers	2	2	3	3	4	4	6	6	8	10
Yorkshire Terriers	2	2	4	5	6	8	8	9	9	11
Boston Terriers	2	2	4	4	6	7	8	9	13	14
Bulldogs	2	2	4	4	8	8	12	11	19	20
Chow Chows	2	2	3	3	4	4	6	6	12	8
Dalmatians	2	2	4	4	6	6	8	11	10	14
Keeshonden	2	2	3	3	4	4	7	5	9	7
Lhasa Apsos	2	2	3	3	4	5	5	7	8	8
Poodles (Miniature)	3	3	8	7	14	12	17	15	22	19
Poodles (Standard)	2	2	4	4	7	7	10	9	13	12
Schipperkes	2	2	3	3	4	5	5	8	7	9
ALL OTHER BREEDS OR VARIETIES	2	2	3	3	4	4	5	5	6	6

SCHEDULE OF POINTS FOR DIVISION 3 - EFFECTIVE MAY 15, 1968

State of California

	1 POINT		2 POINTS		3 POINTS		4 POINTS		5 POINTS	
	Dogs	Bitches	Dogs	Bitches	Dogs	Bitches	Dogs	Bitches	Dogs	Bitches
Pointers (German Shorthaired)..........	2	2	7	7	15	15	21	22	24	28
Retrievers (Golden)...................	2	2	4	5	10	8	11	10	12	11
Retrievers (Labrador).................	2	2	6	4	10	7	12	9	13	10
Setters (English)....................	2	2	5	4	8	7	11	8	15	10
Setters (Gordon).....................	2	2	4	3	5	5	6	6	7	7
Setters (Irish)......................	5	5	14	15	26	26	32	31	37	40
Spaniels (Brittany)...................	2	2	5	4	9	8	12	12	13	13
Spaniels (Cocker), Solid Color, Black..	2	2	5	5	8	10	10	12	11	13
Spaniels (Cocker),Any Solid Color other than Black, including Black and Tan..	2	2	5	5	9	9	11	12	12	15
Spaniels (Cocker), Parti-Color........	2	2	5	5	7	9	9	12	10	17
Spaniels (English Springer)...........	3	3	6	7	11	11	14	15	15	18
Vizslas..............................	2	2	3	4	4	6	5	7	6	8
Weimaraners..........................	2	2	7	6	14	10	16	15	19	25
Afghan Hounds........................	7	6	17	15	25	22	30	28	35	30
Basenjis.............................	4	6	9	12	12	16	17	18	18	19
Basset Hounds........................	6	4	12	9	21	16	23	19	26	22
Beagles (13 inches)..................	2	2	3	4	4	9	5	12	6	13
Beagles (15 inches)..................	2	2	6	4	8	7	9	8	11	9
Bloodhounds..........................	2	2	4	3	5	4	7	6	9	7
Borzois..............................	2	2	5	4	10	8	14	10	17	12
Dachshunds (Longhaired)..............	2	2	5	5	9	9	10	11	11	12
Dachshunds (Smooth)..................	3	3	7	8	11	14	16	21	18	25
Dachshunds (Wirehaired)..............	2	3	3	6	6	9	8	12	11	15
Greyhounds...........................	2	2	3	3	4	4	5	6	6	7
Irish Wolfhounds.....................	2	2	3	4	5	5	7	7	9	8
Norwegian Elkhounds..................	3	3	8	7	15	10	17	12	19	19
Salukis..............................	2	2	3	3	5	5	6	7	8	8
Whippets.............................	2	3	6	7	10	10	13	13	18	18
Alaskan Malamutes....................	2	2	6	5	11	9	14	11	15	12
Belgian Sheepdogs....................	2	2	4	3	5	4	6	5	7	6
Belgian Tervuren.....................	2	2	3	3	4	4	5	6	6	7
Boxers...............................	7	6	15	15	23	22	27	26	30	35
Collies (Rough)......................	5	5	13	15	26	32	40	42	49	62
Collies (Smooth).....................	2	2	3	3	4	5	6	6	12	12
Doberman Pinschers...................	7	7	19	22	29	33	36	44	45	52
German Shepherd Dogs.................	7	6	19	23	47	39	54	58	61	60
Great Danes..........................	6	6	19	18	36	34	39	38	43	43
Great Pyrenees.......................	2	2	5	5	8	9	9	12	11	14
Newfoundlands........................	2	2	3	3	4	4	6	5	7	6
Old English Sheepdogs................	2	3	5	7	8	11	9	13	11	14
Pulik................................	2	2	4	4	7	8	9	10	11	12
Rottweilers..........................	2	2	3	4	4	6	6	11	7	12
Samoyeds.............................	5	4	13	9	21	14	26	17	30	19
Shetland Sheepdogs...................	4	4	10	12	17	20	22	25	26	29
Siberian Huskies.....................	2	2	5	4	7	7	8	8	9	9
St. Bernards.........................	5	5	10	10	17	15	21	19	24	21
Welsh Corgis (Cardigan)..............	2	2	3	3	4	5	5	6	6	7
Welsh Corgis (Pembroke)..............	3	3	9	7	13	12	17	20	21	27
Airedale Terriers....................	2	2	4	4	7	7	9	8	11	10
Australian Terriers..................	2	2	3	3	4	4	5	6	6	7
Bedlington Terriers..................	2	2	3	3	5	5	6	7	7	8
Cairn Terriers.......................	2	2	4	4	6	6	8	8	9	10
Fox Terriers (Smooth)................	2	2	3	3	4	5	6	8	7	11
Fox Terriers (Wire)..................	2	2	4	4	6	6	7	8	8	11
Kerry Blue Terriers..................	2	2	5	4	8	7	11	9	15	11
Lakeland Terriers....................	2	2	3	3	4	4	5	6	6	8
Schnauzers (Miniature)...............	3	3	7	7	10	11	12	18	13	20
Scottish Terriers....................	2	2	5	6	8	10	11	13	15	15
Staffordshire Terriers...............	2	2	3	3	4	4	5	5	6	7
Welsh Terriers.......................	2	2	3	3	4	5	5	6	6	7
West Highland White Terriers.........	2	2	3	3	4	5	6	7	7	9
Chihuahuas (Long Coat)...............	2	2	5	5	10	8	12	12	15	13
Chihuahuas (Smooth Coat).............	2	3	6	7	8	12	10	14	11	18
Italian Greyhounds...................	2	2	5	5	8	9	9	12	10	16
Japanese Spaniels....................	2	2	3	3	4	4	7	6	8	7
Maltese..............................	2	2	4	5	7	8	8	10	9	11
Manchester Terriers (Toy)............	2	2	3	4	4	6	5	7	6	8
Papillons............................	2	2	3	4	5	6	6	8	7	10
Pekingese............................	8	8	8	8	10	10	14	12	16	14
Pinschers (Miniature)................	2	2	4	4	6	7	7	8	8	9
Pomeranians..........................	3	2	7	5	10	8	15	10	19	11
Poodles (Toy)........................	4	4	10	11	18	18	23	24	24	26
Pugs.................................	3	3	8	6	13	10	16	12	18	14
Silky Terriers.......................	2	3	6	6	11	10	13	13	18	14
Yorkshire Terriers...................	2	3	4	7	7	11	8	13	9	14
Boston Terriers......................	2	2	4	5	7	8	11	12	14	19
Bulldogs.............................	3	3	8	8	15	13	19	21	21	29
Chow Chows...........................	2	2	3	3	5	5	6	6	7	8
Dalmatians...........................	4	5	10	11	14	20	17	24	21	27
French Bulldogs......................	2	2	3	3	4	5	5	6	6	7
Keeshonden...........................	4	2	9	5	14	8	16	11	20	13
Lhasa Apsos..........................	2	2	6	5	13	8	15	10	16	11
Poodles (Miniature)..................	6	6	15	10	23	18	26	21	28	22
Poodles (Standard)...................	2	3	6	8	10	13	11	15	12	16
Schipperkes..........................	2	2	3	3	4	4	5	5	6	7
ALL OTHER BREEDS OR VARIETIES.........	2	2	3	3	4	4	5	5	6	6

SCHEDULE OF POINTS FOR DIVISION 4 - EFFECTIVE MAY 15, 1968

Division 4 is comprised of: North Dakota, South Dakota, Montana, Wyoming, Utah, Nevada, Idaho, Oregon, Washington.

	1 POINT		2 POINTS		3 POINTS		4 POINTS		5 POINTS	
	Dogs	Bitches	Dogs	Bitches	Dogs	Bitches	Dogs	Bitches	Dogs	Bitches
Pointers (German Shorthaired)	2	2	6	5	10	10	11	12	14	13
Retrievers (Golden)	2	2	3	3	6	5	7	6	9	8
Retrievers (Labrador)	2	2	4	4	6	5	7	6	10	10
Setters (Irish)	2	2	6	6	9	10	11	11	12	13
Spaniels (Brittany)	2	2	4	3	7	5	8	6	10	7
Spaniels (Cocker), Solid Color, Black	2	2	3	3	4	6	7	7	8	8
Spaniels (Cocker), Any Solid Color other than Black, including Black and Tan	2	2	3	3	5	5	8	6	9	7
Spaniels (Cocker), Parti-Color	2	2	5	4	7	8	9	9	10	10
Spaniels (English Springer)	2	2	3	4	4	6	5	7	6	8
Weimaraners	2	2	3	3	4	5	5	6	6	7
Afghan Hounds	3	2	9	6	12	12	14	14	16	15
Basenjis	2	2	4	5	7	9	10	11	12	12
Basset Hounds	2	2	6	4	11	8	13	9	14	10
Beagles (13 inches)	2	2	3	3	4	4	5	5	6	7
Beagles (15 inches)	2	2	3	3	6	4	7	5	8	6
Dachshunds (Smooth)	2	2	5	5	9	8	13	9	16	11
Dachshunds (Wirehaired)	2	2	3	4	4	5	5	10	6	12
Norwegian Elkhounds	2	2	5	4	8	7	12	9	13	11
Whippets	2	2	3	4	5	6	6	8	7	10
Alaskan Malamutes	2	2	4	3	6	6	9	10	10	11
Boxers	3	3	8	8	13	14	17	20	19	21
Collies (Rough)	2	3	6	7	10	13	12	15	15	17
Doberman Pinschers	2	3	8	9	16	14	18	22	19	23
German Shepherd Dogs	4	4	14	13	28	24	32	32	39	37
Great Danes	3	3	8	9	11	14	14	15	16	18
Old English Sheepdogs	2	2	3	4	4	5	5	8	6	9
Samoyeds	2	2	6	4	10	7	12	10	14	12
Shetland Sheepdogs	2	2	5	6	10	11	11	12	13	13
Siberian Huskies	2	2	5	4	7	6	9	8	11	9
St. Bernards	2	2	5	5	9	9	11	10	12	13
Welsh Corgis (Pembroke)	2	2	4	5	7	8	8	10	9	11
Airedale Terriers	2	2	3	3	4	4	6	6	7	8
Bedlington Terriers	2	2	3	3	4	4	5	6	6	7
Cairn Terriers	2	2	3	4	5	6	6	8	8	9
Fox Terriers (Wire)	2	2	3	4	4	6	6	7	7	8
Schnauzers (Miniature)	2	2	5	5	9	7	10	8	11	9
Scottish Terriers	2	2	4	4	6	6	8	7	9	8
West Highland White Terriers	2	2	4	3	5	5	6	6	8	7
Chihuahuas (Smooth Coat)	2	2	4	5	7	7	9	8	10	9
Italian Greyhounds	2	2	3	3	4	4	5	6	6	7
Maltese	2	2	3	3	5	5	7	6	8	7
Pekingese	2	2	5	4	8	7	10	8	11	9
Pinschers (Miniature)	2	2	3	3	4	4	5	5	6	7
Pomeranians	2	2	4	4	7	7	8	8	9	9
Poodles (Toy)	3	3	7	7	12	12	14	14	18	16
Pugs	2	2	4	4	7	8	8	10	9	11
Yorkshire Terriers	2	2	3	4	5	6	7	10	8	11
Boston Terriers	2	2	4	4	6	6	7	8	8	9
Bulldogs	2	2	6	5	10	8	14	10	15	12
Chow Chows	2	2	3	3	4	4	5	5	6	7
Dalmatians	2	2	4	3	6	5	10	13	11	14
Keeshonden	2	2	4	3	7	4	8	5	9	6
Lhasa Apsos	2	2	4	3	5	4	6	5	7	6
Poodles (Miniature)	4	5	8	9	13	14	17	17	18	18
Poodles (Standard)	2	2	4	4	6	7	7	9	8	11
ALL OTHER BREEDS OR VARIETIES	2	2	3	3	4	4	5	5	6	6

SCHEDULE OF POINTS FOR PUERTO RICO - EFFECTIVE MAY 15, 1968

	1 POINT		2 POINTS		3 POINTS		4 POINTS		5 POINTS	
	Dogs	Bitches	Dogs	Bitches	Dogs	Bitches	Dogs	Bitches	Dogs	Bitches
Boxers	2	2	3	3	6	4	7	5	8	6
German Shepherd Dogs	4	4	9	10	17	21	18	22	19	23
Poodles (Toy)	2	2	3	3	4	5	5	6	6	7
Poodles (Miniature)	2	2	3	3	4	5	5	6	6	7
ALL OTHER BREEDS OR VARIETIES	2	2	3	3	4	4	5	5	6	6

dog is capable of winning at shows where, because enough dogs are entered, you can reasonably expect to find an entry representative of the breed. Let's take up that business of "under at least three different judges." The major wins must be under two different judges, and one or more of the balance of the points must be won under some other judge or judges. In other words, no dog can become a Champion by winning under only one or two judges—there must be at least three.

Points are awarded to the dog who goes *Winners Dog* and to the bitch who goes *Winners Bitch*—and to *these two only*. There are five regular classes in each sex in each breed: Puppy, Novice, Bred by Exhibitor, American Bred, and Open. (The definitions of each of these classes are given in full in the Appendix and are also explained later in the text.) The winner of each of these classes competes for Winners Dog or Winners Bitch. For example: the winner of the Puppy Dog Class, the winner of the Novice Dog Class, the Bred by Exhibitor Class, the American Bred Class, and the winner of the Open Dog Class will, immediately after the judging of the Open Dog Class, come into the ring to compete for Winners Dog and Reserve Winners Dog. Then the classes for bitches will begin. The winners of the Puppy Bitch Class, Novice Bitch Class, Bred by Exhibitor Bitch, American Bred, and the winner of the Open Bitch Class will, immediately after the judging of the Open Bitch Class, compete for Winners Bitch and Reserve Winners Bitch. The judge, immediately after judging winners, also names a Reserve Winners Dog and a Reserve Winners Bitch, and this dog, the Reserve Winner, will receive the points if for any reason, usually infraction of certain rules of eligibility, the points are taken away from the winner.

The Winners Dog and the Winners Bitch, immediately after the judging of Reserve Winners Bitch automatically go into the Best of Breed Class, the class in which Champions are entered, and will then compete for Best of Breed together with any champions of that breed that may be entered in the show. Immediately after choosing Best of Breed, the judge will choose his Best of Winners from the aforementioned Winners Dog and Winners Bitch in the event that neither of these two was placed Best of Breed. After selecting Best of Winners, the judge will choose a Best of Opposite Sex to Best of Breed. In other words, if the judge puts up a dog (male) to Best of Breed, he will choose a bitch and award her Best of Opposite Sex

SCHEDULE OF POINTS FOR ALASKA - EFFECTIVE MAY 15, 1968

	1 POINT		2 POINTS		3 POINTS		4 POINTS		5 POINTS	
	Dogs	Bitches	Dogs	Bitches	Dogs	Bitches	Dogs	Bitches	Dogs	Bitches
Setters (Irish)..........................	2	2	3	3	4	5	5	6	6	7
Basset Hounds.........................	2	2	3	3	5	4	6	5	7	6
Beagles (13 inches)...................	2	2	3	3	4	5	5	6	6	7
Beagles (15 inches)...................	2	2	3	3	5	4	6	5	7	6
Alaskan Malamutes....................	2	2	4	3	5	4	6	5	7	6
Collies (Rough).......................	2	2	4	4	7	7	8	8	9	9
German Shepherd Dogs..................	2	2	8	6	14	10	15	11	16	12
Great Danes..........................	2	2	4	3	7	4	8	5	9	6
Great Pyrenees.......................	2	2	3	3	5	4	6	5	7	6
Samoyeds.............................	2	2	5	3	7	4	8	5	9	6
Shetland Sheepdogs....................	2	2	3	4	4	5	5	6	6	7
Siberian Huskies......................	2	2	3	3	5	6	6	7	7	8
St. Bernards.........................	2	2	3	3	4	5	5	6	6	7
Pomeranians..........................	2	2	3	3	4	6	5	7	6	8
Poodles (Toy)........................	2	2	4	3	6	5	7	6	8	7
Poodles (Miniature)..................	2	2	5	4	8	6	9	7	10	8
ALL OTHER BREEDS OR VARIETIES..........	2	2	3	3	4	4	5	5	6	6

SCHEDULE OF POINTS FOR HAWAII - EFFECTIVE MAY 15, 1968

	1 POINT		2 POINTS		3 POINTS		4 POINTS		5 POINTS	
	Dogs	Bitches	Dogs	Bitches	Dogs	Bitches	Dogs	Bitches	Dogs	Bitches
Setters (Irish).........................	2	2	3	3	4	5	5	6	6	7
Spaniels (Cocker), Solid Color, Black..	2	2	5	3	8	6	9	7	10	8
Spaniels (Cocker),Any Solid Color other than Black, Including Black and Tan..	2	2	3	4	4	8	5	9	6	.10
Spaniels (Cocker), Parti-Color........	2	2	3	3	4	6	5	7	6	8
Basenjis.............................	2	2	3	3	6	4	7	5	8	6
Basset Hounds.......................	2	2	3	3	5	5	6	6	7	7
Dachshunds (Smooth)..................	2	2	3	5	6	8	7	9	8	10
Boxers...............................	2	2	5	7	9	12	10	13	11	14
Collies (Rough).......................	2	2	3	4	4	7	5	8	6	9
Doberman Pinschers...................	2	2	3	3	4	6	5	7	6	8
German Shepherd Dogs..................	6	4	18	14	33	24	34	25	35	26
St. Bernards........................	2	2	3	3	4	6	5	7	6	8
Welsh Corgis (Pembroke)..............	2	2	4	3	7	4	8	5	9	6
Fox Terriers (Wire)..................	2	2	3	4	6	6	7	7	8	8
Poodles (Toy).......................	2	2	4	4	7	8	8	9	9	10
Poodles (Miniature)..................	2	2	5	6	9	13	10	14	11	15
ALL OTHER BREEDS OR VARIETIES..........	2	2	3	3	4	4	5	5	6	6

to Best of Breed. If he puts a bitch up to Best of Breed, he will choose a dog for Best of Opposite Sex. Should the Winners Dog be placed Best of Breed, he automatically goes Best of Winners and the same is true of the Winners Bitch—if she goes Best of Breed, she is automatically Best of Winners. If the Winners Dog is placed Best of Breed, the Winners Bitch is eligible for Best of Opposite Sex. If the Winners Bitch is placed Best of Breed, the Winners Dog is eligible for Best of Opposite Sex.

This process of elimination goes on in each breed—always winding up with one dog of each breed—the Best of Breed. All the winners of Best of Breed compete in the group judging (there are six groups: Sporting, Hound, Working, Terrier, Toy, and Non-Sporting) and the winner of each group competes for the Best in Show—again a process of elimination. The list of American Kennel Club breeds eligible for registration and show competition found on page 207 in this book will tell you in which group the various breeds belong.

To go back once more to the subject of points I repeat, only the Winners Dog and the Winners Bitch get points. However, should there be more dogs competing than bitches, and therefore more points awarded to the Winners Dog than to the Winners Bitch, and the Winners Bitch goes on to win Best of Winners, she gets the same number of points Winners Dog received; not in addition to the ones she had won but instead of. He, the dog, does not lose the points he had won. For instance: Suppose the dog wins two points when he goes Winners Dog and the bitch wins one point when she goes Winners Bitch (based on the number of dogs competing that day) and the bitch goes on to Best of Winners—her show record will then show that she won two points; the dog's record will show that he won two points. If the bitch goes on to win Best of Breed, even though she may beat three or four Champions when doing so, she does not get any more points for that win. However, should our example bitch go on to win the group she will get the maximum number of points awarded to any breed in the group that day. Suppose our example bitch is an Afghan Hound and she wins the Hound Group. If there were enough Beagles entered that day in one sex to produce a four-point show, our Afghan Hound automatically takes on four points instead of the two she had won in the breed. Now suppose she goes on to win Best in Show, and there were enough Boxers entered that day to produce a five-point show, she automatically gets those points, not in addition to, but instead of, the four from the group or the two from the breed. As a Best in Show winner she would get the maximum number of points in the entire show that day. However, once a dog becomes a Champion he or she no longer counts points. A Champion may go Best of Breed twenty times, or win the group a dozen times or go Best in Show a dozen times, but it has no bearing on the points. He stops counting points as soon as he wins the title Champion.

CHAPTER 4

TERMS AND DEFINITIONS

There is something we should discuss before we go any further. You must learn to speak the word "bitch" without hesitation and to hear it without flinching. There is no other correct word to take its place in the dog world. You would not think of saying you were going out to milk the female bull; you say milk the cow. You do not get eggs from a female rooster; you get them from a hen, although the rooster and the hen are both chickens. Probably the main reason for the confusion is that the word "dog" has more than one meaning. Following I will give you the dictionary definitions of two words, "dog" and "bitch," and since "dog" has two meanings I will place one meaning above the other and place the second usage where it belongs—next to its counterpart "bitch":

DOG: any of a great variety of
domesticated quadrupeds

DOG: a male of the dog.   BITCH: a female of the dog.
When speaking of the species you are correct in using the word "dog." When speaking of the sex of the species dog, you use either male and female or you use dog and bitch. Since the words male and female may pertain to anything—cats, cattle, birds, dogs, fish, or people, we take the two words which definitely mean male or female *dogs* and use them entirely when speaking of the sex of the animals.

At shows we refer to the Puppy Bitch Class, never the Puppy Female Class. Puppy female what? Puppy female fox? No! We are speaking of dogs, so the correct word is bitch (denoting sex), and we refer to the class as the Puppy Bitch Class. The class for males is called Puppy Dog Class. If it were called Puppy Male, we could ask

Ch. Sharonellen's Skibbereen, Kerry Blue Terrier, owned by Mr. and Mrs. F. W. Rogers, Jr. and handled by Mrs. Rogers, has scored top-drawer wins from one end of the United States to the other. A solid threat in any company, he has won well in breed, Group and Best in Show competition and has also proven his worth as a producer of quality Kerries.

Ch. Mahogany's Socair Buacaill (Cochise), Irish Setter, pictured winning Best of Breed at the 1969 Bronx County Kennel Club show. Cochise is an international champion. Helen Olivio owned and handled this fine example of the breed.

the same question—puppy male what? Since dog means male of the dog (species), we refer to the class as Puppy Dog Class.

In breeding we refer to our females (female what?) as bitches. Correctly you say, "I will bring my bitch to be bred to your dog on Wednesday," or, "You own a very lovely bitch," or, "Yes, she is a wonderful brood bitch."

It is unfortunate that the word bitch has another meaning not so nice as its true definition—a female of the dog. However, do learn to speak the word bitch around dogs and dog people and know that when you do so you are correct.

A word commonly misused is "thoroughbred." Thoroughbred is the name of a breed of horse. You should not say, "I have a thorough-bred dog" any more than you should say, "I have a Great Dane cat." The correct term is purebred. While speaking of purebred, it goes without saying that all dogs who are exhibited at shows must be purebred.

Following are a few words or expressions you should know in order better to understand this book, but the meanings or definitions given here will apply only to their usage in the breeding or showing of purebred dogs. Words or expressions explained elsewhere are not included here, nor are words which have but one definition. Following the definitions I have listed the classes. You will find the full rule regarding these classes in the Appendix, but when given here I am attempting to point out the little things a novice may not gather when reading the technical wording of the official rule.

All Breed Club. This club may be a member club of the American Kennel Club (represented by a delegate), or it may be licensed by the American Kennel Club. Either a member club or a licensed club may hold an all-breed show at which championship points are awarded. It may hold obedience trials and field trials at which championship points are awarded. Its main interest is in purebred dogs in general, all breeds. Most of the large shows you read about are run by all-breed clubs.

Specialty Club. A club formed for the improvement of any one breed of purebred dogs. It may hold specialty shows and trials at which championship points are awarded, sanctioned matches, social functions, et cetera.

Ch. Brithedd of Cambria, Cardigan Welsh Corgi, posed at an open-air dog show on the West Coast. Cambria Kennels in Santa Ana, California own and manage this champion.

The prize-winning attributes of this champion Irish Setter are not fully displayed in this relaxed pose. However, the array of prizes seen here is ample evidence of the excellent traits he possesses. Photo by Louise Van der Meid.

Specialty Show. A show given by a Specialty Club at which championship points are awarded. This show would be for one breed only, as the Specialty Club is formed for the improvement of one breed. Such a show may be held in conjunction with an all-breed show (by designating the classes at that show as its Specialty Show) or it may be held entirely apart from any other show.

Sanctioned Match. A sanctioned match is an informal meeting at which purebred dogs may compete but not for championship points. A sanctioned match may be held by any club or association whether or not a member of the American Kennel Club by obtaining the sanction of the American Kennel Club.

Point Show. A term used to designate a show where championship points are awarded. Actually the correct term is all-breed show. Since a match is also for all breeds if you said, "My dog won at an all-breed show," you might be asked, "Point show or sanctioned match?"

Puppy Match. The correct term should be sanctioned match, but since a sanctioned match (several different plans are acceptable) is not limited to puppies, a puppy match is usually more of a social event where puppies are exhibited. For instance: I have invited my friends in my breed to come to my home with a picnic lunch and their puppies and asked a friend in the breed to act as judge. This would be called a puppy match.

Sponsored Entry. Frequently a Specialty Club will wish to sponsor the entry of its breed at an all-breed show and will offer additional prize money and/or trophies. This is usually in addition to the one or two specialty shows it runs in a year.

Best of Variety. In any breed with more than one recognized variety, the winner of that variety is called Best of Variety instead of Best of Breed. The breeds divided by height, such as the Beagle, or

The Borzoi is a dog that no one can ignore, especially in the show ring. This champion is literally flaunting everything it has. Photo by Louise Van der Meid.

A Best of Breed winner, Ch. Dorey's Declared Dividend is seen here at a New England Cocker Spaniel Breeder's Club show. This beautiful dog was owned by Mrs. Blanche Dorey.

Ch. Lucky of Pheasant Hill, a German Shorthaired Pointer owned by William J. Stopplebein, was sired by Ch. Zitt v d Sellwide Import. Bred by Eugene L. Keeth and handled by Durwood Van Zandt.

color, such as the Cocker Spaniel, or by coat, such as the Dachshund or Collie, are the only ones concerned with this term. Each variety is treated as a breed when being judged, having all the regular classes and sending its Best of Variety into the group judging. The American Cocker Spaniel has three varieties—Black, Any Solid Color Other Than Black, and Particolored—and all three go into the group. The Dachshund has three varieties—Smooth, Wirehaired and Long-haired—and all three go into the group. It would be incorrect to say that the winner of any variety or division was the winner of the breed, we say he is the winner of Best of Variety.

Registration Certificate. All dogs shown at dog shows should be registered, and after these definitions I will go into more detail on registrations, but for the present I just want to tell you that the registration certificate is that piece of paper issued to the *owner* of a dog by the organization with which the dog has been registered when the dog has actually been registered. On the certificate is listed all the pertinent information regarding the dog, such as name, number, date whelped, sire, dam, breeder, owner.

Pedigree. A pedigree is that paper usually given to the owner of a dog by the breeder. It gives the names of the sire and dam, the grandparents, great-grandparents, and usually the great, great-grandparents. A four-generation pedigree is to be expected when purchasing a purebred dog; however, many breeders issue a five- or six-generation pedigree.

Owner. The owner of a dog is the one whose name (or names) appears on the registration certificate as owner, not necessarily the one in possession of a dog. It is possible to have more than one owner, but the names of all owners should appear on the registration certificate.

Breeder. The breeder of a dog is the owner or lessee of the dam at the time when the dam is bred. Bear in mind that the person who owns the dam when she whelps is not necessarily the breeder and

The Pointer Champion Moscows William shown to his championship by his amateur owner Dr. Stephan Stephanic.

Ch. Lockerbie Sandylands Tarquin, Labrador Retriever, owned and handled by Mrs. James Warwick. This dog has proven his quality in England as well as in the United States and is pictured winning the breed and placing second in the Sporting Group at the Chester Valley Kennel Club under judge Fred Hunt.

will only be the breeder if he also owned her when she was mated. You might hear the word breeder used in another way. "When purchasing a show dog it is advisable to go to a good breeder." This really means to go to someone who raises dogs as compared with a pet shop or puppy-selling establishment.

Whelped. Whelped means "gave birth to"; therefore, "the litter was whelped on July 4th." However, the word is frequently used in slightly different ways. "When is she due to whelp?" means when is she due to give birth to her puppies? "She is in whelp" means she is carrying a litter. You could also say, "He is a good whelp," meaning he is a good puppy, but this expression is rather passé.

Get. Around dogs the word "get" means offspring, children, or progeny. Special non-regular classes are sometimes offered at specialty shows called Stud Dog Class or Brood Bitch Class. The stud dog (or brood bitch) is entered in the class "to be shown with

Fashions, styles, types, change in dogs just as in anything else. Compare the picture of a champion Cocker Spaniel around the turn of the century with a modern day Cocker. They scarcely look like the same breed! The second picture is of the American Cocker Spaniel Champion Highomar Hallelujah owned and shown by Lester Wallack.

two of his get, the get only to count." To explain this: three dogs are brought into the ring; one is the sire or stud dog, the other two are his get; or one is the dam or brood bitch and the other two are her get. Since the two get need not be under a year old the word puppies is not used. They need not be male, so the word dog is not used. Get is the correct word. Incidentally, in the judging of either the Stud Dog or Brood Bitch Class only the two get are judged. The two get need not be out of the same bitch or the same litter for the Stud Dog Class, nor will the two get have to be by the same sire or litter for the Brood Bitch Class. The winner of the class is the stud dog (or brood bitch), even though he (or she) was not considered in the judging.

Type. You will hear references to the type of a dog. This is a rather difficult expression to explain to a novice because first the novice must know that there are different types within a breed. It is only after you know your breed thoroughly that you begin to realize that these different types exist. Also, to different people the word has different meaning. With some people, type means size or shape of body. They will say, "I do not like his type, he is too small and racy." Here they are referring to size, and when they say "racy" they mean shape of body. Usually a racy dog is one who is slight for the breed in question and also, in addition to being slight, the dog may have a top line which slopes rather more than usual for that breed. (See drawings on page 184.) Then, again, you will hear, "I do not like his type, he is too houndy in head." This will mean that the person is referring to type as expressed by the head. I believe most dog fanciers think of type as head. However, there is still another "type" referred to. You will hear someone say, "I like a terrier-type Beagle." Here he will be referring more to the bone structure in the shoulders and foresection. You will also hear a judge say, "I really liked that dog I placed Winners today, he is so typey." The judge will mean that the dog, in his opinion, was typical of the breed. Please note I used the words, "in his opinion." We will take this expression apart in great detail later, as it doesn't rightly come under the heading of definition of the word "type."

Pace. A pace is a gait or manner of moving, such as a trot or gallop, in which the legs on the same side move in the same direction simultaneously. A pace is a very undesirable gait in a dog.

Steward. The steward is actually a judge's assistant. He does not, however, have anything to do with the judging. He only helps in such things as notifying the judge when the dogs are all in the ring for the proper class, getting together the correct and necessary ribbons or trophies for the class, sending messages to officials upon the judge's orders, marking the blackboard in the ring, notifying the judge of a known absentee, et cetera.

Classes. There are many classes in which dogs may be entered at shows. Some are called regular classes, some are non-regular. These classes are more than just names. They have a definite meaning, and all dogs are not eligible to compete in all classes. I suggest you familiarize yourself with the *complete* definitions found in the Appendix; here are some explanations of those definitions.

Puppy Class. The Puppy Class shall be for dogs (except champions) six months of age and over, but under twelve months. The age of a dog shall be calculated up to and inclusive of the first day of a show . . . This class shall be open only to puppies whelped in the United States or Canada. If you import a puppy from Europe, do not enter him in this class just because he is under one year old. If you do, and he should win, the win would be canceled.

Novice Class. The Novice Class shall be for dogs six months of age and over which have not won three first prizes in the Novice Class, a first prize in Bred By Exhibitor or American Bred or Open Class nor one or more points towards championships. Only dogs whelped in the United States or Canada shall be eligible. The two things about this class that confuse the novice exhibitor are: even if you are alone in your class and you win it, the dog has won a first prize; and if he wins a Puppy Class and goes on to win Winners with one point, he is no longer eligible to compete in this class.

Bred by Exhibitor Class. This class shall be for all dogs (except Champions) six months of age and over, which are owned by that identical person (or persons) who was the breeder of record. Dogs entered in this class may be shown in the ring in this class only by an owner or member of his immediate family. Read this rule carefully if you have any intentions of exhibiting in this class. A good friend of mine lost the points won by his dog for the wrong entry of his dog in this class. He was the breeder of record, Mr. John Smith, and later put the dog in joint ownership of Mr. and Mrs. John Smith, so that the breeder and the owner were no longer identical and the dog was not eligible to compete. It was a major win (three points), and

This champion Bulldog without doubt possesses the desirable traits of the breed. Note that his legs are wide apart and his feet are planted firmly. Photo by Louise Van der Meid.

since major wins are hard to find, it hurt to have the points taken away.

American Bred Class. This class shall be for all dogs (except Champions) six months of age and over, whelped in the United States, by reason of a mating which took place in the United States. If you import from Canada a bitch in whelp who whelps her puppies here, the puppies are not eligible to compete in this class, since they were not the result of a mating which took place in the United States.

Open Class. The Open Class shall be for any dog six months of age or over. Some people are under the impression that because their dog is a puppy he may not be entered in this class. This is not so. A puppy may be entered in any class for which he is eligible, and it is not true that a puppy must advance through the other classes before he may compete in the Open Class. In the Open Class, since nothing is said about the United States or Canada, is where you will find dogs from foreign countries competing and, since nothing is said about Champions you may, particularly in some breeds, find Champions competing in this class.

Winners Class. There is no entry fee in this class, and if your dog wins any one of the five regular classes he is automatically eligible to compete in this class.

Best of Breed Competition. A class in which only Champions of Record may be entered. Dogs entered in this class pay an entry fee and with the addition of the Winners Dog and Winners Bitch compete for Best of Breed. If your records show your dog has the neces-

The Toy Poodle Champion Cartlane Once shown to her championship before she was one year old by her amateur breeder-owner Miriam Hall.

The German Shepherd Dog Canadian and American Champion Damon V Rickwood Acre. He was bred by and shown through to his championships in Canada and America by his amateur owner Mrs. Fred Richter.

sary points, you may enter in this class before receiving confirmation from the American Kennel Club, but entering is limited to 90 days. After that you must wait for confirmation of the dog's Championship.

Best of Winners. This is not really a class and there is no entry fee. The only dogs eligible to compete for this award are the dog who won Winners Dog and the bitch who won Winners Bitch.

Exhibition Only. A dog may be entered for exhibition only but without the privilege of competing in any class. He must have won a first prize in a regular class prior to the show. At benched shows a dog so entered will have a bench provided for him, since the benching rule states that all dogs present at a show must be benched. There are occasions when you might have a dog present at a show but not entered in one of the regular classes. For example: Suppose you own a stud dog someone wants to see. The dog is out of condition and you do not want him to compete because you feel he is not ready. You are going to be at the show anyway, showing another dog, so you advise the interested party that he can see the dog at the show. The dog is present at the show and must be benched—entering for exhibition only provides that bench for your dog.

Miscellaneous Class. This class is open to such breeds of dogs as may be designated by the American Kennel Club for which a show-giving club may choose not to offer a regular classification. This class may be judged on a divided sex or a combined sex basis, and the dogs are not eligible for further judging. Usually the breeds shown in this class are foreign breeds who are not yet in this country in sufficient numbers to have a regular classification offered to them. When the Weimaraner first came to this country he was shown in this class.

There are a great many terms used in dogs which may not be found in any dictionary. Mostly they are words used to describe faults or desirable qualities of one sort or another (remember that what constitutes a fault in one breed may be a desirable quality in another) and the word will be so descriptive that everyone in the breed will know what you are talking about. Such words are: flashy, shelly, good-going, substance, slab-sided, snipey, coarse, apple-

This man is showing off all the trophies of his English Springer Spaniel in this informal photo. This breed, well known for retrieving and hunting, can easily be trained for show purposes as well. Photo by Louise Van der Meid.

Ch. Wood's Lou Lou, Boston Terrier, owned and shown by Mrs. Anna M. Griffing, proved a consistent winner during her career in the show ring. Here she is pictured winning Best of Breed at the Saw Mill River Kennel Club under the late George M. Beckett.

headed, et cetera. There are many words to describe the type ear that a particular breed should have: rose ear, prick ear, et cetera. There are many words used to describe the type coat a breed should have: smooth, rough, wirehair, feather, apron, fringe, et cetera. You can see that if I defined each one of these words we would never get on to the main section of this book, so I leave it up to you to find the definitions of the words pertaining to your particular breed. Before we talk about how to show your dog, a few words on the various organizations that hold shows, register dogs, or run field trials.

The American Kennel Club, 51 Madison Avenue, New York, New York, 10010 is the principal organization that establishes and administers the rules for the registration and showing of purebred dogs. It is made up of a group of member clubs, each of which sends a delegate to New York to the American Kennel Club meetings. The American Kennel Club has established records for 115 breeds of dogs for registration and dog-show purposes. It issues rules and regulations, licences judges and handlers, and approves dates for clubs to hold events under its rules, such as dog shows, sanctioned matches, trials, et cetera. It is necessary that the 368 member clubs and the well over 500 licensed clubs clear their show dates through some main clearing house, otherwise too many might choose the same date.

The American Kennel Club keeps a complete record of every dog's show career and can tell where and how many times a particular dog was placed first, second, third, or fourth, and just how many points he has. There were 1,010 shows held in 1967 with 5,855 dogs gaining their championships on the bench, 529 completing their field championships, and 5,927 titles issued in obedience trials. More than 440,300 dogs are shown annually and more than 885,800 were registered in 1967, so it is no surprise that the Show Department and the Registration Department are two of the busiest at the American Kennel Club offices.

The American Kennel Club publishes a monthly magazine, *Pure Bred DOGS—American Kennel Gazette*, which lists its officers, the delegates from the member clubs, show dates, the show records, information pertaining to trials, registrations, and a list of new Champions. Also appearing are monthly columns for most breeds. New rules are written in full, applications for judge's licenses are made known, and licenses granted are listed. Handler's license and kennel name applications are also published monthly.

The men who hold office in the American Kennel Club are all persons who have been associated with dogs for most of their lives, and they try to keep the rules not only up to date but applicable to the entire country. Field trials are also run under their supervision as well as obedience trials. It is the ambition, as well as the duty, of the American Kennel Club to keep the dog registrations and pedigrees in order, to keep the dog shows and trials running smoothly and, most of all, to keep the sport clean and decent.

As you read through these pages you will find many references to the American Kennel Club. Bear in mind that it is doing a mammoth job exceptionally well and for your benefit. Refer frequently to the rules and become familiar with them. Each one has a reason for its being there and, while it is not the wish of the American Kennel Club to impose fines on people for infraction of these rules, it is the only way it can see to it that each of us obeys them.

Brigitta of Gertase Rottweiler started off her show career with a proverbial "bang." The first time in the ring, at the age of only six months, she scored a five-point major and went on to Best of Breed at the Beverly-Riviera Kennel Club. She was handled to this win by her owner, Mrs. John E. McIntyre, and the judge was Dr. Frank Porter Miller.

Here is a typical rule pertaining to dog shows: Chapter 18 of *Rules Applying to Registrations and Dog Shows* states that dogs must be on their benches during the advertised hours of the show. The reason for this rule is that if the dogs were not benched, the spectator who pays admission to the show would not be able to see the dog he is most interested in. If each exhibitor copied the other and absented his dog from the bench, soon there would be no dogs on the benches at all. This rule works the biggest hardship on handlers because of the great number of dogs they take to shows, but they, too, must obey this rule else it would not be fair to the one-dog exhibitor. His dog might be more tired from being benched than the handler's when the two dogs met in the show ring.

Warnings, of course, are given offenders, but occasionally you run into a person who will not heed a warning. If the offense is repeated, the individual is fined and the notice of such fine is printed in the *Gazette*. The fine is usually $25 for each offense (of the benching rule), with subsequent infractions dealt with in more severe manner. In fairness to all, the rule must be obeyed.

Here is another example of a rule: Chapter 16, Section 9-B states that a dog's color or marking may not be changed by the use of any substance. Would you as a beginner consider it fair if one of your competitors, with great knowledge and ability, changed the markings on his dog from poor to good by the use of applied color and won over your dog whose markings were excellent without the artificial change? A busy judge in a poor light may not notice the artificial change, and his placement would not be fair. In the past this rule was difficult to enforce, but there have been changes and now under this rule the judge shares the responsibility of altered color and since the penalties are high you will find practically no artificial changes being made today. Years ago it was not uncommon to see a dog's marking completely altered by the use of stove blackening or mascara. The experienced "painter" had an unfair advantage over the novice in those days, but by the application of proper rules, this practice has been eliminated.

The American Kennel Club library is an unusually fine one containing more than 9,500 books on dogs. The walls of the offices are hung with famous paintings of dogs, mostly donated by past owners. The staff are courteous and helpful to all who need their advice.

The United Kennel Club, Incorporated, with offices at 321 West

Cedar Street, Kalamazoo, Michigan, 49006 also registers dogs and issues rules and regulations pertaining to dog shows and field trials. They publish a magazine, *Bloodlines Journal*, every two months. Such breeds, to name a few, as the Toy Fox Terrier, The American Bull Terrier, English Shepherd Dog, six breeds of Coonhounds and Miniature Boxers are registered with them. They license clubs to hold bench shows as well as field trials, and recognize Champions in both events. Championships (bench show) are obtained by the winning of points but the manner in which they are obtained and the number necessary to receive the title are different from the American Kennel Club rules. So as not to confuse you, the American Kennel Club rules pertaining to registrations and dog shows, being lengthier, are given in full in the Appendix but the United Kennel Club rules, much shorter, follow in their entirety.

UNITED KENNEL CLUB LICENSED BENCH SHOW RULES

1. A U.K.C. Licensed Bench Show is a distinctive gathering of dogs and their owners of certain recognized breeds for the purpose of identifying the winners and making a nationally known record of such winnings. When a dog has won (100) points at such Licensed Bench Show it shall receive the degree of National Bench Show Champion.

2. An application for a U.K.C. Licensed Bench Show may be made in writing, giving the name of the organization and its officers and the date or dates desired. The application must be accompanied with the fee of $5.00. This fee will be returned if the application is not granted. Application must be made thirty days ahead of date of Bench Show. No license will be granted if dates interfere with a License already granted. Holidays, distances apart, etc., will be taken into consideration.

3. A U.K.C. Licensed Bench Show must be advertised as such in Bloodlines Journal, the official publication of the U.K.C. and other publications desired.

4. The name, sex, color and U.K.C. registration number must be given on the entry blank, also the complete name and address of the owner. If the dog is entered by another person than the owner, then his name and address must also be given.

5. The Management must refuse entry to such dogs and owners that have been disqualified for cause, in present or past Bench Shows.

6. Official U.K.C. pedigrees must be shown by the owner or handler upon making himself known to the Secretary of the organization for proof of age of dog and pure breeding, from this pedigree and from the small registration certificate the Secretary shall copy all information pertinent to the information necessary for each and every dog entered. The registration certificate shall show the same name as that of the owner; if names are different then the Secretary will know that the dog has not been properly

transferred to the new owner and shall not accept this dog for entry, if entry fee is paid, it is to be returned to the person making payment of the fee.

7. No dog shall be accepted for entry where the owner or handler cannot show proof of registration, age and of pure breeding (excepting) U.K.C. registered puppies. Usually the owner does not have a pedigree on the puppy and the registration certificate is sufficient proof of U.K.C. registration.

8. There shall be at least one U.K.C. Licensed Judge and he shall be known as Chairman of Judges, he will look after the interests of the U.K.C. and shall be responsible for the rules and regulations covering the show, the signing of the application blanks for points, he shall have the authority to disqualify any dog or owner for misconduct or a fighting dog, any misrepresentation of dog or owner or for any cause that he deems proper. He shall report the name and address of owner, handler; and the U.K.C. registration number of said dog or dogs and their complete registered name to the offices of United Kennel Club Inc.

9. The Secretary of the organization sponsoring the U.K.C. Licensed Bench Show shall keep two copies of the entries and the winnings, furnishing the U.K.C. Licensed Judge with one copy; signed by both himself and the U.K.C. Judge which the Judge will mail to the offices of the United Kennel Club Inc. along with the application blanks of the winners for points. (The applications must be signed by the Secretary of the Organization and the U.K.C. Licensed Judge.) These application blanks must be mailed with the complete show report, winnings, number of dogs entered; to the U.K.C. for recording, (ten days) will be allowed following the date of Show for them to reach the U.K.C.

10. The Management will forward a check to the U.K.C. for the full amount (based on the number of dogs entered in the entire Bench Show), charging 25 cents per dog; this amount is sent to the U.K.C. to pay for the recording and Bench Show Champion, after 100 points have been won.

This will allow the U.K.C. to immediately record the points and notify the owners to the effect. When a dog has received 100 points his owner will be notified immediately to send in the small registration certificate on his dog, he will be issued a new registration certificate and pedigree showing the number of points, also the "Degree of National Bench Show Champion."

POINTS TO BE ALLOWED FOR U.K.C. LICENSED BENCH SHOWS: BEGINNING APRIL, 1950.

Classes: Male under 1 year old; 1 year and under 2 years; 2 years and over. FIRST IN CLASS (Male) 10 points.

Female under 1 year old; 1 year and under two years; 2 years and over. FIRST IN CLASS (Female) 10 points.

BEST MALE OF BREED 15 points.
BEST FEMALE OF BREED 15 points.
BEST MALE OF SHOW 10 points.
BEST FEMALE OF SHOW 10 points.

Classes with no points allowed:

U.K.C. Champions may compete against each other in this (special) class and no point be allowed. Males and females compete against each other for title: GRAND CHAMPION OF SHOW.

The organization holding the Licensed Bench Show may place whatever prize or prizes they see fit for the winner.

DEFINITION OF CLASSES—Males and females shown separately (except) in Special Class where Champions are shown and no points are allowed.

PUPPY CLASS—shall be dogs under one year of age. The winner of this class will be awarded 10 points.

JUNIOR CLASS—shall be for dogs one year of age and under two. The winner of this class will be awarded 10 points.

ALL AGE CLASS—shall be for dogs two years of age and over. The winner of this class will be awarded 10 points.

BEST OF BREED—shall be composed of the winners of the Puppy, Junior and All Age Classes. The winner of this will be known as BEST OF BREED and shall be awarded 15 points.

BEST OF SHOW—shall be composed of the BEST OF BREED winners and the winner shall be known as BEST OF SHOW and awarded 10 points.

The American Field, with offices at 222 West Adams Street, Chicago, Illinois, 60606 also registers dogs and supervises the running of field trials. All purebred dogs are eligible but most dogs registered with this organization's *Field Dog Stud Book* are hunting breeds, such as Pointers and Setters. American Field issues rules and regulations pertaining to field trials, recognizes Field Trial Champions, and for 94 years has printed a weekly newspaper *The American Field*. This newspaper gives the results of trials and lists the names and numbers of dogs who have won the title of Champion. Any dog registered with the American Kennel Club is eligible for registration with this organization, and most of the purebred dogs registered with American Field are eligible for registration with the American Kennel Club.

CHAPTER 5

GETTING READY FOR THE SHOW

After you have purchased your first dog you will wish to register it. You should have received from the seller either a *Registration Certificate* (needing only to be transferred to your name) or an *Application for Registration of Dog of Registered Litter*, both forms requiring the seller's signature. If you received a *Registration Certificate*, the dog will have already been named and will have a registration number, and all you need do is to sign the transfer of ownership on the back and send it to the American Kennel Club with the proper transfer fee. The amount of the fee is printed on the back of the certificate.

If you received an *Application for Registration of Dog of Registered Litter*, you should check to see that all the information needed is filled in, particularly the litter registration number and after filling in the first and second choice of name of dog, sign it on the back and send it to the American Kennel Club with the registration fee. Bear in mind that once a dog has been registered, his name can never be changed. Of course you may give him any *Call* name you wish, but the registered name remains the same.

Since this book is primarily on showing your dog, and since the American Kennel Club rules applying to registration are available from the A.K.C. for the asking, we will not go any further into the how's and why's of registration except to say that if you have a specific problem, read the rules very carefully and I'm sure you will find your answer there.

We have been leading up to getting your dog entered at a dog show. Included here is a facsimile of an entry blank. Across the top of the blank will appear the name of the club holding the show, the date of the show, and the place where the show will be held. Also

Ch. Puttencove Gay Valentino, Miniature Poodle, ready for the show ring.
Photo by Evelyn Shafer.

on top of the blank appears the entry fee, the person to whom the check should be made payable, where to send the entry with fee, and the closing date and hour before which the entry must be in the hands of the person so noted on the blank.

All the information asked for on the entry blank must be given. You should have no difficulty filling it out if you read the instructions carefully.

Breed. Write in the name of the breed you are going to show.

Variety. If you are going to show a breed divided by varieties you would write the breed, such as Dachshund or Beagle, under Breed, and under Variety you would write smooth, wire, or longhaired for the Dachshund or under 13″ or 13″ to 15″ for the Beagle. If your breed is not divided by varieties, you leave the space blank.

Dog Show Class. Under Dog Show Class you write in the name of one of the regular classes in which you wish to show the dog. If the class is divided, such as Puppy 6 to 9 months and Puppy 9 to 12 months, you write in which one you are entering your dog. If the class is divided by color or weight, you write the color or weight.

Obedience Trial Class. If you are not entering your dog for Obedience, you leave the space blank. If you are entering your dog for Obedience only, you leave Dog Show Class blank and write in under Obedience Trial Class the class in which you wish your dog entered. If your dog is to be entered in both Obedience and the Dog Show, you write in the names of the classes in both spaces.

If Dog is entered for Best of Breed. If your dog is a Champion of Record (or if your records show he has completed his championship) and you wish to show him for Best of Breed, check the box and omit any Dog Show Class.

Additional Classes. This space is filled in only if you wish to show the dog in more than one class. If so, in this space write in the name of the Additional Class. You may enter in two or more of the regular classes or in one regular class and one non-regular class, provided your dog is eligible for entry in those classes.

Name of Actual Owner. The Name of Actual Owner must be written exactly as it appears on the registration certificate, and if there is more than one owner, both names or all names must appear.

Name of Licensed Handler. I assume you are not using the services of a handler so leave this space blank. However, if your dog is being shown by a handler, write in his or her name.

OFFICIAL AMERICAN KENNEL CLUB ENTRY FORM

I ENCLOSE $............. **for entry fees.**

● **IMPORTANT—Read Carefully Instructions on Reverse Side Before Filling Out**

Breed	Variety (if any)	See Instruction #1, reverse side	Sex

Dog Show Class	See Instruction #2, reverse side (Give age, color or weight if class divided)	Obedience Trial Class

If dog is entered for Best of Breed (Variety) Competition —see Instruction #3 reverse side—**CHECK THIS BOX.** ☐	Additional Classes

Name of Actual Owner(s)	See Instruction #4, reverse side
Name of Licensed Handler (if any)	[handler] ●
Full Name of Dog	●
A.K.C. Reg. Number OR Litter Number	(OR I. L. P. Number) ILP ●
OR Foreign Reg. Number	(and country) [ ] ●
Date of Birth	Check Place of Birth *(Do not print in catalog)* ☐ U.S.A. ☐ Canada ☐ Foreign ●
Breeder,	● By
Sire	▬
Dam	●

Owner's Address — Street ....

City.............................. **State** .... **Zip Code**..............

I CERTIFY that I am the actual owner of this dog, or that I am the duly authorized agent of the actual owner whose name I have entered above. In consideration of the acceptance of this entry, I (we) agree to abide by the rules and regulations of The American Kennel Club in effect at the time of this show or obedience trial, and by any additional rules and regulations appearing in the premium list for this show or obedience trial or both, and further agree to be bound by the "Agreement" printed on the reverse side of this entry form. I (we) certify and represent that the dog entered is not a hazard to persons or other dogs. This entry is submitted for acceptance on the foregoing representation and agreement.

SIGNATURE of owner or his agent ●

duly authorized to make this entry..

81

The West Highland White Terrier, English, Canadian and American Champion Cruben Dextor, shown to his Canadian and American championships by his amateur owner Mrs. Henry J. Sayres.

Full Name of Dog. The Full Name of Dog must be written exactly as it is on the registration certificate. If there is an apostrophe in the dog's name, be sure it is in the right place.

A.K.C. Reg. Number or Litter Number. The A.K.C. registration number should be written as it appears on the registration certificate or the litter number as it appears on the litter registration.

I.L.P. Number. This applies only to breeds entered in the Miscellaneous Class and refers to an Indefinite Listing Privilege number.

Foreign Reg. Number. This applies only to imported dogs who have foreign registration numbers and are not yet registered with the American Kennel Club. If your dog is an import, use this number and name the country of the dog's birth.

Date of Birth. Written as it appears on the registration certificate.

Place of Birth. Check the proper box.

Breeder. The name of the breeder is written exactly as it appears on the registration certificate. If the certificate states the breeder was Mr. and Mrs. Elmer Jones, do not write Elmer and Mary Jones.

Sire. Dam. Write the names of sire and dam exactly as they appear on the registration certificate. The only change that may be made in filling out this information is if you are positive that the sire or dam of the dog has completed his or her championship and received official notice of it, you may write the letters "CH." before the name of the sire, if he is the new Champion, or the dam if she is the new Champion.

Information at Bottom of Blank. Print the Owner's Address exactly as it appears on the registration certificate. The person making out the entry blank signs his or her name on the very bottom line. This person need not be the owner but *the owner is responsible* for any mistakes made on the entry blank by his or her agent. Any fines imposed for wrong entry of a dog are payable by the owner regardless of who made out the entry.

There, now, the entry blank is made out. Just be sure it gets to its destination on or before the closing hour.

A beautiful German Shepherd, or Alsatian as this breed is known in England, photographed in a deserted dog show ground there. This particular dog is Ch. Eveleys Ailsa of Brinton. Photo by C.M. Cooke.

Perhaps you are wondering why all this information must be sent in and why it is so important that there be no mistakes. The most important reason is that the American Kennel Club will go by this information in compiling its show records and the show catalogue goes on file in its office for future use. At a show, if I want to know what dog you are showing, I need only look at the number you will be wearing, which corresponds to the number listed in the show catalogue for your dog, to find out all about him. If you are showing a good dog, everyone will want to know who bred him, who his sire is, his dam, and how old he is. Also all the exhibitors and breeders will use the show catalogue for their records. Years after you have stopped showing the dog, fanciers will refer to the catalogue to find out all about him. They want correct information!

The most logical question now is, "Where do I get these entry blanks?" There are only three or four places where entry blanks may be secured: The American Kennel Club office; the show super-intendent's office (or by mail from him when you are on his mailing list); the office of the show-giving club (if it has one); or from a member of the show-giving club who might be trying to get entries for the show. Occasionally a show superintendent will have entry blanks for a show other than one he is going to superintend, but this is unusual. Dog-show superintendents usually have a supply of entry blanks for future shows at their office on the dog-show grounds.

The entry blank is attached to what is called a premium list. The premium list tells you everything about the show: the name of the club giving the show; the officers of the club; the location of the show; the names and addresses of the judges who are officiating in each breed; the prizes offered; the classes; the entry fee; and it also includes entry blanks for that show. The premium list is actually what you would ask for when you want an entry blank for a particular show.

Now you will be asking, "How do you know when or where a show will be held?" In each issue of *Pure Bred DOGS—American Kennel Gazette,* and in almost every other dog magazine, you will find a list of coming shows with the name of the show secretary and the show superintendent, and from them you may secure premium lists with entry blanks attached. At almost every dog show the superintendent can tell you about his future shows and supply you with the premium list. Another way to know when and where the shows are to be held is to be active in the dog game; join a dog club!

Good side view of a champion Pug in show stance owned by Glen McDebitt, Canoga Park, California. Some dogs assume this pose with pride at the slightest command. Photo by Louise Van der Meid.

I would advise everyone interested in dogs to join at least one club. There are the specialty clubs, interested in just your one breed, or the all-breed clubs, interested in all breeds of dogs. You will hear from the other members about the activities going on all about you. Many of these clubs hold sanctioned matches (the practice shows I mentioned earlier) and frequently at these matches announcements are made over a public address system giving you the location and dates of other matches and shows coming up soon in the nearby area. At these matches you will find young stock from good kennels getting a little preliminary training, as well as novice dogs and owners trying out their "sea legs." You will enjoy these matches and get lots of help; the judge will take time to tell you just what to do, and other exhibitors will be glad to give you a few pointers.

Whether you join a specialty club or an all-breed club (if possible, join both), if you have the time to spare offer your services on one of the committees. Ask to be placed on a committee where you think you will be of some help. Some of the committees are:

Publicity. This might involve typing some press releases for newspapers or magazines regarding the club's activities.

Advertising. This might mean that you would solicit advertisements from local merchants and kennels for the show catalogue.

Trophy Committee. Here you might write a few letters soliciting

Ch. Katanga's Cameo Caprice, Italian Greyhound; these sleek, diminutive dogs seldom bark and have found great favor among apartment dwellers. Photo by Evelyn Shafer.

Star de Severac, Bichon Frise, winning Best of Opposite Sex Puppy at the Bichon Frise Club of America Show in 1971. This breed is now recognized by the American Kennel Association.

trophies either for your own particular breed or for the entire show.

Hospitality. If you are a good handshaker and like to meet people, any club would appreciate your help in this direction. Or because many clubs hold an informal buffet supper the night before or after their annual show, you might be asked to prepare and/or donate some food toward the event.

Grounds Committee. Most clubs must "borrow" a location for their show, and after the big event is over, someone must see that these grounds are left in good condition so that the club may "borrow" them again next year. A husky man with a rake is a welcome man the day after a show! Or on this committee you might be asked to help direct traffic on the grounds the day of the show.

Working on any committee will help you to get to know your fellow members and for them to get to know you, and it will also help to acquaint you with the problems of running a show. You will not be a novice in the dog game for long after working on any committee for any club.

Getting back to the premium lists. The best way for you to receive them regularly is to give your name and address to the dog-show superintendents in your section of the country. Tell them you would like your name put on their mailing list. Here is a list of annually licensed dog-show superintendents:

ANNUALLY LICENSED DOG SHOW SUPERINTENDENTS

BEHRENDT, Mrs. Bernice
470–38th Avenue
San Francisco, Calif. 94121

BRADSHAW, Mrs. Jack
727 Venice Blvd.
Los Angeles, Calif. 90015
    Barbara Bradshaw
    Jack Bradshaw III

BURKET, Mrs. Helen Rosemont
20 Sycamore Street
San Francisco, Calif. 94110
    Bruce R. Burket

FOLEY, George F.
2009 Ranstead Street
Philadelphia, Pa. 19103
    Mario Fernandez
    Howard H. Foley
    Thomas J. Gillen
    Joseph H. Spring
    Mrs. Joseph H. Spring

JONES, Roy J.
P.O. Box 307
Garrett, Ind. 46738
    Mrs. Elizabeth F. Jones

MacIVER, Allan P.
P.O. Box 2042
Grand Rapids, Mich. 49501
    Raymond Loupee
    Mrs. Audrey F. MacIver
    Jack Onofrio

ENGELKE, Mrs. C. B.
200 Trimble Lane
Exton, Pa. 19341
    Lewis C. Keller
    Durwood Van Zandt

MARING, Mrs. Helen D.
2650 S.W. Custer Street
Portland, Oregon 97219

MOSS, Edgar A.
P.O. Box 20205
Greensboro, N.C. 27420
    Ralph Cox
    Mrs. Nina R. Crowe
    Tom Crowe
    Walter A. James
    Mrs. Barbara Moss Mulvey

SEDER, Miss Helen
9999 Broadstreet
Detroit, Mich. 48204

    T. N. Bloomberg
    Herbert H. Evans
    Paul A. Ferguson
    Robert G. Foster
    Richard C. Heasley

THOMSEN, Jack
Box 731
Littleton, Colo. 80120
    Mrs. Ann Thomsen
    Mrs. Nancy L. Walden

WEBB, Marion O.
507 South Jackson Street
Aubrun, Ind. 46706
    Mrs. Betty Dennis
    Mrs. Dorothy Webb

MATHEWS, Ace H.
11423 S.E. Alder Street
Portland, Oregon 97216

Ch. Jen-Araby's Huntsman, a Saluki owned, bred and handled by Wayne Jensen, is being coaxed here to assume a show stance. Salukis, like Afghan Hounds and Borzois, always impress people with their graceful elegant appearance. Photo by Louise Van der Meid.

Some superintendents have more than one mailing list: one list would send premium lists to you for shows in the state in which you live; another list for shows in the surrounding states; and still another list for shows held anywhere in the country that the superintendent had a show. Remember, the American Kennel Club does not mail out premium lists. The officers of a show-giving club have only premium lists for their own shows.

When you get your premium list, read it through from beginning to end. The first page will tell you where the show will be held, the date, which superintendent. It may also tell you that there is another show being held the day before or the day after this one. You may want to go to both, as they are usually within comfortable driving distance of each other. The premium list tells you the closing date

Ch. Adam's Rib of Rocky Run, German Shorthaired Pointer, finishing his championship at Lancaster, Pennsylvania. He was one of four champions in a litter. Rib finished his championship in four straight shows and has also placed in five derbies. Robert H. McKowen is his proud owner.

on which your entries must be in the hands of the superintendent or show secretary—this is usually two to three weeks before the show. Through the pages of the premium list you will find the following information: the officers of the club, the names of people on committees, the judges' names and addresses and which breeds they are going to judge, the cash prizes and trophies offered in each breed, the name of the veterinarian in charge, the nearest available hotels and motels.

Under the title of "Notice to Exhibitors" you will find such interesting and necessary information as: the time the show starts, the time the judging begins, the time the dogs should arrive and the time they may leave, and any other information pertaining to this particular show.

Study the classes available in your breed. Aside from the division by height, color, or weight, there are many other changes that may occur. If you have a puppy, there may be more than one puppy class available. Instead of one class for puppies six months to twelve months old there may be two classes: one for puppies six to nine months old and one for puppies nine to twelve months old. Check the trophies offered. If your dog is eligible to compete in any one of the five regular classes, it may be that you would like to enter him in a class where there is a special trophy offered.

When you have checked the premium list thoroughly, make out the entry blank. Print or type the information, as you will want it to be correct when it appears in the show catalogue. Attach your check or money order in the proper amount to the entry blank. Follow the instructions on the top of the entry blank about where it should be mailed. Remember mail moves slower over a weekend—be sure to mail your entry *in plenty of time* to reach the superintendent or secretary before the closing time. Do I seem to be stressing this point? Well, I have good reason. So many entries are returned because they do not get in on time, and the owners are always so disappointed, although it was no one's fault but their own.

Approximately one or two weeks after you mail the entry, or about one week before the show, you will receive an identification card and an admission ticket to the show. The identification card is for your dog, the admission ticket for you. Each dog entered will get an identification card, but the number of admission tickets you will receive varies, and depends on the number of dogs you enter. The number of tickets sent to you, the amount of cash prize money offered, the closing hour of a show are all decisions which are made by the show-giving club.

CHAPTER 6

EARLY TRAINING

In several different places in this book I mention that certain things could have, or should have, been done while you were waiting for your puppy to grow up. Let's take just a little time right now and discuss how to do some of these things.

Let's start with the lead-breaking of your puppy since it is so important to the sound attractive stylish gait of a show dog. Let's assume that when you bought him he had never been on a lead.

There are many methods advocated by dog enthusiasts. Some allow the young puppy to drag a lead for a few days so he won't object to it. (Just be sure he doesn't learn to chew it while he is learning not to object to it.) Some folks attach a light weight to a short lead around the puppy's neck and let him carry it around so that he will learn to hold his head up high. Some use the reward method giving the dog a tidbit if he does the job well and withholding it if he does not. Once the puppy is well lead-broken it does not matter which method was used in the training since the outcome is all we are interested in. After trying many, here is the method I like best.

Start training the puppy just as soon as you get him. If you keep him in a run or pen, every time you take him on a lead you should keep in mind that this will be his training period. However, if the puppy lives in the house with you and, at least in the beginning, has to be taken out on a lead to relieve himself, there should be a difference in the manner in which you and the puppy behave while he is on the lead. Don't try to lead-break him for shows when he has other and more important business on his mind. Allow the puppy to sniff the ground and use a longer lead, giving him ample time to take care of his duties. If he is allowed to roam where he wants to and when he

Ch. Silvermine Jackpot, English Setter, owned and handled by the author, proved to be a handy winner in the ring. This photo shows the show animal's relaxed confidence that is the direct result of intelligent training.

wants to he will scarcely be aware of the fact that he is on a lead and the duties will be taken care of quickly. With that important business out of the way you can then settle down to the training.

Now tighten up on the lead. (Shorten it by crumpling it in one hand as I advise you to do under the subject of helpful hints.) Put the collar as far forward under the dog's jaw as you can. He will resent it —perhaps fight it—some dogs jumping into the air and screaming as though they had been hurt. Wait until he quiets down and then start walking in the direction you want to go and talk to the dog. Call him by name and keep your voice pleasant. Don't drag him but keep the lead taught so he can feel in which direction he is being coaxed to go. As soon as he takes a few steps with you, praise him loudly and keep encouraging him to go along. After he goes along, try releasing the lead a bit and if he keeps going—fine! If not, use short jerks to keep him going. After the puppy goes along a reasonable distance, stop and pat him, praise him to the skies. Then start out again. Repeat this performance several times and until he goes along with you without your having to tug at him. Then praise him some more, reward him

A lovely English Setter puppy receiving some early show training at home.

Start show posing your puppy as early as possible. He will soon learn to stand still, and the training pays off when his show career starts.

with a tidbit if you wish and stop the training on a pleasant note. You should not have to do this too often before your puppy will be lead-broken. While he is a puppy he is so easily led and he is so anxious to please that it pays dividends if you master this early.

If at any time during the training the puppy sits down or lies down and refuses to go along with you, use short tugs on the lead until he is on his feet and in a position where he *can* go along, and then keep tugging. Keep encouraging him, be firm not rough, and you shouldn't have any trouble. If it seems difficult at first, think of how much easier it is to do while he is small—picture yourself lead-breaking a frisky Great Dane puppy and then picture yourself lead-breaking a fully-grown, stubborn Great Dane! Need I say more?

A word of caution: few people buy expensive or perfectly fitting collars for puppies because they outgrow them so quickly. If you are using a collar that does not fit the puppy well, check it frequently during training periods to see that it does not tighten and choke the puppy. The best collar for training is a light weight chain choke collar. Just be sure it slips through the ring correctly and easily. Employing tugs or jerks on this collar will insure that the collar will never be too tight as it will loosen itself as soon as you stop pulling or the puppy stops pulling. If it is well chosen for size the chain choke collar will fit a puppy for a long time and it has the added advantage of being long lived since the puppy cannot chew it.

After your puppy is lead-broken, remember to make a distinction whenever you take him on a lead: slow when he is taking care of himself or when playing; faster, livelier and in the direction of your choosing when practicing for shows.

Another thing your puppy can be trained to do while he is growing up is to stand still for trimming and grooming. The grooming should be done while the puppy is standing in a show pose and this will help in your training him to pose. The main exceptions to grooming while in a show pose are breeds such as the Poodle, Afghan Hound and the Old English Sheepdog; and oddly enough it is these exceptionally heavily coated or long haired breeds who most of all need to behave well for trimming and grooming. Let's take the Poodle first. He should at a very early age, be taught to allow the use of clippers on his feet and face without any fuss. If you do this often enough, perhaps every week or two whether or not he needs it, the puppy will not be afraid of the clippers and eventually it will mean no more to him than the combing or brushing. When brushing the Poodle puppy, lay him on his side and insist he stay in that position until you have finished, then turn him on the other side and again insist he stay until you allow him to get up. Then go over him when he is in a standing position—a show pose position —and insist on his behaving until you are finished. Perhaps then you could take him on a lead and go through his lead work before stopping for the day.

With breeds having relatively small coat problems, the trimming and grooming should be done while the puppy is in a show pose. I recommend that a puppy always be trimmed and groomed while in a show pose on a table or crate top as it is easier for you to work on him and because of the height involved the puppy is more inclined to stand still. Never allow the puppy to determine when the chore is finished—keep him on the table until you have finished for the day and keep him as much as possible in the show pose. You will be glad you spent the time training him to do this when at an important show some day and in a great hurry, your dog stands perfectly still while you give him that final going over before entering the ring. Don't forget to get him used to clipping or filing his toe nails—that's important!

Getting your puppy used to people and strange places is another thing you can do for him while he is growing up. Take him with you as often as you can. After he is lead-broken (so you know he won't embarrass you), take him with you to the market, or the post office or to buy some cigarettes. This is even more important if you live in the country where his own back yard is all he would get to know without your help. Take him in the car with you when you go to the railroad station, airport or bus depot; if possible take him through a revolving door and in an elevator. Then when he runs into these things at a dog show, they won't faze him a bit. If you take your puppy with you in your car often enough while he is still a puppy and continue to do so while he is growing up, you will never have to car-break him or clean him up upon arrival at a show—he will be so used to traveling. Also you will never have to watch him shake and tremble at the sight of a lot of people—he will expect that each and every one is a great friend—it will reflect in his behavior and will benefit him greatly in his show career.

By all means, don't forget the best training grounds of all—the Sanctioned Match. Whether he wins or loses at the Match, the training he gets there will stand him in good stead. When you go to a Match, go through all the motions just as though it were a big and important show, for the experience is good for you too. Here is where your dog will get used to being shown, handled and gaited with a strange dog beside him. I have seen well trained and well behaved puppies go all to pieces at a Match when perhaps for the first time in a long time they see many strange dogs. Remember, your dog will be expected to behave without thoroughly investigating each and every new arrival. Of course, if you have two or more dogs at home your puppy may be fairly used to company but he may expect that he can play with the new acquaintances just as he does with his friend at home and the new dog may not feel like playing or the new dog's owner may not be inclined to allow his youngster to indulge in puppy foolishness at a Match. If you have used the short, quick tugs on the lead when you lead-broke your puppy, resort to them at the

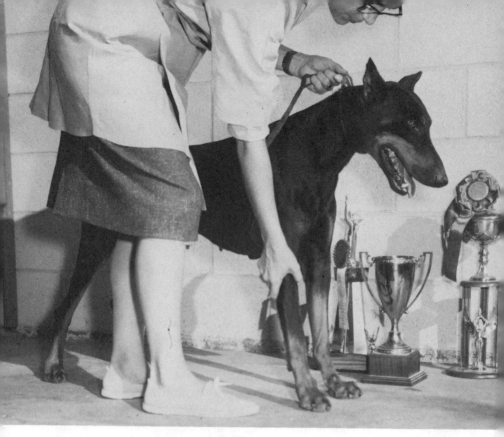

A properly set front leg is important in showing. Even champions like this Doberman need to practice posing prior to an important show. Photo by Louise Van der Meid.

Match when he gets too frisky. The puppy will soon remember that he is on a lead and is expected to perform for you. The word, "No" in a sharp tone of voice used at the same time as the sharp jerk on the lead will also help, particularly if you have used this word whenever he displeased you or you wanted him to stop doing whatever he was doing.

Talking of the use of the word, "No"; whenever you give a command to a puppy (or any dog for that matter) remember that the tone of your voice is almost more important than the word you use. Try this and see if you don't agree with me. Say the word, "No," as you would if a friend asked you if you went to the movies last night and you wanted to give a negative answer. A puppy won't know the difference between that "No" and the word, "Yes," spoken in the same tone of voice. Now think of how you might say the word, "No," if you were in a large and very noisy room and you were being accused

Here is a photograph of Mrs. Claude Decker with one of her Champion English Setters. This is a very good show pose. The picture was taken on a hot day and the dog is panting but it is a good example of a well trained show dog in a show pose. Compare this photograph with the one below.

Here is an English Setter who had not been trained to pose. Notice she is fighting the posing enough to be off balance, the handler has pulled the head too close to him, throwing the dog out in front. (If you look carefully at the leg closest to the camera you will see that the dog appears out in elbow. Compare this front with the lovely front on the well posed dog in the picture above.)

of a wrong-doing. Make it low-pitched, fairly loud, slightly angry, clear and emphatic. This is how you should say, "No," to a puppy when you are training him and then always use the same word and the same tone. He will soon recognize and respect the command.

Let us go on from here, assuming that you have a good dog and have made his entry. As I mentioned before, I hope you have investigated carefully, and that your dog has no disqualifications. In certain breeds the Standard of the Breed (by which all judges are supposed to judge) lists certain faults as complete disqualifications. In all breeds cryptorchidism (male with no testicles) or monorchidism (males with one testicle) is cause for disqualification. In some breeds an undershot mouth (under jaw protruding) will disqualify. In some breeds an excess of the color white will disqualify. As well as having no disqualification, it would be well if your dog had no faults listed as serious in the Standard of the Breed. These are the reasons why I advised you so strongly to know your breed before you buy the dog and before you start to show him.

I also hope that you have had your dog inoculated by a competent veterinarian, not only against distemper and hepatitis, but for any other diseases for which vaccines are available at the time you are ready to show.

One very necessary subject that you must learn something about but which I will not go into in this book is trimming. Since practically every breed is trimmed differently—and of course some require no trimming—it is necessary that you know exactly what is done for your particular breed.

If you have studied your breed as carefully as I have advised you to do, you will begin to see that trimming may help conceal certain faults in your dog, or it may be used to emphasize his good points. Watch other people in your breed trim their dogs. Beg, if you must, permission to visit them when they are trimming. If you own a long-haired but flat-coated dog, such as a Cocker or Setter, who is just a shade wide in the shoulders, you could be of much help with a very judicious use of thinning shears. By removing some hair from underneath without interfering with the top hair, you will improve your dog at this faulty spot. If your breed should be well-chiseled between the eyes, a few hairs plucked out with the fingers or stripping knife may help him a great deal. The better you know your breed, the better you will be able to trim your dog for the show ring.

The Kuvasz is a working dog breed that is more well known in Europe than in the United States. The coat of this Hungarian breed is never trimmed, even for show purposes, except for some hairs on the hocks and between the pads. Photo by Dr. Ernest Kubinsky.

The Poodle is probably the most difficult breed to trim, with the Kerry Blue Terrier running a close second. There are many good books available on trimming; get one for your breed. Learning to trim takes a great deal of time, as does the actual task, but it is well worth the time in the long run.

Be sure that your dog's toenails are kept as short as possible. If you have a few months' waiting period before you are going to start showing your dog, do not neglect his toenails. He will have far better feet, and you will never have to go through the distasteful task of having them cut back.

From the time you purchase your puppy until the time you actually take him to a show, you should have been grooming him. Every breed requires grooming. The smooth-coated dogs will shine if rubbed with a hound glove; the dead hair will be removed from a

101

long-haired breed by brushing. Don't neglect the grooming—it pays dividends. Someday your dog will be up against an equally good dog and at that moment it may be the condition of your dog's coat that will sway the judge in your dog's favor.

Know enough about your breed so that you can tell when your dog is in good weight. Try to show him always in the proper weight. You don't want him fat, but you certainly don't want him thin or out of condition. When I speak of condition I do not mean weight only—I refer more to health. A healthy dog has a clear eye, he is alert, and his coat will usually reflect this state of good health. Many a good dog has been turned down in the ring for lack of condition. A dull, dead-appearing coat, or dog a who is "dead on his feet," will not be rated high in the judge's eye.

Getting away from your dog for a moment, let's talk about you— your appearance, your atttude, your general behavior at a show. Your clothes are very important. Remember the saying, "Clothes make the man"? It's something to think about. There is nothing that is going to happen to your very good suit at a dog show that would not happen to it anywhere else. Too many men and women save their old clothes to wear to the shows, and when they are in the ring they look as though they didn't care. Also, if you wear something that is not suitable, you, instead of your dog, will catch the passing eye. Remember you are not at a dog show to show yourself but to show your dog. This is a little more important for women than for men. Men should keep themselves neat, freshly shaven, their shoes shined, trousers pressed, dust or chalk or dog hairs whisked off. And please keep that shirt tucked in. Wearing a tie clasp will keep your tie straight, from flapping in the wind, and also from falling across your dog's head. It is considered better taste to go into the ring without a hat.

To the ladies I have a great deal more to say. Bright colors are certainly permissible, but garish ones detract from your dog. I have found that the judge gets a better picture of your dog if there is a contrast. I remember watching the judging of an all-white dog against an all-white dress—it was very hard to tell which was the dog and which was the dress. Ladies, please wear a neckline in which, shall I say, you will be comfortable. Remember there are times when you must bend over, kneel, stoop, and run. With the running in mind, wear the proper underwear. A well-fitted bra and a sport girdle will

Take your puppy with you as often as possible when he is growing up. This charming young English Cocker Spaniel has gone visiting with her owner on a Sunday afternoon. She is finding out no harm is coming to her from strange places and people.

The two photographs are of the same novice Beagle. The second photograph was taken after just a patient bit of re-posing by the novice handler. The judge cannot help but be more impressed with an animal if he sees her for the first time looking as she does in the second picture instead of the way she looks in the first picture. Frequent handling and show-posing your dog at home before the show career starts will give you and your dog more confidence when the performance is repeated at shows.

not be uncomfortable and you will look a lot better and save yourself the embarrassment of being discussed in all four corners of the show grounds. Wear a skirt that is full enough to be graceful when you are bending or kneeling, but remember that at outdoor shows too full a skirt can be a nuisance, for the wind whips it and blows it, sometimes right over your head. Too tight a skirt, on the other hand, will keep you from gaiting your dog properly. It goes without saying that you should wear the proper heels. I don't mean that "flats" are necessary, but certainly no one can gracefully gait even a medium-sized dog in wobbly high heels. A few words to the wise may be sufficient: check the elastic in your underwear! Check the hooks and eyes and straps! It is very embarrassing in the ring to break both straps on a slip and have it fall to your ankles. I have actually seen this happen. Slacks on women are rarely as becoming as a dress, and you do want to look your best. Above all, don't look sloppy; have yourself as well groomed as your dog.

Regarding your attitude. Don't walk into the show with a chip on your shoulder. Don't have the feeling that your dog is the best and everyone there must realize it, but please, don't go to the other extreme and feel that your dog doesn't have a chance. This latter attitude frequently communicates itself to your dog and to other people. Don't talk in a voice so loud that you can be heard all over the place. Avoid bumping into other people or crowding their dogs in the aisles or in the ring. Avoid placing your belongings on the bench provided for another dog. In other words, be considerate and gentlemanly.

CHAPTER 7

EQUIPMENT

Before you start for your first show there are certain pieces of equipment you will need. One is a strong collar that fits your dog well; either round leather, flat leather, or a chain. Another item you will need, if the show is benched, is a bench chain. A bench chain is just what its name implies—used to chain a dog to the bench, snapping onto the ring in the collar and to the ring provided for that purpose on the bench. When fastening the dog to the bench, be sure to leave enough chain so that the dog can lie down but not so much as to allow him to jump off the bench, as he could possibly hang himself that way.

You will also need a show lead. A show lead is usually much finer than the leads used for walking a dog. Before purchasing a show lead, find out what type is used by the successful exhibitors in your breed. In some breeds the dogs are exhibited on the same chain collar used for benching with a fine leather snap-on lead attached to it. In some breeds the exhibitors prefer leather one-piece leads. I say leather, but this type one-piece show lead is made up in whalehide, lacing, nylon belting, and many other materials. In the toy breeds some exhibitors use a nylon string, which is no heavier than the lead of a pencil. Terriers are almost always shown on a leather collar and lead.

You will need a sponge, and if you have a liking for the synthetic ones, they will do very nicely. You will want to take along a towel—an old one will do. Your dog will have been bathed before being brought to the show, if he is of a breed that requires bathing, but if he becomes carsick and drools over himself, or if he walks through a puddle and then through dust or dirt, the sponge and towel will help you clean him before taking him into the ring.

If you are sure that you have done every necessary bit of trimming

This Basenji, Ch. Circus Boy of the Bambuti, was Best of Breed at Lubbock, Texas. This red and white dog was the progeny of the English Ch. Fleet of the Congo. Photo by Alexander.

at home perhaps it will not be necessary to carry trimming tools with you. However, a great many people find it advisable to carry with them at least a few trimming tools for those last-minute repairs. A pair of scissors, perhaps a small stripping knife, and any other one or two tools for trimming in your breed may come in handy. A comb and brush are necessities, and will be very welcome just before you go into the ring.

Talking of equipment leads me quite naturally to a discussion of crates. A tack crate, with one or two drawers, would have all these tools stored in the drawers ready to go at a moment's notice. It is not at all necessary for you to take your dog to a show in a crate or to have a tack crate; the majority of dog-show goers do not use crates. If your dog rides well in the back seat of your car or even on the front seat next to you, and you enjoy having him there and wish to take him to the shows that way, you will find at least nine tenths of the exhibitors doing it the same way.

If, however, you feel you would like to carry your dog to the shows in a crate, or if you haven't yet made up your mind, I would like to point out these advantages. En route, if you have to jam on your

Here is the author giving her young English Setter a last minute going over before entering the show ring. They are under a tent and the dog is standing on top of a crate in the space provided for crates at an outdoor show.

A pair of good carriers with a couple of Dobermans already enclosed. Photo by Louise Van der Meid.

brakes suddenly, the dog will not tumble from the seat to the floor and perhaps hurt himself enough to be limping when he goes into the ring. Instead, he will scarcely be aware of the sudden stop. If your dog is riding in a crate, he will not be looking out of the window and getting himself all excited at every dog or cat he sees; he will be asleep and resting. If you want to go out for dinner and it is necessary to leave your dog in the car or in a hotel room, you will find that he will soon become so accustomed to the crate that he will be more than happy while you're away and you won't have to worry that he may become bored or angry and start to chew on the upholstery—an expensive pastime.

Suppose you are staying overnight at a friend's home where there is another dog and you can't very well bring your dog into the house. It may be too cold or too hot to leave him locked in the automobile. He can be kept in his crate and the crate placed in the garage, the basement, or even in your bedroom, and you will rest assured that he will annoy no one and will get his proper rest.

The greatest advantage in using a crate is that it gives you an ideal surface on which to clean your dog at the show, and when the dog is on the bench the empty crate is an excellent place in which to store your belongings. At an unbenched show it is ideal and worth its weight in gold.

If you have decided to use a crate and have to purchase one, here are a few things to look for. First of all, be sure the crate is a good one. It is never wise to economize when buying a crate. If you decide to build one yourself, be sure first to examine a good crate and copy it faithfully. Without exception everyone I know who has built a crate has had to rebuild it after using it only once or twice. No one ever makes his first crate strong enough to "take the gaff." Or if he does, it is so heavy that two strong men can hardly lift it, and you soon find the proud owner trying to lighten the crate by removing as much of it as possible.

A good crate is well ventilated with holes or openings close to the top in order to let out the heat. I believe the wooden crates are superior to the aluminum ones for show purposes. The sides and top of a wooden crate can be of plywood for lightness, but the floor and the door should be of hardwood for lasting qualities. If it is a

At some shows exhibitors can use private exercise pens such as the one shown. These have proven to be comfortable as well as useful, but it is wise to check the premium list beforehand to see if the superintendent will allow their use at his or her shows.

wooden crate, there should be a great many ventilation holes, but not so large that the dog can get his teeth in and start to chew. It is preferable to have the door lined with metal; one of the best types is a piece of stamped-out sheet metal, which is very strong and provides good ventilation. If you get a crate with a door with vertical bars, be sure they are close enough together so that the dog cannot chew in between them or get his teeth around the bars. Be sure the fastener for the door is a good one—it has been found that window locks make good fasteners—and it is wise to have a hasp on the door as well. If the crate is a well-made one, all of these things will be incorporated.

The wooden crate may be painted or, preferably, varnished with a good grade of spar varnish. Remember the crate should be washed out after every trip whether or not it has been soiled.

The first few times a dog rides to a show in a crate it is wise to line the floor of the crate with newspapers and then tear some newspapers in strips on top of the lining. If the dog gets carsick you can empty all the papers at one time. The torn strips will help keep the dog clean until you get to your destination. Because of their small size they tend to cover over any moisture or soil. Later on you will probably line the floor of the crate with an old Turkish towel. Newspaper has the one disadvantage of leaving smudges on a light-colored dog.

At some of the shows you will find plenty of assistance in getting your crate out of your car and into the crate space provided. At smaller shows you may have to take care of this yourself. Be sure to tip the boys who help you load and unload your crate, as they are very rarely paid to do this by the club. If they *are* paid by the club and are told not to take any tips, they will so advise you.

At an outdoor show, when placing your crate in the space provided, be sure it is on level ground. The crate that tips is not easy to work on and the dog is uncomfortable in one that jiggles around. Upon your arrival, notice the direction in which the sun is traveling and don't place your crate where the afternoon sun will shine directly on it. At indoor shows watch for drafts from doors which must be opened, and watch out for radiators. Give yourself enough room so that you can work on your dog on the crate top without being crowded, and consider your neighbor; don't crowd him. On the other hand, don't be selfish and take more room than you actually need. This crate space is usually very crowded.

If you do not use a crate, you will have none of these problems to think about. At a benched show just make your bench your headquarters. At an unbenched show, however, let me caution you about leaving your dog in the parked car. While you may park the car in the shade of a large tree upon your arrival, the sun moves, and very shortly the car may be sitting out in the broiling sun. It gets unbearably hot in a closed car, and occasionally a fine animal loses his life due to the carelessness and thoughtlessness of his owner. If the dog does not die of suffocation, he may have a heat stroke. If it is a hot day, take the dog with you and try to keep him in the shade.

Perhaps you think I am dwelling too much on the subject of keeping the dog as cool as possible. However, letting a dog get overheated is one of the big mistakes the novice exhibitor makes at shows. He is never aware of it until it has been pointed out to him, and then it may be too late. I have seen a novice exhibitor stand at the ringside for an hour waiting to go into the ring, and in his effort to keep the dog clean and dry he won't allow the animal to curl up under a chair or in his own shadow, and before you know it the dog's tongue is hanging out a mile. He is panting and getting very restless, and by the time he goes into the ring, the poor dog "has had it." Notice the old-timers and the professionals in this respect. Unless it is a cool day or at an indoor show, you will never see them standing in the hot sun with a dog about to go into the ring. Just remember that in no breed is the expression of the dog enhanced when he is panting.

Now let's get back to the big day. You are ready to go to your first show. Let us assume you have chosen one fairly close to home and will be starting out early the morning of the show. You will have given the dog a bath either the day before or, with some breeds, a few days before the show. Many exhibitors believe a very recent bath takes the natural oils and sheen out of the coat and makes it appear dull. This is particularly true of black dogs. Of course a white dog will have to be bathed just before a show in order to have him really clean. Remember you may not have the best dog in the show, but you can always have the cleanest! Nothing discourages a judge more in his examination of a dog than to have to touch or smell a dirty dog. Incidentally, if you are showing a flat-coated dog, pin a large towel around him after his bath and notice how it helps to lay the coat.

The night before the show you should get together all of the things you are taking with you. While you are still a novice it won't hurt to make out a written list and check it before you leave. If the show is an outdoor one, regardless of weather reports or how the morning looks to you, take along a raincoat and rubbers or boots. The show goes on, you know, no matter what the weather. Even though the judging will be under a tent, you will have to go from either the benching tent or your car to the judging tent, and you may have to do it during a cloudburst. If your dog is too big to pick up and carry under your raincoat, it would help if you took along something to throw over him on his way to the judging ring.

Here are the things to take along which I consider necessities: the identification card and ticket (need I remind you?); a water pan (although you can always use the cardboard ones supplied by feed companies at most shows, I prefer to take my own); a sponge and towel (I hope you won't need them!); a bench collar and bench chain or wire bench crate; a show lead; a comb and brush. If you use a tack crate (a crate with drawers), these very useful and necessary articles may be permanently stored in the drawers and will always be ready to go. If you do not use a tack crate, you will probably "latch on" to an old brief case or small overnight bag which will accompany you to shows, and these things can be stored in it and will always be ready to go.

Here are some things you can also take along if you wish: trimming tools (if you aren't sure you have completed the trimming task right down to the last whisker); a bucket (if your water pan is large enough perhaps you will use that, but if your breed is a large one, which may need a lot of cleaning up, the bucket will come in handy); a first-aid kit (you never know what may happen); a thermos of water or coffee (some exhibitors always carry with them their dog's drinking water, for he becomes less upset internally when drinking the water to which he has become accustomed); lunch (a few homemade sandwiches are very welcome); and a change of shoes for your weary feet. Everything in this list may be prepared the night before and placed with the necessities except the lunch, which you will want to store in the refrigerator until morning. (Ten to one you'll run off and forget it!)

In the morning, exercise your dog carefully. If you have a pen for him, fine; otherwise don't turn him loose; he may wade through a puddle, or, worse, he may chase a passing cat and make you late for your arrival. A very good friend of mine whose dog was extremely well trained had this happen to him: the dog decided to take off one morning before a show and they didn't catch up with him until it was too late to go to the show at all. Watch to see if your dog evacuates; if he doesn't, you will want to give him the opportunity to do so immediately upon arriving at the show. If not then, try again before he goes into the ring. Your dog will show better for you if this act has been performed. However, it happens that no matter how many opportunities you may give a dog to evacuate before he goes into the ring he will decide that right now, in the ring, is the time. If it happens to you, don't die of embarrassment. Remember it has happened before. Just try, if possible without interrupting the dog, to maneuver him to the side or end of the ring and stay there until he has finished. When he has finished, go on with whatever you were doing. If the judge has had to wait for you, you might say very quietly to him, "I'm sorry." That will be sufficient. Usually the judge, or a steward, or the ring runner, will send word to the proper person that the ring needs cleaning. If the cleaning up has not been taken care of after a reasonable period of time, you might advise the show superintendent's office and they will see that it is done.

Back we go again. You are ready to leave for the show. You and your dog and your equipment are in the car. You should perhaps place a cover on the upholstery and some newspapers on the floor of the car if your dog has not been car broken. Don't feed him or give him any water in the morning before the trip if he isn't car broken. Incidentally, car breaking is something you can do long before you start to show a dog. Start when he is a puppy, with short rides daily. He will soon love it, and you will have no further trouble. Some dogs are wonderful riders and never have to be car-broken; others never quite get used to riding. You are lucky if your dog is a natural rider.

I think this might be a good time for me to mention a few helpful hints about staying overnight with your dog when you take him to a show. Years ago it was not much of a problem, as almost all hotels allowed you to bring your dog into your room. However, so many people abused the privilege that the hotels have had to put an end to the practice. There are still some hotels and some motels which will allow the dogs in the rooms, and usually the show-giving club prints the names of these establishments nearest the show grounds in the premium list. You can also obtain a booklet listing the names of hotels and motor courts which offer accommodations for guests accompanied by their dogs by writing to Gaines Dog Research Center, 250 Park Avenue, New York, New York, 10017. Enclose 25 cents and ask for the directory entitled *Touring with Towser*. Listings are given for the entire country, and a preface gives tips on caring for your dog while traveling. Some establishments which accept dogs conditionally require that you sign a form stating that you will be responsible for any damage your dog may do.

No matter how well housebroken your dog is, or how accustomed he may be to staying in your house alone, when he gets in a strange place and is left completely alone he worries and frets and usually gets into trouble of some sort. He may soil the rug, tear the bedspread, chew on the furniture, or just plain bark and howl. I don't know which annoys the management of a hotel the most, but since you are responsible for damages, I guess the barking and howling. The folks in the room next to yours will certainly complain. Now I know you cannot take the dog into a dining room with you and you probably will be hungry after the trip; but see if you can't arrange to leave the dog in your car, particularly if he is accustomed to it and enjoys sleeping in it, at least until you finish eating and until you are ready to go to your room for the night. When you are with him he will probably settle down and be the angel he is at home and you will save yourself a lot of trouble and money. Besides, you owe it to other exhibitors and dog lovers who do manage to keep their dogs out of mischief, to see to it that the few hotels and motels who now allow you this privilege of having your dog with you, continue to do so. If your dog is accustomed to going out early in the morning, leave a call and get up at the same time and take him out. You owe him that much.

CHAPTER 8

ARRIVING AT THE SHOW

You should know before you leave home exactly where the show grounds are located. Just because a club held its show on certain grounds one year is no guarantee it will do so the following year. Check and be sure before you start out. Frequently a club holds a show in a town other than the one appearing in the club's name. For instance, the Ashtabula Kennel Club (Ohio) held its show on the fairgrounds in Jefferson, Ohio, and the Baltimore County Kennel Club its show at the state fairgrounds in Timonium, Maryland. Think of the driving time wasted if you drive into the city of Ashtabula instead of going directly to Jefferson, and although the map shows Timonium only about four miles from the city of Baltimore you will waste an awful lot of time if you first drive into Baltimore and then out to Timonium. Usually the show-giving club will put up arrows directing you to the show grounds, but if the club is lax, you are on your own to find it. Allow yourself plenty of time. Frequently the show grounds or show building will have but one entrance, where the slow task of taking tickets and selling admissions will cause the line of arriving exhibitors to have to wait much longer than they had anticipated in order to gain their entrance. I have seen a late arrival park the car on the side of the road, grab the dog, practically knock down the ticket taker when presenting the ticket, and run into the show ring. This sort of entrance will not help your composure, or your dog's, in the ring.

You should check the judging program before leaving home to find out at exactly what time your breed is due to be judged. The judging may be delayed, true, and as a result your breed may be judged later than the program said, but—and here is a good thing to know—it may never be judged earlier than stated on the program.

Ch. Solidarity Tim, Irish Terrier, is a worthy example of good breeding. He was sired by Ch. Slemish Solidarity. Rudolf Jensen was his proud owner and breeder.

If you have your husband or wife or an understanding friend with you this first time, they can be of great help, particularly if your dog is to be judged early. There is quite a lot to be done at this point: park the car way off in that far lot, watch the dog, produce your admission tickets, watch out for that passing dog, hold on to your brief case or kit containing your possessions, watch the dog, et cetera. Do watch your little bag, for bags have been known to disappear. Perhaps your friend would hold it for you and also take care of the tickets. Then you could devote all your time to the dog. If you want a show catalogue, and if catalogues are sold at the entrance, now would be a good time for your friend to buy one for you.

If it is a benched show, you must find your bench. This will be a partitioned-off stall and on it will be marked your breed and the identification number of your dog. This number corresponds to the number on your identification card which was mailed to you. Now the collar and bench chain. (Except toy breeds; these are usually placed in wire cages.) See that the collar fits well, making sure that the dog cannot slip his head out of it. Don't use a leather lead or a piece of cord to tie your dog to the bench, as a dog can chew either of these in two before you turn around. Use a bench chain. There will be rings placed in strategic points along the chain with snaps at either end. There should be a ring on the dog's collar. Snap one end of the chain to the ring on the collar and put the other end of the chain through the ring on the bench and then fasten the end to the ring on the chain which best fits your dog. I have mentioned this before, but it is important; do not make the chain so short that the dog cannot lie down but—and almost more important—not so long that he can get his head around and into the next stall. He might get bitten by the neighboring dog who doesn't particularly want company. Also a long chain may give your dog the idea that he isn't fastened and if he jumps off the bench when you are not around he is liable to hang himself.

Opposite:
It is quite obvious in this portrait that this Miniature Schnauzer was a consistent champion. Photo by A. Barry, Three Lions, Inc.

Place your packages, toolbox, lunch, or whatever you have with you *under* your dog's bench. If you put it down on the bench next to yours, as soon as the dog arrives who belongs there you will only have to move it, and it might be at a more inconvenient time.

Now take stock of the situation. If you have allowed yourself time, you will not have to rush right into the ring. If you think the dog has to urinate or evacuate, take him to the exercise pen provided for the purpose. There may be two, one for dogs and one for bitches, and so marked; or there may be several pens with no markings. In the latter case, choose any one. On the way to the exercise pen don't let your dog lift his leg on someone's tool kit or crate, and if you have to walk through crowded aisles, watch that your dog does not get stepped on or panicky at the barking of the dogs on the benches. When you get to the exercise pen, give your dog time to take care of himself but don't overstay. Be sure to fasten the latch on the gate securely. Now back to the bench.

If it is a hot day and you think your dog is thirsty, offer him a drink of water; a small one if he is due to be judged soon, all he wants, within reason, if he has a long wait before being judged. Too much water before the judging may make the dog look "pot-bellied." Do not leave the water pan on the bench with your dog. He may upset it and get himself thoroughly soaked as well as the dogs around him, and also your packages under his bench.

Did your dog get dirty on the way? Did he drool over himself, or pick up a grease spot from the car? Look him over now. Did he step in anything in the exercise pen that may be stuck between his pads? If he needs cleaning up, get right to it. A sponge and some soapy water, or just the end of the towel dipped in water, will do the job, depending on how badly soiled he is. Now do that last-minute trimming and grooming. Even though he was thoroughly trimmed, you may see just a little something which could be improved. It is amazing how fast the whiskers grow back in!

When you have the dog cleaned up and you are sure he is ready for the ring—well groomed and with last-minute trimming done—put him back on the bench, properly fastened, and prepare to leave him. If it is his first experience, he will watch you and be reluctant to have you leave him alone in this new atmosphere. But it is best for him if he is going to be a show dog to learn how to stay on a bench quietly. An old trouper will curl up and go right off to sleep. Of course you always run into an occasional "ham," the dog who loves to have an audience and who makes eyes at every passer-by, pawing at them and trying to "shake hands" with them. If he likes attention, it won't bother him just so his admirers do not wear him out. If it is your first show, or his first show, you might feel better if you stay with him or, better still, near him. But remember, there will be times when you will have to leave him, and the sooner you see to it that he knows how to relax on a bench the better off you both will be. One or two barks from the dog will not bother him just so he does not exhaust himself barking. Nor should you allow him to work himself

At benched shows dogs must be in their designated stalls most of the time during the hours of the show. The sooner a dog learns to be comfortable on the bench the better off he will be as a show animal. In the great majority of cases a dog will quickly acclimate himself to rest or sleep while on the bench and in this way appear more refreshed when in the ring.

into a frenzy lunging against the collar. Check to see he does not get himself tangled in the bench chain. Once again, try to keep him from panting, so his expression is not spoiled. If and when he quiets down and you decide to go and leave him, remind your family that he might become upset if they awaken him, and then leave him again. Once you have gone off, only go to him if it is necessary. Check on him often, of course, but try to do so from where he will not see you or pick up your scent. When your show dog learns to relax on the bench, one of your big battles has been won.

If you haven't already discovered its location, now is the time to find the ring where your dog will be shown. Some shows will have only a few rings, and finding yours will not be difficult. Some shows have a great many rings, and they are not always laid out in numerical order.

If you did not buy a catalogue, and you want one, now is the time to get one. Often the show-giving club runs out of catalogues toward the end of the day, and you may have to do without one if you do not get it early.

It might also be a good idea at this point to check your entry in the catalogue. Be sure the dog is listed there correctly and in the class in which you intended to enter him. If there is any mistake, now is the time to check it with the show superintendent. If you have entered him incorrectly, the chances are that the dog cannot be shown. However, if it is a matter of wrong sex or if the mistake was in the printing of the catalogue, the superintendent will correct the entry in the judge's book, and you may then show in the proper class.

While you are looking in the catalogue you will find out how many dogs are in your class, how many classes before yours, and also, *who* will be in the ring with you. When you remember that at every show the classes are always judged in the same order: Puppy, Novice, Bred by Exhibitor, American Bred, Open, first in dogs and then in bitches, you will have some idea of when you will be called. However, you must realize that there may be classes with no entries at all, and therefore a shorter waiting period before your class is called. Very often a novice exhibitor will be found sitting right at the ringside with his dog while the loudspeaker is blaring his number or while the ring runner is searching the benches, the exercise pen, and the crate section trying to locate him. If you know *who* is to be in the ring with you, it may help you know your class is being called when you recognize the person entering the ring. Don't depend on the steward, the ring runner, or the loudspeaker, for if they do not function properly, your dog will be marked absent after a suitable waiting period.

If your dog is resting quietly and you have the time you might like to watch some of the judging. It would be a good idea, if possible, for you to watch the judge who is going to judge your dog later on. From watching him you will pick up a few pointers about his ring technique, such as: where he poses the dogs, at one end of the ring or at the side; if he gaits the dogs down the center of the ring or across the ring; whether he looks at all the dogs in the class and then gaits all the dogs in the class, or whether he looks at one and gaits him and then goes on to the next dog and then gaits him; or whether he has each dog brought up to him for examination. As a novice exhibitor you will feel more at ease in the ring when you have some idea of what to expect from the judge.

Before you actually go into the ring, here are a few more pointers. There are lots of rules around dog shows and, like all rules, they should be obeyed. The benching rule is an important one. Your dog is supposed to be on his bench at all times except when he is being judged, being exercised, or being prepared for the judging. The rule allows a dog to be off his bench one hour before he is due to go into the ring, and the people who use crates for their dogs may take the dog off the bench and after he is "done up" for the ring they may put him in the crate until the judging actually takes place.

If I did not stress it before, let me do so now. Use extreme care in walking your dog back and forth from the ring, the bench, and the exercise pen. Another dog may not have the best disposition in the world and might snap at your dog as he passes. He could be hurt, but even if he were not, it might frighten your dog. Keep an eye on him. Make sure that your dog is not guilty of snapping at another dog. Keep an eye out for lit cigarettes—if your dog steps on one he will have a very sore foot when he goes into the ring. Once you have had a dog go lame from a cigarette burn you will come to have a strong dislike for the person who does not stomp out his discarded cigarette. Don't be guilty of this offense yourself.

Your class is about to be called. Take the dog out of his crate, or off his bench, and put the show lead on him. Do not leave your bench chain and collar on the bench, as a great many chains and

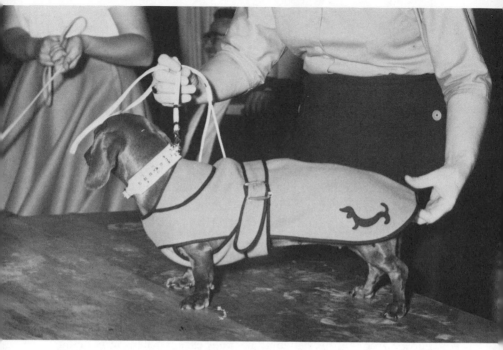

Many commercial firms use dog shows for advertising and selling their products. Shown is a fashion show featuring a coat designed for Dachshunds. Photo by Louise Van der Meid.

collars have disappeared when left there without the dog. Run the comb through his coat, or wipe him off with a towel, or give him a last-minute brushing. Take your dog to the entrance to the ring. You should be calm and poised at this point, and while I know you will not be, try to give the outward appearance of being so. If you are nervous or upset, your dog will sense it and perhaps reflect it.

If it has not already been done while you were waiting at the ringside, as you come into the ring the steward or ring runner will give you an arm band on which will be printed your dog's identification number. Check to be sure it is the correct number. The person giving it to you will probably assist you in putting it on. Arm bands are usually worn on the left arm. Some arm bands come equipped with rubber bands and they stay in place and fit almost everyone in any type of clothing. If you're lucky enough to be using this type, you will have no trouble. However, with other types of arm bands, if a woman is handling the dog and is wearing a short-sleeved dress,

In this photograph the arm band is held in place by the fold of material in the sweater. This will apply to any heavy material such as in men's or women's suit jackets. This is the best way to wear an arm band if you are sure it will stay in place.

Here is another good method of attaching or holding your arm band in place. The safety pin will definitely hold the arm band but it is a bit difficult to close the pin with one hand. Be sure to have someone help you attach it.

the arm band will slide down around her wrist and will be most uncomfortable. Be prepared to fasten the arm band securely in some fashion. Some people fold over the excess and fasten it with two paper clips; others use a rubber band. With a very lightweight fabric some women use a safety pin to pin the band to the sleeve; still others will place the arm band in the belt of their dress but usually on the left side. A man will not have this problem, as usually the material in the sleeve of his jacket is heavy enough to keep the arm band in place.

From looking in the catalogue you know how many dogs are entered in your class. If you are alone in the class, you walk right into the ring and wait for the judge's instructions. If you know there are to be, let us say, four dogs in your class, glance around the ring. If there are already three there, you know they have been waiting for you, and as soon as you enter the ring the judge will at once ask

If the fabric of the dress is so fine that a safety pin may damage it or if the costume is sleeveless, try bending over the excess arm band and encircle with a strong rubber band as shown here.

Here the belt of the dress or skirt is run through the arm band. This is a good method as the arm band is seldom in the way and almost always visible.

An example of the wrong way to wear an arm band as it can easily be knocked out of the pocket when running or posing the dog.

Another example of the wrong way to wear an arm band as it will greatly interfere with the proper handling of the dog. It will fall over the hand and slide down the lead— or it may hit the dog as the handler attempts to pose the dog.

With the tail up, the head high, this Sealyham seems to enjoy posing for a show. Photo by Orlando, Three Lions, Inc.

everyone in the class to go around the ring. I will describe this procedure later. When you come up to the ring for a class in which there are four dogs entered, if there are only two dogs in the ring, go into the ring and then wait for the arrival of one more dog. When he arrives, be prepared for the judge's instructions. If you hear that the fourth dog is being marked absent, the class will proceed as soon as the judge has marked the absentee in his book.

CHAPTER 9

THE BIG MOMENT — JUDGING IN THE RING

Do not talk to the judge, or attempt to talk to him, while you are waiting for the class to begin. Even if you have met the judge socially this is no time for a cozy chat. Don't strike up a conversation with the steward or with anyone sitting on the ringside—be ready to start.

While waiting in the ring for the class to begin it is a good idea not to let your dog get in a sloppy position. Frequently a judge's eye will roam over the waiting entries, and it is to your dog's advantage if he looks well at this moment. However, it is not necessary that your dog be in a show pose, unless the judge is actually making an attempt to judge the dogs while he is waiting.

This is important! I don't care which of the breeds you may be showing, never hold your show lead with two hands! The lead should always be held completely in the left hand, either looped, crumpled up, or folded. There is nothing in showing a dog that points out inexperience so quickly and looks less graceful in the ring than a lead stretched between the left hand and the right hand in front of the handler's body. It looks as though the handler expected the dog to run away and he was prepared to "hold on with both hands"—a bad impression to give. Actually, the right hand is not doing a thing except holding on to the end of the lead, and with the lead in this poor grasp the handler's arms are in an ungraceful position; he does not have complete freedom of wrist movement without which he cannot as easily control the direction in which the dog is traveling nor the proper gait of the dog.

The correct way is very simple; try it. Put the lead on your dog. Hold your left arm at right angle to your body and ball up in your

Ch. Pixietown Serenade of Hadleigh, a Pomeranian, was judged Best Toy at the Westminster Kennel Club Show in 1962. Photo by Evelyn Schafer.

In this photograph the lead is held incorrectly. Note both hands are used to hold the lead, one actually doing nothing. Compare with the correct hold as shown in the next photograph.

Here the lead is held in one hand leaving the other free if it is needed. This is the correct way to hold a lead. See next photograph.

The extra or unneeded portion of the lead is crumpled inside the hand (one fold may be wrapped around the hand or around one finger). Most of the pressure or pull should be on the fatty side of the hand near the third knuckle of the small finger.

left hand all the excess lead necessary to make the lead taut between the dog and your hand. I cannot tell you how much lead will be exposed, as it will depend on the height of your breed. It will be longer for a small dog, shorter for a tall dog. For the rest of this demonstration I will assume that your dog has been properly lead-broken, which certainly he should have been long, long before you take him to his first show. Now you gait your dog. First, let us suppose he is going along next to you at the proper speed, in the proper direction, and with the proper head carriage, and that the lead is crumpled up in your left hand as directed. To relax the tension on the lead you need only to lower the left arm and immediately your dog is gaiting "on a loose lead," a request you will hear frequently in the show ring. More and more judges insist on seeing the dogs "gait on a loose lead, please."

Now suppose your dog drops his lead or lags behind. All that is needed are a few short, quick tugs on the lead, all done with the left arm, and he will soon go along at the proper speed or raise his head. If the dog veers to the left, a quick pull will bring him back in line. If he gets too close to you, an outward jerk on the lead will set him straight. I mentioned short, quick tugs on the lead. Never use a pulling motion, always the short, quick, jerking motion. The dog will respond much more readily.

Now what to do with that useless right arm. Just forget it entirely. If you do not think about it, your arm will automatically assume a graceful position as you run or walk with the dog. It will also be free to give the dog a little pat on the shoulder as you make a turn at the end of the ring should he require it.

Back once again to the crumpled-up lead in the left hand. Should you feel it desirable that you travel a slightly greater distance from your dog after you have started to gait him, all you need to do is relax the fingers of the left hand and the lead will pull itself out a little bit at a time. To stop its pulling-out action, you just tighten your grip on the lead. When you are gaiting the dog, if he is too far from you and you want to shorten the lead without changing the dog's gait, you simply take up a hitch or two by winding the lead around the fingers or by a few simple twists of the wrist. It is just that simple and quick.

This is a photograph of the late Charles Palmer, when he was a top professional handler, showing his dog in actual competition. Notice the lead held completely in one hand. The dog is going along in a business-like manner but still happy (you can see the wagging tail!). If the dog should drop his head, the handler need only raise his hand a bit to remind the dog to get his head up. When the dog goes along with his head held up, the handler lowers his hand and the dog is automatically "on a loose lead."

This proper holding of the lead is one of the easiest things to learn, but until it is pointed out to you, you may not realize that the best handlers are doing it this way. Watch any good handler show a dog and you will see what I mean.

We have talked quite a good deal so far in this book about gait; do this when you gait your dog, see where the judge gaits the dogs, do that when gaiting, and so on. Just what is gait and why do you gait your dog in the show ring? When a judge is asked to choose the best dog in the ring, he looks at them standing still to see where they excel and where they could be improved. But if he made his decision on just this basis, it is conceivable that the dog he chooses would be a cripple. In the show ring you are always striving for perfection, and certainly even a slightly crippled dog is not a perfect dog. So the judge asks that each handler gait, or "move," his dog, and he watches closely to be sure that the dog is free from defects, which now show up. The judge's opinion is then based on both standing-still and moving dogs.

A dog who is cow-hocked may be able to stand still and not show the fault too much, but when he "moves" away from the judge, it shows up at once. It is the same with a poor front. If the dog is "out at elbow," it will show up when he gaits. The judge can also tell at a glance if the dog is made correctly in the shoulders, or any number of other places, by seeing him gait.

Along with looking for faults the judge is also looking for good points when he asks to see a dog gait. It is now that carriage, elegance, symmetry, and style show up. These attributes count heavily when the judge makes his decision, as indeed they should. The Standard of almost every breed gives them a high point rating.

Now that you know why you are asked to gait your dog you must realize that the better your dog gaits, the better opinion the judge will have of him. The judge will want to see the dog gait around in a circle so he can see him from the side—see the style and flash of the dog and then he will want to see the dog go away from him and come toward him—in a straight line. This is when he will be checking for soundness. It is important that the handler not be forced to tug and pull on the show lead, for if he does, he might possibly cause the dog to throw an elbow or a hock in such a fashion as to make the judge think the dog is faulty. Remember the judge's time in the ring is limited, and he cannot take all day to make a decision. Frequently

Small mincing steps look awkward and are rarely of the correct speed for any breed.

Normal walking steps, a trot or a run, will give you and your dog a far better gait than tiny "get-nowhere" steps.

the first impression he gets will be the only one he has time for. Gaiting is so important that it will pay you to learn to do it right.

Aside from the incorrect holding of the lead, as pointed out earlier, the biggest mistake the novice makes is in gaiting his dog too slowly. The mincing steps of the novice handler are a dead giveaway. Your dog cannot gait properly if you do not move fast enough yourself to give him the opportunity to reach out and take normal strides, and there is nothing more awkward than a grown man or woman taking little, bitty steps, usually on tiptoe. Even if you are showing a small toy, you should be able to walk at a normal walk. With the larger breeds it may be necessary for you to move at a fast walk or trot, or even a run.

As you gain more experience, and if you will follow this advice—watch the good handlers—you will soon learn what is correct and you will acquire the proper gait for your dog. But when you first start, please avoid the mistake of going too slowly and with too small steps.

You are in the ring, and the one dog the class has been waiting for has finally arrived. The judge, with perhaps a circular motion of his arm and a nod to the exhibitors, or an "O.K., let's go," makes it known that he is ready to judge the class. Unless otherwise told you will be expected to take your dog, along with the others, in as large a circle as the ring will permit, moving in a counter-clockwise direction. The dog should be on your left side with the lead in your left hand, your left hand only. Usually the judge stands in the center of the ring so that he can see each of the dogs as they go around. If, however, the judge stands slightly to one side or remains in one corner of the ring, unless he tells you to do otherwise you should continue to show as stated, go around in a circle with the dog on your left side. Continue in this fashion until the judge tells you or motions you to stop. Some judges have you go around only once or twice but there is no definite number of times you will be expected to circle the ring.

As far as the speed with which you make this circle is concerned, be governed mostly by your dog's best gait. The dog should be

Ch. Gosmore Wicket Keeper, Miniature Schnauzer, is seen here in show pose. This photo was taken at an English dog show by C.M. Cooke.

The Affenpinscher is a toy dog and should not exceed 10 inches at the shoulder in height. A black coat is preferred; very light colors and white markings are considered faults in show Affenpinschers. Photo by Louise Van der Meid.

moving at a brisk or animated trot. Be sure he doesn't pace, and try to keep him from going into a gallop. If he has been properly lead broken, with showing in mind, he will be going around the ring with an easy but lively step, his head held high. Remember the judge wants a pleasing picture. Try to have your dog look the proud aristocrat he is. The dog should be gating on a loose lead and you should not have to choke him with the lead to keep his head up. Try not to lag, and if you find yourself getting too close to the dog in front of you, slow down a bit. If, in slowing down, you feel you will throw your dog off his best gait, it would be better to stop for a moment, in a corner, and let the dog in front of you get ahead or, better still, if it is possible make a slightly larger circle. This will give you more ground to cover and will keep your dog gaiting at his best speed. Unless the judge or the handler asks you to pass the slower dog, it is not quite cricket to do so.

If you are showing a dog whose tail should be wagging and held rather high, it will encourage him to do so if you talk to him or cluck to him as you are going around. If, however, you are showing a breed whose tail should be dropped when gaiting, it is best not to speak to him.

Be on the lookout for joints in the matting or carpeting at an indoor show which might trip you. Be on the lookout also for numbers that are placed in the ring designating First, Second, Third, and Fourth placing. These are very easy to trip over and always seem to be in your way. At outdoor shows watch for holes, roots, and rough terrain.

Glance quickly and occasionally to see what the judge is looking at. If you see that he is looking at your dog, be sure you keep going. Don't slow down until the judge's eye has left your dog—even though you have been around so many times you think you are going to drop. You can rest later. You probably will wish that you had been born with many pairs of eyes: one pair to keep on your dog, one on the dog in front of you, one on the ground, and one on the judge. But don't despair. You will see all these things at once rather automatically, once you have done it a few times.

When the judge motions with his hand, or speaks to you or one of the other exhibitors, telling you to stop and line up in front of him, or over there, or here, do so with the attitude that you know what you are doing and where you are going. If you didn't hear the judge's orders, glance to see in which direction the others are going and follow them. Don't stand in the middle of the ring waiting for more definite instructions as, chances are, there will be none.

If yours is the first dog stopped, go slightly to the side of the ring and pose your dog, unless the judge gives other instructions. If you are alone in the class, the judge may ask you to pose your dog in the center of the ring. In the ring always do as the judge tells you to do, whether or not it is standard procedure. If yours is not the first dog stopped, line up in the order in which *you went around the ring*, and pose your dog. If yours is the first dog, attempt to get him in a good show position as quickly as possible, since the judge's eye will probably be on your dog. If yours isn't the first dog in line, you will have a little more time to get him in what you consider his best show position.

Some judges will go immediately to the first dog in line and start

These two photographs were taken when the author was judging English Setters at Morris and Essex. Notice in the first picture how the handlers, Charles Palmer and Harold Correll, are out of the way of the judge and also give themselves an opportunity to reset the rear if necessary. Notice in the second picture, when the judge looks at the rear, the handler is in front holding the dog's head.

to examine him. However, there are a great many judges who will stand in the center of the ring while the dogs are lining up and watch as the handlers pose the dogs. The judge may just glance up and down the line or he may walk up and down several times, looking from dog to dog. If the judge does this, he is not looking for fine points but trying to get the general over-all picture of the dog or dogs. Have yours looking his best as soon as you can.

In your breed, if the good handlers remove the lead when posing, now is the time to take the lead off your dog. Don't throw it carelessly to one side, it may become entangled with another lead, or, at an outdoor show, be hard to find in the grass. Place it carefully close by. If you are showing a breed usually baited in the ring, you will leave the lead on and stand in front of your dog. If he has been correctly trained, he will stand still with his head raised, looking at you, or, I should say, at the liver, meat, or playtoy in your hand.

Let us hope that when the judge comes to your dog for a close examination he will approach him slowly or at least carefully. If not, forgive him, for at this time he has a lot on his mind; he is making all sorts of mental notes about the dogs he is judging. Your dog should have been prepared in advance of the show for the approach of a stranger. Sanctioned matches are a big help in this direction and your good friends will understand if you ask them to approach the dog in your living room some evening while you are doing some training in show posing.

The judge will usually examine the head first, looking at skull, ears and ear placement, eyes, teeth, expression. If yours is a breed whose ears should be erect, try very hard to have them erect when the judge approaches him. If yours is a breed whose ears should be low-hung, be calm and try to have your dog's ears relaxed. Some judges will look for themselves, but more and more frequently they are asking the handlers to show the dog's mouth. This keeps the judge's hands from coming in contact with germs in the dog's mouth and spreading them from one dog to another. He may ask, "Let me see his mouth," but he really means his teeth, his bite. He is not interested, as some people still believe, in the roof of the mouth (there are exceptions such as Chow Chows), but in the dog's teeth and how and where they meet. Don't try to conceal anything—show the dog's bite as well as you can. Your dog may need a bit of special training before he will let you or anyone else touch him around the mouth

Although French Bulldogs are not a very popular breed, a few of them have been top winners like the one pictured here surrounded by many awards and trophies. Photo by Louise Van der Meid.

without dancing all around. The well-trained dog will stand perfectly still while his mouth is being examined.

If the judge places both his hands on your dog's head, it is best if you remove your hand from the dog's head. Be alert, however, and ready to grab the dog should he try to get away from the judge. Many dogs go along perfectly all right until this time, when they suddenly realize they are being touched by a stranger. I said, "grab the dog." Perhaps "clasp him firmly" would be a better expression. Sometimes a really sudden grab, even from the dog's owner, will frighten the dog even more. Soothe your dog as best you can; the judge will realize he is frightened and give you the time; then, as calmly as possible, re-pose your dog.

If when the judge approaches your dog he throws his key ring, a pack of cigarettes, or matches, or any other object to attract your dog's attention, don't be in the way. Try to have your dog see the object, or hear it, and react to its being thrown. That is what the judge wants to see—the dog's reaction, his expression. If he doesn't react—throw some small object of your own. If you are in a breed where this practice is customary, you will never go into the ring without carrying with you something which you can toss or hold in front of your dog to get his attention.

It is possible that as the judge approaches he will be more interested in the dog's front and will examine that before he looks at the head. Try very hard to have the front in the correct position for your breed before the judge approaches. By "front" I mean the dog's two front legs. If the two front legs are in the very best possible position *before* the judge approaches you, you will have time to concentrate on other

The coat of a Yorkshire Terrier requires especially meticulous grooming prior to entering a dog show. The condition of the coat is an important factor in judging the breed. Photo by George Heyer, Three Lions, Inc.

things which may need your attention. Just check with a quick glance to see that the dog has not shifted one or the other leg without your knowing it, and, as the judge approaches, be ready to turn the entire front end of your dog over to him if he wishes it.

The setting up of a dog's front depends a great deal on the breed and a great deal on the dog's front—how good it is or how bad it is. First let us take up the breed differences. In small, straight-legged breeds, such as most of the Terriers, you will find the good handlers lifting the dog's front by using the collar and letting the front drop naturally. In large, straight-legged breeds, because the weight involved is so great, this natural dropping is difficult, and usually each leg is placed in the proper position. In breeds where the front legs are not perfectly straight, such as the Basset Hound and the Bulldog, the best idea, particularly in the beginning, is to place the legs in the proper position. The best advice in this respect is, once again, watch the good handlers in your breed. None of this placing of fronts will be necessary if the dog, of his own accord, places his feet in exactly the spot you want them to be in. You can help your dog do this by leading him up to the spot slowly and carefully.

Now let us talk for a moment about how good or how bad your dog's front is and how it concerns placing a front. If you have a dog with a very good front, you want the judge to see it. With a medium-sized dog it is possible to drop the front as the Terrier people do, except do not use the collar to lift the weight of the dog. Place one hand under the brisket of the dog, the other hand holding the dog's head, and lift the weight of the front part of the dog off the ground, then let it drop. The front will come down right! A judge loves to see a front dropped as I have described, but only if it is a good front. If it is not good, it might come down all wrong, and the judge would see what you are trying to keep him from seeing—a bad front. If the dog has a good front, try walking him up to the exact spot you want him in, moving slowly so that you can stop just where you want to be. Perhaps you will only have to move one leg, and that is better than having to move both legs when you have so many other things to do. Check frequently while reading this section on the photographs showing fronts and the placing of fronts.

In placing a front, first one leg and then the other, you will find it is almost impossible to do if you attempt to touch the feet and place them. You must grasp the dog's elbow and place the leg by directing the foot to the proper spot. Hold on to the dog's head or his lead with one hand and place one leg at a time with the other. You may stand in front of the dog or on the side when placing the front, but don't take both hands off the dog's head while you are doing it. One hand on the dog's head, or his lead, will keep him from feeling uncontrolled and perhaps from deciding to leave the spot.

If the judge has first examined the head and then directs his attention to the front, try to check to see if the front is still as you left it when the judge approached you. Often when a judge is examining the head he will throw the dog slightly off balance and the dog will move one leg. If so, and you can fix it without interfering with the judge, correct it.

Different judges have different ways of examining a dog's front. Some will just look it over from a distance, depending on the dog's gait to show any faults. Some judges will just press on the shoulders

In this photograph the dog is being dropped in front. The legs are coming down correctly and will probably drop well enough. The dog's left foot (on our right) may possibly be turned slightly inward, in which case she can be redropped. Notice one hand lifting weight under brisket and the other holding the muzzle. When holding the muzzle or head and dropping the front, have the head pointing straight ahead and the front is more apt to drop correctly.

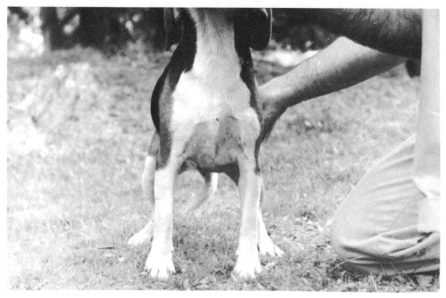

A Norwegian Elkhound winner with a few of his prizes. A minimum of grooming is needed for this breed, although the beauty of the thick fur is greatly enhanced by regular care.

and sway the dog from side to side, watching the legs while doing so. Others will examine the front very carefully, picking up first one leg and then the other. They probably will be very interested in watching each leg drop back to its position naturally. Do not interfere. If the leg comes down in what you consider a bad position, do nothing until the judge is finished. Some of these judges will be careful to leave the dog in a good position but some, after the examination, will leave the dog in any position he happens to be in. Check as soon as possible after the judge leaves the front, and if all is not as it should be—correct it.

Some judges examine the dog's shoulders rather carefully, others depend on seeing the shoulders in action when the dog is gaiting. If your judge pays attention to shoulders, either from the front of the

Never try to pose or reset a front by holding the foot. Instead firmly grasp the elbow and direct the foot to the correct spot. You can also better control a slight toe-in or toe-out by grasping the elbow and slightly turning the leg in the right direction before the foot touches the ground.

It would be difficult even for a novice handler to pose a dog as badly as either of these two photographs show. However, after you have set the dog up in front correctly, or dropped him correctly, if he is off balance it is possible for him to step into one or the other of these positions. Check frequently to be sure he is standing as you want him to be.

dog or from the side, just be careful not to get in his way. The same is true if and when he checks on the "middle piece"—the ribs, brisket, back, loin. While the judge is examining the shoulders or "middle piece," you could be holding the dog's head to be sure he didn't turn around and at the same time you could stretch it ever so slightly or turn it ever so slightly to make his neck fit into the shoulders as well as possible. By now you should be prepared for the judge's examination of the rear.

While the judge was going over the front of the dog, you should have had ample time to set up the rear if it was necessary. If the dog has not moved, you will not have to touch it again. As the judge finishes looking over the body, just check once more to see that he has not moved and that the two back legs are set as well as you can possibly have them.

In the first photograph the hind legs are not back far enough, in the second they are back too far. The third picture shows the hind legs as they should be.

For almost every breed the two back legs will be posed the same. The main exception is for the German Shepherd Dog, and I advise you who are interested in this breed to study the other exhibitors and handlers of Shepherds. In other breeds the two back legs are spread apart so that the bone that goes from the hock joint to the back foot— the hock—is perfectly perpendicular whether viewed from the side or from the rear. This shows very well in the accompanying photographs.

If your dog is cow-hocked (knock-kneed in rear legs), setting up the rear will not be too easy, but lots of practice will show you how best to set it up so the fault is concealed as much as possible. I hope you start out with a dog who does not have this fault, for although it is a common fault, it is one of the easiest for the judge to find. Now, it is quite possible that your dog will have a good rear, but as a result of being in a strange place he will tend to appear cow-hocked. A frightened dog will often look cow-hocked. If this happens to your dog. I can only recommend that you take him around with you as much as possible until he begins to lose his fear of shows and judges and really enjoys them.

If you have a dog with a really good rear, it is possible that you will never have to set him up—he will set himself up. Good! You cannot improve on that. Just be sure he does not place his hind legs in such a spot that his body is turned. If so, just move them and let the dog readjust himself.

There are many ways of moving or of setting up a rear. Watch a few of the handlers. Some will lift the dog by the tail; some will place a hand under the dog between the two hind legs; some will place their arm under the loin of the dog; and still others will place each leg by grasping the hock joint and directing the foot to the correct spot. Here again, as in lifting the dog for dropping the front, size and weight of the dog will make a difference. Yes, in a very small dog, such as some of the small Terriers, you can lift the dog by his tail just long enough to take his weight off his back legs and then

Here are two photographs showing the right and wrong methods of "setting up" a rear. Most dogs will object and squirm about if the foot or lower part of the leg is touched. It is far better to direct the foot to the correct spot by grasping the leg firmly at the stifle joint as shown in the second photograph.

146

Ch. Quibbletown Good Time Charli, Great Pyrenees, receiving an award.
Photo by Evelyn Shafer.

This English Doberman is in a good show pose on a loose lead. The handler is in front of the dog and is alert for any movement the dog may make. Photo by C.M. Cooke.

drop the rear in the correct spot. But I wouldn't advise trying it with a larger dog. Be governed quite a bit by the weight of your breed. A large breed will be uncomfortable if all the weight of his rear is held in one hand even for a short time. A male of a large breed will not enjoy being lifted with one arm under his loin. Find the way which is easiest for you and is most commonly practiced by the good handlers in your breed.

While the judge is looking over the hindquarter you should be up around the head of your dog, holding it or at least watching to see that the dog does not turn around. If yours is a breed usually baited in the ring, do so now. The dog will stand much better if he sees you or you hold him while the judge makes his examination. Also, you might direct the head at this time to give the dog his best appearance in neck and shoulder. In some breeds the Standard calls for an arched neck. Experiment with your dog to find out just how

The dog here is being dropped in front. Notice the weight of the dog being held under the brisket while the head is held with the other hand. The legs are coming down too close together. See result in next picture.

Notice how the legs are coming down parallel. This usually means that the front will be correctly dropped.

The handler looks down and sees that the feet are too close together. In the following two photographs the dog is being dropped correctly.

Here the front has dropped correctly. Now the handler can devote his time to setting up the rear.

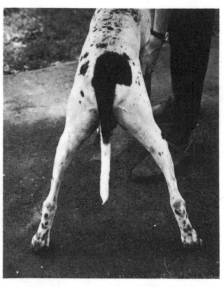

In this photograph the dog's hind legs are too far apart.

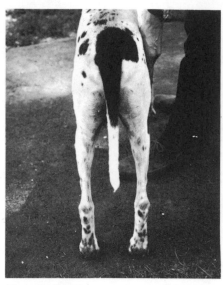

Here the hind legs are too close together.

In this photograph you will note that the dog's left hock appears to turn in. This is known as "cow-hocked".

In this photograph the dog's rear is well set up.

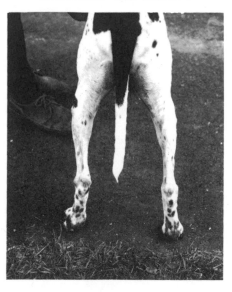

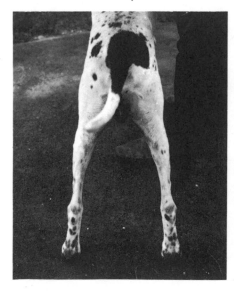

150

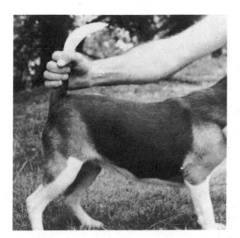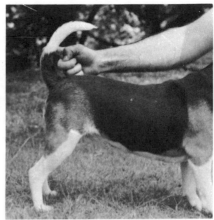

Many hounds and terriers are posed with the tail held erect. The touch of a finger is usually enough to hold the tail upright and it looks much better than grasping the entire tail.

to show this good point to your best advantage. When the judge looks up, you want him to see the dog in his best pose.

When the judge completes his examination of the hindquarters, you may expect one of two things. Either he will go off to examine the next dog or he will continue to go over yours. He may stand off and look at your dog for an "all-over" picture. Try to give him the best picture of your dog that you can. If your breed has the tail usually

If you are careless about checking your dog after you think he is posed, he may move and the judge might see him looking as he does in the first photograph instead of as he CAN look in the second photograph.

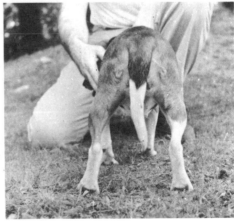

This picture was taken during the actual judging of a very large Open Dog Class, English Setters, at Morris and Essex. Notice the first few handlers are busy setting their dogs up for the judge to go over. The last few handlers—knowing it will be a long time before the judge gets all the way down the line to them—are not tiring their dogs out by keeping them posed but still have them under control and looking well. They will keep a close watch on the progress of the judge and will have the dogs posed when he reaches them.

held, hold it now in the proper position. Glance occasionally to see if the judge is still looking at your dog, but *do not stare at him*. So many novices think they can wish the judge into putting their dog up by staring at him. If it does anything at all, it will make him a bit angry. A quick glance should tell you what you want to know and that is, is he still looking at my dog and where is he going next. As long as the judge looks at your dog, keep him in the show pose. If he goes on to another dog, you can relax a bit, but keep the dog posed, as he may look at your dog again for a comparison with the next dog in line. Some judges tell you as they leave the examination of your dog to let the dog relax. If the judge tells you this, do as he says, let the dog relax. If the lead has been removed, put it on. I said let the dog relax, but don't let him "raise Ned" with another dog and do not let him curl up for a little nap. The judge will be with you shortly and you want to be ready. How long you will have to wait will depend on the size of the class.

If the class is rather large, check once in a while to see how the judge is progressing. As you see him going over the last dog, re-pose your dog. Most judges, after the examination of all the dogs in the class, will stand off for another look at the dogs to refresh his memory as to which ones he liked and which ones he did not. After this look, be prepared to gait your dog. If the lead has been removed again, as soon as the judge stops looking put it on and be ready to gait.

A great deal of what we have just been going over will not apply to the showing of the toy breeds. Some are posed, yes, but you will find the majority of the good ones shown au naturel on the end of a lead. So long as the dog is standing in a good pose, let him alone. If not, move him slightly and let him re-pose himself. Almost all of the toy judges will have you pose your dog for them on a table, otherwise they would have broken backs at the end of the day. If it is a large class, the judge may call you up to the table one at a time; if the class is a small one, perhaps all the dogs in the class will be on the table at one time. If many dogs are on the table at once, all I will say is that the end of the table is the easiest to get around, but since there are only two ends, some of the exhibitors will have to take the middle spots. Try to get on the end, but if it falls your lot to take a center spot, do so gracefully. Most of the toy judges will pick your dog up

Notice how much better the neck looks on the dog in the first photograph. The lead is well forward underneath as well as on top and it does not tend to cut in half the lovely, long-necked appearance. In the second photograph the skin and hair are bunched up. Besides looking sloppy it tends to make the neck appear shorter and, incidentally, offers the handler less control of the dog.

in their hands to estimate the weight, to feel the coat, to study the expression. Try to have your dog accustomed to being handled by strangers.

We have discussed the individual examination of your dog, now let us take up the individual gaiting of your dog. The judge will ask each exhibitor to gait his dog alone. When you came into the ring you went around in a circle and the judge was looking for general all-over appearance, now he will be checking for soundness. The judge will probably stand in one certain spot and have all the dogs, one by one, start their gait from this particular spot. If he has definite instructions, or instructions contrary to the following, he will give them to you as you approach him. If there are no instructions, you will gait your dog in as straight a line as possible away from the judge and then back to him. Look at the six drawings. Number One is the path you will

Collapsible wire crates are good carriers particularly for small breeds like Boston Terriers. Photo by Louise Van der Meid.

Here is an interesting series of photographs taken during the actual judging of Specials Only Class, English Setters, at an important show. The author is on the right showing her International Champion Silvermine Wagabond. In the first photograph the dog is fairly well set up but she realizes that his head is not at the best possible angle nor is the grip quite right. In the second picture she is changing the hold on the head. In the third, she feels the dog is standing as well as she can pose him. There was only a slight improvement but important in close competition. In the fourth picture the judge is going over the dog. This series of pictures points out several things I have advised you to do or not to do in the text. For better control don't kneel on the ground and you will be able to move about easier, faster and more gracefully. When the judge is looking at your dog's front, you go to the rear, check to see that it is as well posed as possible. Notice in these photographs that a well trained dog will not squirm about when waiting for the judge and will stand still for the judge to go over him.

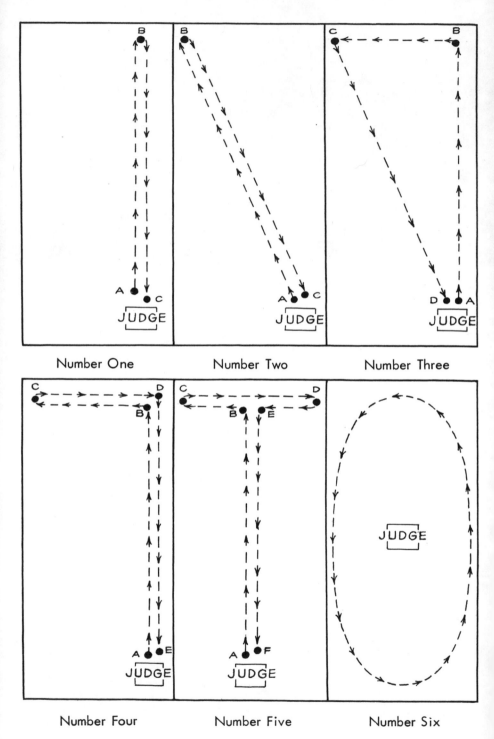

Number One

Number Two

Number Three

Number Four

Number Five

Number Six

follow now. For the sake of these drawings we assume the judge to be standing in the lower right-hand corner of the ring and in the same spot for each path (except for path Five and the circle and for the circle he could be standing any place), but if he is on the opposite side of the ring, you just do the same thing but your starting point will be immediately in front of the judge. Remember, if the judge wishes you to take any path except Number One, he will tell you.

Do you recall our earlier discussion regarding gait? The reason the judge wants to see the dog gait? How the dog should go and how you yourself should go? Now is the time to put those words into practice. Try to have your dog going along at a brisk, animated, but steady gait, and, if possible, don't let him break his gait for a look at another dog, shake, sneeze, or any of the other things he may decide to do at this time. Before you start to gait, check the lead to see that it is on properly and not, for instance, caught on one ear, or, as has happened, in the dog's mouth.

Let's look again at the drawings of the six paths. If the judge wishes you to take any but Number One he will let you know, but if he does not tell you by word of mouth he may motion with his hand, assuming that you know what he wants you to do. It will be one of these paths, and if you are familiar with them you will have no trouble deciding which one he is motioning for you to take. In a few breeds the judge may ask you to go in a circle for the individual gait. If he asks you to, of course you will do so.

In following the pattern in drawings Number One and Two there is not much to worry about except to keep the dog in his best gait in as straight a line as possible with no interference. In following drawings Number Three, Four, or Five, remember that when your dog is traveling broadside, or sidewise, to the judge, the judge will again be checking on general appearance. Keep him going and looking his best, head up and alert.

Remember what I told you about the lead being held in one hand? Now is the time you will be glad you learned to hold it this way. When you are following path Number Three, between points B and C, be sure to have the dog between you and the judge. In following path Number Four, between points B and C, have the dog between you and the judge, and then when you make the turn and you are between points C and D, you still want the dog to be between you and the judge. Just change the lead from your left hand to your right hand and the dog will be in the right place. The same is true of path Number Five—whenever your dog is sidewise to the judge, have him between you and the judge no matter how many times you change the lead from one side to the other. Watch the experienced handlers make this quick change. It's easy; practice it a few times. Incidentally, path Number Five is most apt to be called for in group judging or in exceptionally large rings.

When you have completed the individual gaiting of your dog, unless you have definite instructions from the judge, go back to the spot where you originally posed your dog, re-pose him, and be prepared for another individual examination. Some judges will know exactly what dogs they are going to place as soon as the individual gaiting has been completed, but others will want another look.

When the judge takes this other look, it is possible that he will ask for changes in the places where the dogs are posed: he may have several dogs change places; he may ask that all the dogs face another direction; that all dogs be posed in the center of the ring; or he may take two or more dogs off to a corner and spend extra time on them. However, whatever happens at this time will be entirely up to the judge and he will let you know just what he wants. Occasionally, in very large classes, as you complete the individual gaiting of your dog, the judge will ask you to go to the opposite side of the ring from the side you were on; he may be dividing the class in two parts, half on one side of the ring and half on the other side. If there are no special directions, as I said before, return to the same spot you were in before, and pose your dog. If the judge walks up and down the ring looking at the dogs, just be sure you have your dog ready for this second examination. If all the dogs are facing the center of the ring and the judge is around back looking at hindquarters, check to see that your dog's rear is posed correctly. If not, fix it. When the judge comes around front and looks at all fronts, see that your dog's front and his head angle are as good as you can possibly have them.

Don't get in the judge's way. Make it as easy as possible for the judge to see *your* dog. I want to emphasize this point. If you watch the top handlers carefully, you will notice that they never—and I mean never—stand between the judge and their dog. They may move back and forth a dozen or more times, but let the judge's eye, regardless of where he is standing, wander to their dog, he will see the dog and not the handler's body. This takes a bit of practice as

Ch. Haydenhills Brian of Catharden, Doberman Pinscher owned by Mrs. Hayden, standing alongside his trophies. Photo by Louise Van der Meid.

you are so intent on having your dog in the proper pose, showing nicely, that it is sometimes difficult to remember that the judge is walking around. Follow the technique I described earlier—quick glances to see where the judge is and in what direction he is going. Do not stare at the judge, for if your dog moved you would not be aware of it. Quick glances keep you posted on the judge *and* the dog. Whether gaiting your dog or posing him, never be between your dog and the judge. On this second posing of your dog be careful not to get so close to the dog next to yours that you cannot move from one side of your dog to the other quickly and gracefully while keeping out of the judge's view of your dog. If the judge asks you to bring your dog up next to another dog—or has another dog brought up next to yours—keep your dog in his best show pose until the judge decides between the two and leaves the examination.

Earlier in this book I mentioned that I would tear apart the phrase, "in his opinion." Here I go, and to me it is most important. To me it explains dog shows and judging. There is only one other phrase in judging that can come near to it in importance, and that one will enter into our discussion of this one. What I am about to say is in spite of the fact that all breeds are judged by a Standard of perfection which has been described by the breed fanciers themselves, and all dogs are judged by comparison—one against the other.

A judge at a dog show is a human being, with intelligence, integrity, and knowledge of the breed he is judging, and he always tries to judge the dogs to the best of his ability. Now it will happen that you will see at a show certain dogs judged, and the very next day the very same dogs will be judged by another person and the placings will be different. "How," you will say, "can such a thing happen and still be correct and sincere?" Or you might say, "One judge was wrong, which one?" Well, there is no law that says we must all like exactly the same things. One man likes blondes, another prefers brunettes; one man can't stand women who jabber constantly; another abhors untidy women. I'm not being facetious. I realize that dog judging is important, but we all have our likes and dislikes and we are entitled to them, even in the dog game. One judge might be absolutely repelled by a dog with a bad bite whereas another judge will overlook the bad bite but cannot stand a light eye, and although a judge may realize that either of these are fairly insignificant faults (in some breeds), his intense dislike of one or the other cannot help but interfere with his placement of a dog who has such a fault.

By the same token, judges who also *breed* dogs may find it extremely difficult to get certain qualities in their own dogs and when they judge they are taken with, or at least swayed by, dogs who excel in those certain qualities which they find it almost impossible to breed into their own dogs. The hard-to-get certain quality is unknowingly magnified in the judge's mind. Isn't this a natural reaction? Judges are human, remember?

Some judges are convinced that the beauty traits of a breed—all of them taken as a whole—the things that make one breed different from another—are more important than the structural soundness of a breed, and just as many are convinced that the reverse is true. The advocates of both sides are convinced they are right, and when they judge, their sincerity impels them to follow what they believe to

The prize-winning Dalmatian Duke of Elbaref being set into show pose. Photo by Louise Van der Meid.

be correct, often to the scorn of their opponents. But both sides are honest, both know the breed very well, and both are correct *in their opinion.*

Now it may also happen that you will see, let us say, four dogs judged by two different judges. The second judge will place the first judge's winner last and his last dog first. Are either of these judges wrong? No. And I point out this example of how it can happen. I have actually been in a class of four dogs where any one of the four could have won the class and the judge would be correct. All four of the dogs were good. In fact, I found out afterward that any one of the four that won that day would have received the necessary points to complete his championship. So they were all good! They varied, yes, but each dog had only minor faults which were each about as important as the next. I'm sure the judge would have liked to have been able to say he would award first to each dog but, of course, that is impossible. The judge must place one dog first, one second, and so on. He must decide which one, on the day, is best *in his opinion.*

There, now, I have used the other phrase I said was important—*on the day.* You will hear it used often. A certain dog does not show as well one day as he does another; or his coat is not in so perfect condition one day as on another; or his weight; or he has not quite reached the high of perfection in some way *on the day* as he will on another. But a judge must judge the dogs as he sees them right now —as they are in the ring—*on the day.*

You may also notice that a certain judge will place a dog very high at a certain show and the next time he judges that particular dog he will apparently ignore him. This happens frequently in Group and Best in Show judging, but let us concern ourselves with how this can happen in breed judging. Mr. Jones gives Best of Breed to Dog A at a certain show. Two months later Mr. Jones is judging the breed again and everyone is convinced that Dog A will again win. But they are surprised when Mr. Jones puts Dog B up to Best of Breed. They shouldn't be surprised. It could be that Dog B was not present at the first show and therefore Mr. Jones did not have the opportunity to place him over Dog A. Or it could be that at the first show Dog B was not feeling up to par or was not in good condition. At the second show Dog B is in the pink of condition and, as we say, showing like a million, and Mr. Jones sees him in a different light. Mr. Jones will place the dogs as he sees them *in his opinion—on the day!*

You should also remember that "comparison" is an important word. A judge may tell you he likes your dog and then, when you show your dog under him, he turns you down. Well, he does like your dog, but in his opinion, on the day, he liked another dog better.

As you sit around the ringside at shows you will hear the judge criticized in loud voices by other judges, by breeders, by exhibitors. They will call him everything from crazy to crooked; from senile to stupid. Don't you believe it. There will always be differences of opinion. All the art critics do not agree on which of Van Gogh's paintings is his best and all the music critics do not agree on Chopin's Preludes. Disappointment at a dog show, however, does seem to make some people want to exercise their vocal chords in public.

As far as dog shows or judges being crooked, or fixed, or influenced, is concerned take it as so much nothing from a few bad losers. I have talked to a great many people who have been in the dog game for more than ten years and every one of them agrees that the dog game is 95 per cent on the square. Not that they know the other 5 per cent exists, but they just don't want to make a definite statement they may not be able to prove. You will hear someone say, "Give me a horse race—you can always tell by the photograph which horse really wins." Hog wash! What they can't tell, or don't know or don't want to know, is which jockey is pulling which horse. And so it is in all sports, in music, arts, et cetera. But take it from me, the dog game is as clean a sport as you will find in which you can actually participate. And it's up to you, once you get in it, to keep it clean.

Now just a few more words on *in his opinion* and *on the day*. After you are in dogs for a little while you will realize that it is a good thing the same dog does not always win. For if he did, there would be no more dog shows. Who would show his dog if he knew in advance the same dog would win every time? No one but the winner —and he wouldn't show for long if he was always all alone.

In looking at dogs which are doing a lot of winning, or at dogs which have beaten your dog, don't always be looking for faults. There never was and there never will be a perfect dog—there is always a spot or two which could be improved. It seems that with some people, as soon as they realize they are able to recognize a fault in a dog without first being told by an expert that it exists they must talk constantly about that fault. Instead, look for and be able to recognize the good points a dog possesses. If he is a constant winner, he must be a good dog whether or not you personally think so. All of the judges who put him up can't be wrong. So try to look for the good in a dog—see him as a whole instead of a lot of minor parts held together by wire or string. This reminds me of a saying—see if you don't think it is applicable. "Quibbling over the minutia is indicative of failure to grasp the entirety."

Always be courteous to the judge. Tardiness is a discourtesy; a dirty or messy dog is not only a discourtesy to the judge it is also a disgrace to you; bad manners of any sort or sloppy clothes in the ring are a discourtesy. The dog-show judge when he is in the ring deserves and usually gets the same respect paid to him as a judge sitting in a court of law.

I remember attending a meeting, I've forgotten whether it was a debate or just a discussion, run by the Amateur Dog Judges Association. The exhibitors were putting all sorts of questions to the judges and one in particular has always remained in my mind. The exhibitor said to the panel of three judges, "Isn't there any way you judges can arrange to be more on time in your judging? Sometimes you are running behind and you go off for lunch and come back later than you should. I think it is rude of you, and I don't think it's fair to us exhibitors who have prepared our dogs for the ring to have to keep them waiting for the judge."

Mrs. George B. St. George answered the question. (In political life Mrs. St. George was then Representative Katherine St. George of New York State.) In general she said, "On the contrary, I think it is you exhibitors who are unfair to the judges. We arrive on time and start judging on time but you delay, for one reason or another, the starting of every class. We need our lunch, and most of us make every effort to down it quickly and return to our assignments, but we cannot help it if the caterers are overworked or shorthanded. We give up our whole day and are not paid or even rewarded with a ribbon—sometimes not even by a 'Thank You.' You are sometimes extremely rude and offensive to us. However, always remember this, you can choose your judges, we cannot choose the exhibitors who will show under us. You get a premium list which tells you just which judge will officiate in your breed on the day and if you think that judge is rude or unfair *you need not show under him: no one forces you to*. But we judges never know who will be entered under us and whether or not we like the exhibitor we have no choice, we must judge his dog."

These words of Mrs. St. George are very true. No one forces you to show your dog under any particular judge. We are fortunate that we have so many shows to choose from that we need never show under anyone we consider unjust or offensive. Further along in the chapter on "tricks of the trade" I suggest that you keep a little notebook with you at all times. If you find a judge you do not like, you can write in your book next to his name: "Never show under him again." However, I'll bet that if you do write such a thing, years later you will look back at it and laugh and cross it out. The judge may by that time be a good friend of yours or at least you will have decided he is a good judge and you'll show under him any day.

You may have taken exception in several places to my saying

A Doberman in excellent show stance. She is standing still, front legs straight and square, and the hind legs pulled slightly behind.

something about "The judge being a good friend of yours," or, "This judge was a friend of mine," or, "The judge told me later." You may say to yourself, "Some people know all the judges—I don't know any judges personally. Will I win?" First let me tell you that there are just as many judges, *if the dogs are equally good,* who will lean over backward in order *not* to put up a friend as there are judges who will try to place a friend, and I mean that sincerely. Now I want to ask you a question. Would it not be an extremely peculiar person who was in the dog game any length of time who *didn't* have friends in the game? And those friends could be judges, other exhibitors, show officials, professional handlers, et cetera? If you are a normal person, sincere about dogs, you too, will very soon be friends with lots of people in the game.

CHAPTER 10

THE AWARDS

With your eyes on your dog, glancing up occasionally to see what the judge is doing, be prepared for the judge to call out or point out his placing of the dogs. If he says to you, "first," or "One," or points to you and holds up one finger, go at once to the first-place number marker in the ring. If you are showing a very tiny dog, it would not be amiss to pick him up and carry him to first place. If you have a large dog and the lead has been removed, put it on him quickly and go to first place. If the judge calls to you "Second," "Third," or "Fourth," or points to you or catches your eye and holds up two, three, or four fingers, go at once to the proper marker. Now is the time for you to give your dog a great big pat and/or a tidbit. Let him know he has performed to your satisfaction and you are pleased with him. He'll come to look forward to this moment of glory in the ring and will eventually love the applause. At first it may frighten him a bit, so be prepared.

If the judge does not advise you in some fashion that your dog has been placed in the class, leave the ring. If you want to watch what is going on, do so from the outside of the ring. If you are not placed, you remain in the ring only if the judge specifically asks you to or if you are entered in the next class with the same dog, and then you should go to the side of the ring and wait until the dogs who have been placed in this class leave the ring.

Let us assume, however, that your dog has placed in his class. If the judge has gone to his table to mark his book, or if he has his book in his hands and is writing in it, just be sure that he can see your arm band. The band may have slipped around so that the number is not visible. Make it as easy as you can for the judge to see the number.

Ch. Mueller Mills Valentino II, German Wirehaired Pointer, finished his championship with a three-point major at the age of eight months. The handler is Evonne Chashoudian. Photo by Bennett Associates.

Before marking his book, however, if the judge should hesitate or take another look at the dogs, which are now standing in front of the numbers one, two, three, and four, be sure to keep your dog in a show pose. If the judge hesitates, it may mean that he has not completely made up his mind and he may change the placings. Once he writes down his placings in his book, he will not change them, but a class is not considered judged until it has been written down by the judge. If he hesitates and you are standing in front of the Number One spot with your dog in a sloppy or poor position, and the Number Two dog is looking his very best, that dog may catch the judge's eye. He may change his mind, changing you from first place to second and the second-place dog to first. If you were in fourth place and the third dog at this moment looked inferior, the judge might decide that he liked your dog better and move you up to third place before marking his book.

It is a good idea, anyway, to keep your dog looking his very best all the time he is in the ring. The spectators will be watching, and among them may be sitting the judge who will pass on your dog at another show in the near future. Some of these judges have remarkably good memories! Also, among the spectators are other exhibitors and breeders—let them go away with a good picture of your dog in their minds.

If you have placed in your class, wait at the designated number until the judge hands you the ribbon. I hope he will also hand you a trophy or some prize money! All prize money and trophies won by your dog should be received by you in the ring. There is only one exception: the judge or steward will tell you the trophies are on display and by presenting your ribbon or a card which they will give you you may pick up your trophy at the display stand.

Regardless of whether your dog was placed first or fourth, say "Thank you" when the judge hands you the ribbon. Do not linger in the ring; do not ask the judge why he placed your dog where he did; just say "Thank you," and leave, unless, of course, the judge wants to talk to you about your dog. The judge has other classes to judge and he must complete his task so the show can go on. As you leave the ring, remember the other judges and breeders sitting on the ringside. Let your dog leave the ring looking like a winner!

In the last few paragraphs we talked about what to do if your dog placed in his class. Now let us assume that your dog has won his class. Regardless of which class your dog wins, or if he is alone in it, he will have to return to the ring for the judging of Winners—Winners Dog if you were showing a male, Winners Bitch if you were showing a female. If you win the Open Class, do not leave the ring at all. If you win the Puppy, Novice, Bred by Exhibitor or American Bred Class at a small show, or if there are only a few entries in your breed, it will be a very short wait before you have to go back, so don't go too far away from the ring, for it will delay the judging if you have to be located. If you have won the Puppy or Novice Class, and there are very large entries in the Bred by Exhibitor, American Bred, or Open Classes, you could put your dog back on the bench, or in his crate, or off in a quiet spot where he can get a little rest while waiting for the Winners Class to be called; but keep an eye on the ring and be ready.

In the judging of the Winners Class the judge may go through the same procedure he went through in the judging of the regular class. He may have you circle the ring, pose the dog, individual gaiting, and a second pose; or he may just glance at the dogs to remind him of how well he liked them during the judging of the regular classes. At any rate, he will choose one dog (or bitch) as his Winners and will then choose another dog as his Reserve Winners. Before he judges Reserve Winners he will have another dog brought into the ring.

If your dog wins second in a regular class you should stay fairly close by the ring until after the judging of Winners has been completed, as your dog may be eligible to compete for Reserve Winners. The correct procedure after Winners Dog has been chosen is for the judge, or the steward or ring runner, to call the dog who placed second in the class from which the Winners Dog came. This second-place dog is eligible to compete for Reserve Winners, as he has not yet been defeated by the winners of the other regular classes. For instance, if the winner of the American Bred Dog Class goes Winners Dog, the dog who placed second in the American Bred Dog Class goes into the ring to compete for Reserve Winners against the winners of the other regular classes.

I purposely used American Bred Dog Class for the above example because so often the novice exhibitor feels the judge will find his Winners Dog in the Open Class. It is true that often the Open Dog is a bit more mature or a more finished performer; a little older, perhaps; or handled by an experienced handler; and very frequently it *does* go Winners. However, too often the handler of the dog going second in the American Bred Dog Class thinks he is finished and he disappears. Remember that the winner of *any* class may be the one the judge chooses for his Winners Dog. Do *not disappear !* The judge is not supposed to wait for a dog to be located, and if the dog does not show up, the judging of Reserve Winners will go on without him.

After the judging of Reserve Winners Bitch, the dog going Winners Dog and the bitch placing Winners Bitch come back into the ring and along with any Champions entered compete for Best of Breed.

Remember, too, that there is an award named "Best of Opposite Sex to Best of Breed." If a male from the Best of Breed class goes Best of Breed, the Winners Bitch and all Champion bitches in the class are eligible for Best of Opposite Sex. If a bitch from the Best of Breed class goes Best of Breed, then the Winners Dog and all male Champions in the class are eligible for Best of Opposite Sex. The Winners Dog or the Winners Bitch may be placed Best of Breed, in which case Best of Opposite Sex is chosen from the remaining dogs of the opposite sex. If the Winners Dog is chosen as Best of Breed and the Winners' Bitch is chosen as Best of Opposite Sex, the Winners Dog is automatically named Best of Winners. The reverse is also true—the bitch would automatically be Best of Winners if she had been placed Best of Breed. In the event that a Champion is placed Best of Breed, Winners Dog and Winners Bitch compete for Best of Winners before Best of Opposite Sex is judged.

If your dog should be Best of Breed, he is eligible to compete in the group judging. As a novice you may believe this is something that happens only to the experienced. Nonsense! If you have a good dog in good condition, well trained, well shown, it is quite possible for you to go Best of Breed even though it may be your first show or your dog's first show. Or, as sometimes happens (and no slur is intended), you may have the only dog of your breed entered that day at that show. Yes, if yours is the only one of his breed, and as long as the judge thinks he is representative of the breed, you will get Best of Breed and be eligible to compete in the group. There is no rule saying you *must* compete in the group, but you are eligible, and it is usually a good idea to compete in the group even though you feel you do not have a chance to win it or place in it. It is good experience for you and for your dog to show in the group, and no harm is done if you are ignored.

The German Shepherd Dog is shown in greater numbers, in the United States, than any other breed of dog. Consequently he has the highest point rating of all breeds. But whether you show a Shepherd or any of the other fine breeds recognized by the AKC you will get more out of dogs if you are aware of what the dog sport is all about from the beginning.

Showing in the group is just the same as showing in the breed, except that the ring is usually a great deal larger and you will be competing with other Best of Breed winners instead of dogs of the same breed as yours. The larger ring means that you will have a lot more ground to cover when gaiting your dog around the ring. Frequently in group judging—and I've seen it done many times— the judge will stand in one position and have each dog brought up to him for examination and then he will ask for the individual gait, following path Number One on the drawings. If the judge did not get a good opportunity to see the dogs as they were going around the ring, or if the circling of the ring was dispensed with, when he asks for the individual gait he will probably have each dog gait twice: once he will be standing at the end of the ring watching for soundness, and the other time the dog is gaited the judge will move to the side of the ring and watch the dog's over-all appearance. Just remember to change the lead from one hand to the other, keeping the dog between you and the judge.

The alternatives to having the dog brought up to the judge for individual examination and gaiting would be for the judge to go down the line of dogs, examining each one and gaiting each one before he moves on to the next dog for examination; or he might examine all the dogs and then gait all the dogs.

You will be a little more nervous in the group ring, but if it's any consolation to you, so is everyone else in there with you. The same procedure is followed as in the breed classes when the judge places your First, Second, Third, or Fourth.

I do not think I need say that should you win the group you will be eligible to compete for Best in Show. Excited though you may be, you will instinctively know this. However, you may not know that the rule states that the winner of a group *must* compete for Best in Show.

On page 173 is a picture of me winning my first Best in Show. I was so nervous that my hands shook when I accepted the red, white, and blue rosette from the judge. The trophy was very large, and I didn't know whether to drop the ribbon and take the trophy, or to let go of the dog so I could hold both the ribbon and the trophy. The kind judge saw my predicament and helped me by placing the ribbon inside the trophy. I was so excited I forgot that photographers would want a picture of the big event and the late William Brown, who got

The author Virginia Tuck Nichols winning her first Best In Show with her International Champion Silvermine Wagabond.

this picture, was ever so patient, waiting until I got myself and my dog back under control. Just as we would get all set, the dog would move and "Brownie," as he was affectionately known, smiled and said, "Take your time, take it easy." He picked up the sign proclaiming our win and moved it to a more advantageous spot; and we tried again. He eventually got a really nice picture.

I have since found out that when a picture is taken by more or less regular (official) dog photographers, they want a more or less show-posed photograph. However, when the picture is taken by press photographers, you and the dog and the photographers can relax a bit and up comes something like the one of me on page 174 standing next to my dog, with the rosette pinned to his lead, which was taken by the New York *Daily News* photographer and used in their news-

An informal press photograph of a winning dog and his owner. This is a
New York *Daily News* photograph of the author, Virginia Tuck Nichols,
with her English Setter, Champion Silvermine Messenger.

paper after an important Best of Breed win at the Westminster Kennel Club show.

We have now gone through the technical parts of what I call ring performance. There are many more fine points discussed in the next chapter. Before we go on, this seems as good a place as any to mention a word about breed popularity.

The 115 breeds and the 127 varieties are listed in the Appendix under their proper group headings. Some of these breeds are little known around the shows—some are very well known. Usually the number of dogs registered in a breed in one year has a direct bearing on the number of dogs shown in that breed in the same year. (This does not seem to hold true of Beagles—Beagles are usually 2nd, 3rd or 4th in number of registrations but never hold that position in show popularity.)

In 1967 Poodles held the number one position in registrations— 255,862 Poodles were registered, an increase, by the way, of almost 20,000 over 1966! German Shepherd Dogs held the number two position with 107,936 registered, an increase over 1966 of almost 15,000. Boxers were in 18th position with 9,570 registered. There were only 74 Greyhounds and only 1 Sussex Spaniel registered. You will find the show popularity of these breeds reflected in the Schedule of Points shown on pages 47 to 52. It takes 33 to 37 German Shepherds, 15 to 17 Boxers but only 4 Greyhounds to make a three-point show.

CHAPTER 11

TRICKS OF THE TRADE

Before going on I want to point out that when I use the word "handler" I do not necessarily mean a professional handler. The handler is the person actually in the ring with the dog. He is a professional only if showing dogs is his profession and he gets paid for being in the ring with the dog. You who are not familiar with the word may misinterpret some of my statements. When I say, "watch the good handlers," I do not necessarily mean the professional handlers. There are good handlers who are strictly amateurs.

Along with the two main mistakes a novice exhibitor makes, that of holding the show lead in two hands instead of one, and of taking tiny, little mincing steps when gaiting his dog, there are many small things, not exactly mistakes, which should be pointed out to him in order to improve his handling. These are not in any particular order of importance, for when it comes right down to fine points, they are all important.

When showing your dog, use a firm hand—firm but not rough. The rough handling, if you have a hardheaded dog, should be done at home during the training period, certainly not in the show ring. Occasionally it may be necessary to reprimand a dog in the ring if he seems to have forgotten all his training, but when it is necessary, you should speak harshly to him, perhaps using a few light taps where they will do the most good. A hard smack will give the judge and the spectators the impression that you do not love your dog, that the win is more important to you than the dog, and that you have done no training at home. The gasp that goes up around the ringside whenever a dog is loudly spanked in the ring, even though the dog is not hurt, will convince you that I am correct. It is necessary that you acquire a firm hand so that the dog knows what you expect

The Best of Breed trophy of this Papillon stands higher than the dog itself.

of him. A wishy-washy touch with a dog is as bad as a wishy-washy handshake. The limp handshake might lose you an expected friend and a too-light touch with a dog might lose you an expected ribbon.

Don't get down on both knees when you pose your dog. In order to get out of this position you must shift all your weight to one knee while you are bringing the other foot into position to stand on it. Frequently you lose your balance getting out of this position. I will admit that sitting on your heels during a large class is better than having nothing to sit on, but in the long run you will find the position has more drawbacks than it has comfort. In showing a great many breeds you will be standing upright all of the time, but if you must get down lower, try the squat, or try placing only one knee on the ground and keep the other leg bent. Whichever you choose, keep your back as straight as possible. Either of these two positions allows you to get on your feet quickly and gracefully without the danger of losing your balance.

When you are in the show ring, don't waste your time looking aimlessly around. While waiting for the class to begin, glance at your dog frequently to be sure he has not assumed a grotesque pose or that he is not getting into some mischief with another dog while you are staring into space. While the dog is in a show pose, check on him frequently to be sure he has not stepped into a less attractive stance. If he is maintaining the correct pose, *don't fuss with him.* Unless there is something that needs correcting, don't spoil the picture your dog is making by nervous fussing with him which will accomplish nothing.

These words remind me of a story told by the late Charles Palmer, a very well-known professional sporting-dog handler. Charlie was watching the judging of Best of Breed in a fairly popular breed. There were twelve or thirteen dogs competing, all quite well known and all well above average for the breed. Since it was at the Westminster Kennel Club show, each owner or handler wanted desperately to be given the nod, saying his dog had won. The ringside was very quiet, the mood tense, the perspiration flowing freely from the brows of every exhibitor in the ring. Charlie leaned toward a friend and said that he noticed that all the handlers were fussing with their dogs to the point where the judge was not getting a decent picture of any. Only one handler, pointed out Charlie, had his dog properly set up in full view of the judge; only this one dog was correctly posed *every time* the judge looked at him. "I'm not saying *he is the best dog,*" said Charlie, "but if those other fellows don't watch out, THEY'LL CONVINCE THE JUDGE HE IS." The judge took his time going over each dog many times, for they were all good ones, but every time his eyes passed over the lot, only one dog stood out. This dog finally got the award amid great applause. Do you get the lesson I am trying to point out? If not, reread this paragraph again after you have been showing for a time; you'll get it then, I'm sure.

If you are showing your dog at a summer show out in the broiling hot sun and you are entered in a very large class which must, of necessity, take the judge a long time to do, here is a little tip. For you, as the handler, there is no way out of it, but you could try to cast a shadow with your body to give your dog a little comfort while waiting for the judge. If it is a very large class, don't pose your dog until the judge is just two or three dogs away from yours. Your dog will be just a little less tired of it all when the judge gets to him, and these little things count quite a lot in hot competition.

I have advised you many times in this book to watch the good handlers in your breed. I have also advised you to know your breed well. Here is one very good reason why this is important. A novice watches a good handler show a dog. He sees the handler place his hand on the dog's rump, between the hipbones and the tail set. The handler makes sure the judge has seen him do this. The judge looks at the same spot on the other dogs in the class and gives the first prize to the handler of whom we're speaking. The novice, if he doesn't know *why* the handler acted as he did, mimics the handler when he shows his dog but with disastrous results. Why? The novice did not know he was pointing out a fault in his dog whereas the handler was pointing out a good spot on his dog. The Standard of perfection for the breed in question states that this breed should have a medium-high tail set. The smart handler noticed when he came into the ring that his dog had a very good tail set but the other dogs in the ring were faulty at this spot. Where the competition is keen, these things count quite a lot. The handler placed his hand on his dog's good spot, the judge saw it, recognized that the dog excelled here, looked at the other dogs, realized that they were faulty here, and gave the award to the handler. The novice, if he doesn't know his breed, does the same thing, but instead of pointing out his dog's good spot, he points out what may be his dog's main fault, a poor tail set. The same situation might exist regarding throat on a dog, or clean-cut shoulders, or good feet, or any number of spots where a dog excels; when pointed out, it may help the decision come your way. But unfortunate may be the results if you, not knowing, point out a dog's fault.

It is best if you do not try to point out good or bad parts of your dog until you know very well what they are and how best to point them out, and until you are able to recognize as soon as you enter the ring whether or not it is to your advantage to point them out. When you feel you do know, please don't be obnoxious about it. If you cannot do it in a nice way, don't do it at all. I have been in the show ring between two excited handlers who decided to show the judge how good their dogs were. They got so intent on what they were doing, each trying to outdo the other, that the judge became annoyed. He said they were insulting his intelligence—that he could and would find the dog of his liking without any further help from the handlers. Because I realized what the handlers were attempting to do, I set my dog up, knew he was set up correctly, and never made another move. It gave the judge the impression that I was not worried, that my dog was there looking his very best, and that I was sure he, the judge, would find him to his liking. I didn't win that class, but I felt very good after the judge made his remark and I knew he was not talking to me. He preferred another dog to mine that day but he was certainly not criticizing my handling. Years later this judge remarked to me about this particular class and how annoyed his was watching those handlers "make fools of themselves." So if your dog is well posed and showing well, don't fuss with him.

One very good piece of advice I'll pass on to you was given to me the first time I showed a dog. "Keep your nose clean, your eyes and ears open, and your mouth closed until you know what it is all about." Keep your eyes open and everywhere at once. You will see lots of things, some not intended for your eyes. The same with your ears. You'll hear ever so many things—some complete contradictions of what you are *positive* is right—some-day you will be able to make up your own mind which is correct. When I say keep your mouth closed I don't mean you shouldn't ask questions or ask for help or advice. But don't repeat anything that has been told to you or anything you have seen. As a novice you may incorrectly repeat what you have been told, unintended, to be sure, and cause a lot of hard feeling between friends of long standing, or between persons who would have been friends had you not made enemies of them.

These young Affenpinschers descended from Ch. Walhuf Ivan and Aff-Airn Pretty Picture.

Two good examples of this: I said a friend's stud dog was not right for my bitch—a newcomer said I said the stud dog was not right—I lost a friend. Another example: An exhibitor was told by the judge that his dog "had been kept too close to the kitchen." When the story got around it changed, and the judge reportedly said, "The dog was nothing but a kitchen dog." What the judge meant was that the dog was too fat, had been kept too close to the kitchen and had received too many tidbits. What he reportedly said was "that the dog was no good." You wouldn't want to be responsible for such an erroneous statement, would you? As a novice, not realizing the import of what you are saying or the true intent of the statement you are repeating, you might. As a novice don't pass judgment on people or their dogs around the shows. Invariably the person, or the best friend of the person, will overhear you and you will lose the opportunity to know that person before you have ever had a chance to know whether or not you would like to. When you feel you know the breed well, and you are willing to pass judgment on a dog to the owner's face, then go ahead, but do it in a gentlemanly way.

In asking advice or help on how to improve the trimming of your dog, for instance, don't tell Mr. Jones that Mr. Smith has just told you the completely reverse method. Just make a mental note of both methods and who made each suggestion. Later on you will decide for yourself who was right and who knows more about your breed.

Keep your nose clean. You never heard that statement before? Well, it's just another way of saying, don't do anything you'll be sorry for later on. Don't pull any "fast ones," don't do anything you wouldn't want written up in your biography. You may become an important person in the so-called dog game someday—just be sure you will have nothing to hide. Remember you must live with yourself.

Try not to hurt the feelings of fellow exhibitors. Perhaps you don't realize that a simple phrase such as, "My, you're lucky," could hurt someone. The implication might be that the dog won by luck alone. There are other words that can hurt, and you'll soon learn them, so try to avoid using them.

Don't make a pest of yourself at club meetings. Every novice who enters the dog game attends a club meeting and gets up on his feet and makes a long speech. Usually it is about the Standard of the breed. "It's all wrong! The Standard states that the males should weigh 45 pounds yet the dog who won today was 48 pounds. Let's correct the Standard." Out of courtesy no one interrupts him, and he consumes very valuable time. Later he finds out that this very question was taken up in detail at the last meeting and it was decided that the Standard was correct, would stand unchanged, and little by little the club would try to educate judges to the fact that the desirable weight for the males of this breed is 45 pounds.

Or the novice will ask, at the club meeting, for someone to explain, right now, what the Standard means by "a long, lean head—with ample brain room." He probably has a dog who has been criticized as having a coarse head and he wants to be told exactly, down to the 1/100th of an inch, just how wide a dog's head may be and be within the Standard. Club meeting time is valuable and scarce. A much nicer thing for the novice to do, granted he is sincere about wanting to know more about the Standard, is to ask the club if they have a Standards Committee, or someone who knew the Standard well and who would be willing to explain parts of it to him. The club members will appreciate his desire to learn and all will be most willing to help him. In this way he has antagonized no one and made friends of a great many busy people who must leave immediately after the meeting to take care of other things.

In speaking of Standards, there is one thing I want to point out. Don't be too anxious or too hasty to criticize the Standard. In most breeds this Standard of points, or Standard of perfection, has been worked out by students of the breed, men who have devoted a lifetime to the study of this one breed. The Standard is usually correct; it is the interpretation of it that is wrong; and time will usually take care of the wrong understanding of a Standard. If time does not take care of it—and these things are done slowly—public opinion will.

How can time or public opinion influence a Standard of a breed? Let us take as an example of time influencing a Standard, the English Setter Standard of points. Under general appearance the relative weight given to symmetry, style, and movement (not running gear) is twelve points. That is a lot of points! Under symmetry the Standard states, "Symmetrical dogs will have level backs or be very slightly higher at the shoulders than at the hips." Thirty years ago almost all English Setters had level backs, but it was found that they tended to be sway-backed—a fault. So the breeders attempted to breed their English Setters with backs "very slightly higher at the shoulders than at the hips." In attempting to get the slight slope—and dogs

E.H.HART

with slight slopes to the back line began to win!—they got a back that was *very* sloped. Soon judges and breeders began to say that the English Setter was beginning to look more like an Irish Setter, whose Standard permitted much more slope to the top line. Too much slope was not good, and back the breeders went to some of the level-backed dogs for breeding. The pendulum swings, and has swung from the level-backed Setters to the too-sloped-back Setters and is now coming to rest on slightly sloped top lines which the Standard calls for. But all this takes time!

The drawings shown on page 184 clearly demonstrate the three different top lines we just talked about. All three of these drawings were copied from actual photographs of English Setter Champions!

How can public opinion influence a Standard? Let us take for our example, the Cocker Spaniel. The Standard calls for "speed and endurance"—"quick and merry." If a breeder of Cocker Spaniels disregards disposition—"merry"—and breeds only for looks, soon he will have a bad-tempered dog, and the public will not buy a bad-tempered dog. I once heard a new breeder say, "You can buy temperament in a pet shop—I'm breeding for looks." She found out she was wrong and now she, as well as breeders of all dogs, know they must consider temperament every bit as important as looks. The same thing is true regarding coat. The Cocker Spaniel Standard states, "flat or slightly waved, silky and very dense, with ample Setter-like feather." The coat of the Cocker Spaniel is, at the moment, so dense it is difficult to run a comb through it, and when the breed reaches the place where the public refuses to buy the puppies because of the denseness of coat and the difficulties in caring for it, the breeders will soon have to breed for a less dense coat or find no sale for their excess puppies. Public opinion does and will influence the interpretation of a Standard.

I think this little item, which has not been mentioned previously, belongs under the heading of fine points of showing. Don't get lost in the ring! I don't mean that you will lose your way—even a child can't very well do that in a show ring—but don't get so out of the way that the judge can't find you. This actually happened to someone I know. It was a fairly large class and the judge told the exhibitor to wait over in a certain corner of the ring. It was a dark day, rainy and cold, and the judging was being done under a tent. The exhibitor was showing a black dog and she was dressed in dark clothes. She took the judge very literally and went way, way over in the corner where she disappeared against the dark background of spectators. When the judge looked around the ring to make his final decision on which dogs he would place, our friend, the exhibitor, could not be seen. She should have moved out into the ring slightly and the judge's attention would have been called to her dog. Afterward the judge told me that her dog was one of the best in that class and he would probably have won but unfortunately he never saw the dog or the handler again until after the class was completed, the book marked, and the exhibitors leaving the ring. This exhibitor had to learn this lesson the hard way. Fortunately it was only a sanctioned match, but it could have been an important show. The judge spoke to the exhibitor after the show—there was nothing he could do after the class had been judged—and told her she had a good dog, that he was sorry she missed being placed. I don't think she will make this mistake again, do you? When a judge has completed the examination of the last dog in the class, be on your toes, be ready to re-pose your dog, or to move in if you have been asked to wait in a dim, far corner.

While this is not a fine point of handling, it is a suggestion—you might find helpful. Buy yourself a little notebook and keep your dog's complete show record in it. It is amazing how fast one can forget! On the top of the page write the dog's registered name and number. Next to it write his call name. You know, regardless of what the registered name is, you can call your dog any name you wish. Many a dog is called "Butch" whose registered name might sound something like "Handsome Harry of Sunset Hill." Under the name and the number write the sire, dam, breeder, and owner, and date of birth. Now skip a line or two and begin the show record. If you have taken the dog to a sanctioned match, write it down. Include the date of the match, which club ran the match, who judged your dog, and where your dog was placed. Do this for every match you attend. When you go to an all-breed show, do the same thing. List the date, name of show-giving club, the judge, and where he placed you. If you were fortunate enough to get any points, write them down. If you went Reserve Winners it might be a good idea to include the name of the dog or bitch who went Winners. Just because you did not win under a judge is no reason why you shouldn't try him again some time—particularly if you know that the one dog who beat yours on the previous occasion is now a Champion and out of the classes.

The great Maltese winner Ch. Aennchen's Poona Dancer, being presented with the Best in Show award at a Trenton Dog Show. Owned by F.E. Oberstar and L.G. Ward; bred by Mrs. J.P. Antonelli. Photo by Deulin.

One thing this record will do is keep you straight on just how many points your dog has. You probably feel you could never forget something as important as how many points you win, but you might, and with this list you not only know how many points, you also know where and when and under whom you got them.

Carry the book with you to all the shows. Keep it with your show equipment so you won't forget it. It will come in handy when making out entries while at a show. You'd be surprised how easy it is to forget the dog's number or date of birth when you are making your entries, particularly if you own more than one dog.

In the back of the book you might like to jot down a few little notes on judges; those you have shown under as well as those under whom you have not shown. Your record might read something like this: Mr. Jones: Told me he liked large dogs. Mrs. Smith: Can't stand light eyes. Mr. Black: Likes a good-moving one. Mrs. White: Very particular about hindquarters. As you go along and show your dog, you will know when and where you have the best chance, but in the beginning such notes may prove very helpful.

Here is something you can do if you want to use a tidbit to give your dog at the show after he has done a job particularly well or if you are showing a dog usually baited in the ring. Buy some liver—pork liver is the cheapest and the best—and cook it the night before you leave for the show. Allow it to dry. When all the moisture has dried off the outside, pack it in an empty glass jar with a screw top and place in the refrigerator until you are ready to leave. Dogs love it, but be careful, as it doesn't keep too well in warm weather. After it has been properly dried you can handle it with ease and you will not get yourself or your clothes messed up. While I've known a few persons who have had a pocket lined with plastic in which they carried the meat it isn't really necessary once it has been dried.

Several times in this book I have made references to the latch on the exercise pens at shows. The latch, or lock, will vary depending on which superintendent is supplying the pens, but regardless of the type, always check to see that you have securely fastened it whenever you use it. If you are going into the pen and remaining in there with your dog, and even if you have him on a lead and are the only one in the pen, still, as you enter the pen, fasten the latch. Remember that other people will expect the door to be fastened and someone may lift a small dog over the pen wall and turn the dog

Ch. Robin is dwarfed by her numerous prizes in this portrait. This Chihuahua belonged to the Olenicks of Tuckahoe, New York. Photo by Orlando, Three Lions, Inc.

loose. A slight push on the door by the small dog will give him his freedom. At most shows there is no rule about the use of the pen as far as dogs being on or off leads is concerned. At the few shows I know of where special pens are set up for the use of "dogs on lead only" there is no door on the pen.

Don't let your dog stay too long in any exercise pen. If there is any one place at a show where a dog is exposed to germs or disease it is in the exercise pen. Watch your dog, and as soon as he has taken care of his duties there, remove him. Needless sniffing around in the pen will not do him any good. Of necessity these pens are rather small, and only a certain number of dogs can safely and adequately be taken care of within the confines at one time. Be considerate of the numerous others who want to use the pens. Incidentally, you will accomplish something worth while if you can possibly train your dog to use the exercise pen quickly—almost as soon as he enters. I have done this with one of my dogs, and I must say that this particular dog was always a joy to take to shows for this one reason. The moment he entered the pen he did all he had to do and came to the door of the pen and waited to be taken out. He never paid the slightest bit of attention of any other dogs in the pen and he was not too interested in staying in there. Don't allow your dog too much time to play in the pen. At shows where the pen has a sawdust cover in it, a playful dog gets himself full of the sawdust that will have to be removed before the dog is shown—or gets it all over another dog and then someone else has a lot of last minute, unexpected work to do.

This is as good a time as any to tell you just a little about obedience classes at shows. Somewhere in your neighborhood you will find a dog-training class, usually run by a branch of a show-giving club or by an obedience club. Yes, the obedience trial people have clubs of their own. At these classes the owner or handler is taught how to train his dog for obedience trials. The actual training is done at home. Every house pet can make good use of this training in his everyday life. The dog is taught to heel, which means to follow you on your left side close to your heel; to sit when you stop; to sit and stay on command; to down on command, and to down and stay on command; to come on command; and many other exercises which the dog can use daily. A well-trained obedience dog is a joy to take around with you, for he is trained to obey your commands. At the dog shows they have classes, called trials, to test the dog's ability. A premium list always tells you if such classes are held at that particular show. All breeds may compete, and a dog may be shown in obedience *and* regular classes on the same day. There are quite a few rules governing these trials and also your deportment while in the obedience ring. If you are interested in training your dog to compete in obedience trials, I suggest you contact a training club in your area and attend its classes, which are usually held once a week. The leader or trainer will acquaint you with the rules and the steps you take to acquire an obedience title. There are several titles; the first is the addition of the letters "C.D." to your dog's registered name. C.D. stands for Companion Dog and that is just what your dog is when he has completed the first phase of his obedience training. The second title is C.D.X., which means Companion Dog Excellent— self-explanatory. The third title a dog may acquire is U.D., meaning Utility Dog, a dog who is useful; next comes U.D.T., standing for Utility Dog Tracking, a useful dog on tracking; next and final and highest of the obedience titles is T.T., Tracking Test.

There are a great many books written about obedience training and the people in obedience work are very enthusiastic indeed. You will have fun and be "in the thick of it" very shortly after you locate the nearest training club.

There is another activity in dogs which you may not know about— the Junior Showmanship Class. In this class children between the ages of ten and sixteen compete as the best handler. The dog's quality does not count, only the ability of the child to handle the dog in the ring to advantage. This class is always judged by a licensed professional handler, and this group, the handlers, are not only interested in the work but help in many ways to make the class a worthy one. The handler is never paid to judge the class although it frequently takes him from other work for which he is paid.

Aside from getting a ribbon and perhaps a trophy or some candy, the child winning the Open Junior Showmanship Class at five shows is entitled to enter this class at Madison Square Garden, the Westminster Kennel Club show in New York City. All dogs entered in the breeds must have won major points before entering at Westminster, but the children must have won five firsts in the Junior Showmanship class before they may enter at the Garden. By the time a really interested child has shown in Junior Showmanship Classes for a few years he is quite competent and can and does compete against the best in the game. Many children under sixteen have shown a dog completely through to its championship unaided by adults. Watch these children at any show; you will be surprised how really good some of them are. Besides making good handlers of the children, it teaches them sportsmanship and a great deal about dogs and dog shows. These children are the future of the dog game, they will become the breeders, exhibitors, and judges of the future. Indeed, at certain shows there are also junior judging competitions, the winners going to the International Kennel Club show in Chicago for the finals. Your child will enjoy dogs and enjoy accompanying you to dog shows ever so much more if you can interest him in the Junior Showmanship Class.

Now just a few words about field trials. I am not going into detail, as there have been books, many books, written by truly great authorities on the subject. If you own *any* of the sporting breeds, or Basset Hounds, Beagles, or Dachshunds, and you wish to run them at field trials run under the American Kennel Club rules, I suggest you contact your breed club. They will advise you how and where and with whom to get in touch. If you wish to run your dog at American Field trials, write to that organization and ask for the names and addresses of people in your neighborhood who are currently running dogs, or contact one or more of the sportsmen's clubs in your section of the country. Under American Kennel Club rules a dog becomes a field trial champion of record when he has won a certain number of points under a certain number of judges. There are several different stakes run at each trial; there are sanctioned field trials with no championship points awarded and there are licensed and member-club trials at which championship points may be awarded. The points are based on the number of dogs actually running in each stake. As I said before, I won't go into detail—it would take a book just to write the rules to be followed and the procedure for the running of the several different breeds. But I will say this: Field trials and running your dog in them, or even just hunting over a good dog, is a joy not to be equaled by many other sports. And don't let anyone tell you a show dog won't hunt or can't hunt. He certainly will and I personally know a great many sportsmen who are now hunting over dogs which they or their wives have shown. Some are even bench champions! I knew one man who had a dog that was a bench champion, had an obedience title or two, and who had or was about to get his

Tigner's Miss Cinderella, a beautiful white Bichon Frise, winning a good Miscellaneous Class under Isidore Schoenberg. The dog is owned by Ken and Jessie Tigner, Fairytale Bichons, Tonawanda, New York.

This is a typical group of dog show enthusiasts during the lunch hour at an outdoor show. Each family has brought along their own picnic basket— they find a suitable spot and enjoy lunch together. This is one of those rare moments at a show when everyone has time to compare notes on raising puppies, the latest developments in canine medicine, show careers and future shows.

field-trial championship! This dog was also his house pet! Look into this wonderful sport. I'm sure you'll enjoy it!

Getting back to showing dogs, I can't stress enough the importance of good sportsmanship. Remember that you've gone into the sport as a hobby—for fun! You will have more fun and you will have so many more friends and be so much more welcome if you *are* a good sport that for these reasons alone it would be worth your while. The notoriously poor loser is very rarely invited to join the gang at supper at someone's home, or does he often hear these words, "Let's all jump in the car and go somewhere for dinner." The poor sport is not often seen in such happy and interested groups as the folks having a picnic lunch at a dog show in the photograph above.

Even if your heart is breaking for being turned down, go up to the winner and congratulate him and let him be convinced you really mean it. It takes only a minute, but it makes the winner feel good and leaves a pleasant aftertaste. If you've lost, and you must gripe about it, why not wait until you get home? Your husband or wife, or the four walls in your living room, will not have as poor an opinion of you as your fellow exhibitors will have if you really let go. And when you really know dogs you'll find you have a lot less to gripe about. After you have been invited to judge, and you find out what the poor judge goes through trying to decide between many good dogs, you'll have even less to gripe about. So spend some time watching the judging, and after you have mastered your own breed, and think you understand it and know it thoroughly, learn about some of the other breeds. Then learn to recognize a good one of any breed.

Horse racing is referred to as the Sport of Kings. Well, I think we could refer to dogs and dog shows as the Sport of the Entire American Family. Husbands and wives can share an equal enthusiasm in this hobby, and so can Junior and his little sister. Children love to help raise the puppies, and they love entering in the Junior Showmanship Class.

Go to it, folks, and have a really good doggy time!

The Airedale, above, has won many ribbons and awards for his perfection as regards the American Kennel Club standard. The German Shepherd (Alsatian), below, is being shown in Germany in a Field Trial, where both the dog's physical and obedience abilities are being judged.

This beautiful Beagle is Ch. Pixshire's Texas Tally pictured with her handler, Heather Louise Pixley. Tally is also a house dog and a favorite pet, and she is frequently handled at the shows by Heather. Photo by Lloyd W. Olson Studio.

AKC RULES AND REGULATIONS

The American Kennel Club
Incorporated
Rules and Regulations
and
Extracts from By-Laws
RULES AND REGULATIONS
Reprinted by permission of The American Kennel Club

CHAPTER 1
GENERAL EXPLANATIONS
SECTION 1. The word "dog" wherever used in these Rules and Regulations includes both sexes.

SECTION 2. The words "United States of America" wherever used in these Rules and Regulations shall be construed to include all territories and possessions of the United States of America and all vessels sailing under the American Flag.

CHAPTER 4
DOG SHOWS DEFINED
SECTION 1. A member show is a show at which championship points may be awarded, given by a club or association which is a member of The American Kennel Club.

SECTION 2. A licensed show is a show at which championship points may be awarded, given by a club or association which is not a member of The American Kennel Club but which has been specially licensed by The American Kennel Club to give the specific show designated in the license.

SECTION 3. A member or licensed all-breed club may apply to The American Kennel Club for approval to hold a show at which championship points may be awarded with entries restricted to puppies that are eligible for entry in the regular puppy class and dogs that have been placed first, second or third in a regular class at a show at which championship points were awarded, provided the club submitting such an application has held at least one show annually for at least ten years immediately prior to the year in which application for a show so restricted is made, and further provided that there shall not have been less than 900 dogs entered in its show (or in one of its shows if the club holds more than one show a year) in the year preceding the year in which application is made for its first show with entries so restricted.

When an application for this type of restricted entry show has been approved by The American Kennel Club the only dogs eligible for entry shall be puppies that are eligible for entry in the regular puppy class and those dogs that have been placed first, second or third in a regular class at a show at which championship points were awarded held not less than sixty days prior to the first day of the show at which entries will be so restricted.

However, a club making application to hold a show restricted to entries of dogs as specified above may further restrict entries by excluding all puppies or all puppies 6 months and under 9 months and/or by excluding dogs that have placed third or dogs that have placed second and third, provided the extent of these further restrictions are specified on the application.

Any club whose application has been approved to hold a show with restricted entries as described in this section shall indicate the extent of the restrictions in its premium list.

SECTION 4. A member or licensed all-breed club may apply to The

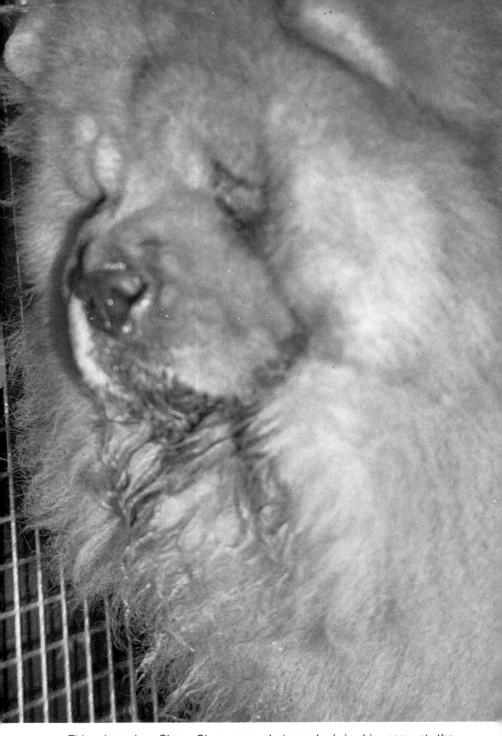

This champion Chow Chow was photographed in his cage at the Westminster Dog Show (1974) awaiting his turn in the show ring.

A beautiful Irish Terrier is posed during a local dog show.

American Kennel Club for approval to hold a show at which championship points may be awarded with entries restricted to dogs that are champions on the records of The American Kennel Club and dogs that have been credited with one or more championship points, provided the club submitting such an application has held at least one show annually for at least 15 years immediately prior to the year in which application for a show so restricted is made, and further provided that there shall not have been less than 1200 dogs entered in its show (or in one of its shows if the club holds more than one show a year) in the year preceding the year in which application is made for its first show with entries so restricted.

When an application for this type of restricted entry show has been approved by The American Kennel Club, the only dogs eligible for entry shall be those dogs that have been recorded as champions and dogs that have been credited with one or more championship points as a result of competition at shows held not less than 60 days prior to the first day of the show at which entries will be so restricted.

However, a club making application to hold a show restricted to entries of dogs as specified above, may further restrict entries by excluding all puppies or all puppies six months and under nine months and/or by excluding dogs that have not been credited with at least one major championship point rating, provided the extent of these further restrictions are specified on the application.

Any club whose application has been approved to hold a show with restricted entries as described in this section shall indicate the extent of the restrictions in its premium list.

SECTION 5. A member or licensed show with a limited entry, at which championship points may be awarded may be given by a club or association in the event said club or association considers it necessary to LIMIT the TOTAL ENTRY at its show due to the limitations of space. The total number of entries to be accepted together with the reason therefor, must be indicated on the cover or title page of the PREMIUM LIST. A specified closing date, in accordance with Chapter 9, Section 9, must be indicated in the premium list together with a statement that entries will close on said date or when the limit has been reached, if prior thereto. No entries can be accepted, cancelled or substituted after the entry is closed. The specified closing date shall be used in determining whether a dog is eligible for the Novice Classes at the show.

SECTION 6. A specialty show is a show given by a club or association formed for the improvement of any one breed of pure-bred dogs, at which championship points may be awarded to said breed.

SECTION 7. An American-bred specialty show is a show for American-bred dogs only, given by a member club or association formed for the improvement of any one breed of pure-bred dogs at which championship points may be awarded to said breed.

SECTION 8. A sanctioned match is an informal meeting at which pure-bred dogs may compete but not for championship points, held by a club

202

or assocation whether or not a member of The American Kennel Club by obtaining the sanction of The American Kennel Club.

CHAPTER 5
MAKING APPLICATION TO HOLD A DOG SHOW

SECTION 1. Each member club or association is entitled to hold one show and one field trial a year without payment of a fee to The American Kennel Club, but must pay a fee of fifteen ($15.00) dollars for each other show and/or field trial which it may hold during the same calendar year.

SECTION 2. Each member club or association which has held a show or shows in any one year shall have first right to claim the corresponding dates for its show or shows to be held in the next succeeding year.

SECTION 3. Each member club or association not a specialty club which shall hold a show at least once in every two consecutive calendar years shall have the sole show privilege in the city, town or district which has been assigned to it as its show territory.

SECTION 4. A member club or association must apply to The American Kennel Club on a regular official form, which will be supplied on request, over the signature of one of its officers, for permission to hold a show, stating in the application the day or days upon which, and the exact location where it desires to hold such show, and sending a copy of any contract, or if verbal, a statement of the substance of the agreement made with the Superintendent or Show Secretary. This application will be referred to the Board of Directors of The American Kennel Club which will consider the same and notify the member club or association of its approval or disapproval of the dates and place selected.

SECTION 5. If a member club or association not a specialty club shall fail to hold a show at least once in every two consecutive calendar years, the Board of Directors of The American Kennel Club upon application may give a license to another club or association which need not be a member of The American Kennel Club to hold a show within the limits of the show territory of the member club or association which has so failed to hold its show.

SECTION 6. If a member club or association not a specialty club shall fail to hold a show within the next calendar year after a licensed show has been held within the show territory of said member club or association, The American Kennel Club will consider such failure sufficient reason to consider an application for membership in The American Kennel Club by any other club or association organized to hold shows within said territory which shall conform to the requirements and conditions of Article IV of the Constitution and By-Laws of The American Kennel Club although said member club or association so in default shall not consent thereto.

SECTION 7. Where there are two or more show-giving member clubs or associations not specialty clubs located in the same show territory, the jurisdiction of said clubs or associations shall be concurrent.

SECTION 8. The use of a club's name for show purposes cannot be transferred.

A champion Great Dane with some of his trophies. Photo by Louise Van der Meid.

Show dogs vary in their capacity to perform and pose satisfactorily within the ring, and some animals are simply better performers than others. Some are "naturals," whereas others have to be trained much more rigorously. The Welsh Terrier shown here is being taught to master the "stand," with the owner using the lead to keep the dog's head up and her palm flat against the tail to maintain it in erect position. Photo by Louise Van der Meid.

SECTION 9. If a non-member club or association wishes to hold a dog show, it must apply to The American Kennel Club on a regular official form, which will be supplied on request, over the signature of one of its officers, for permission to hold a show, stating in the application the day or days upon which, and the exact location where it desires to hold such show, and sending a copy of any contract, or if verbal, a statement of the substance of the agreement made with the Superintendent or Show Secretary. The American Kennel Club is to be supplied with such information with regard to Constitution, By-Laws, names of the officers and members, and the financial responsibility of the applying non-member club or association as The American Kennel Club may request. A non-member club shall pay a license fee for the privilege of holding such show under American Kennel Club rules, the amount of which fee shall be fixed and determined by the Board of Directors of The American Kennel Club. The application will be referred to the Board of Directors of The American Kennel Club, which will consider the same and notify the non-member club or association of its approval or disapproval of the dates and place selected. If the Board of Directors shall disapprove the application, the license fee will be returned to said non-member club or association.

SECTION 10. A member specialty club may hold a show confined to the breed which it sponsors and such show shall carry a championship rating according to the schedule of points of the breed for which the show is given.

SECTION 11. A member specialty club may hold a show confined to American-bred dogs only in which show winners classes may be included and championship points awarded, provided that the necessary regular classes are included in the classification.

SECTION 12. A non-member specialty club may be licensed to hold a show, if the consent in writing that it may be given first shall be obtained from the member specialty club formed for the improvement of the breed sought to be shown which first was admitted to be a member of The American Kennel Club, which member club is commonly known as the Parent Club.

If a Parent Club unreasonably shall withhold its consent in writing to the holding of such show, the non-member specialty club may appeal to the Board of Directors of The American Kennel Club at any time after one month from the time when said consent was requested. A committee of said Board appointed by said Board or between sittings of said Board appointed by the President of The American Kennel Club, or, in his absence, by the Executive Vice-President of The American Kennel Club shall hear the parties who may present their respective contentions, either orally or in writing, and in its discretion may issue a license to the non-member specialty club to hold such show.

SECTION 13. Where a specialty club wishes to consider as its Specialty Show the breed classes at an all-breed show, written application must be made to The American Kennel Club and a fee of $15.00 sent with application. Consent of the parent member specialty club must be secured by the non-member specialty club and forwarded to The American Kennel Club.

206

SECTION 14. A specialty club that wishes to hold a futurity or sweepstake, either in conjunction with a show or as a separate event, must apply to The American Kennel Club on a form which will be supplied on request, for permission to hold the event, whether or not the futurity or sweepstake will be open to non-members.

SECTION 15. The Board of Directors of The American Kennel Club, may, in its discretion grant permission to clubs to hold sanctioned matches, which sanctioned matches shall be governed by such rules and regulations as from time to time shall be determined by the Board of Directors.

SECTION 16. American Kennel Club sanction must be obtained by any club that holds American Kennel Club events, for any type of match for which it solicits or accepts entries from non-members.

SECTION 17. The Board of Directors of The American Kennel Club will not approve applications for shows where dates conflict, unless it be shown that the granting of such applications will not work to the detriment of either show.

SECTION 18. A show-giving club must not advertise or publish the date of any show which it proposes to hold until that date has been approved by The American Kennel Club.

SECTION 19. All clubs holding shows under American Kennel Club rules must have available at each show through their bench show committees, a copy of the latest edition of *The Complete Dog Book* and at least one copy of the rules of The American Kennel Club.

SECTION 20. Any club holding a show for charity if requested must submit to The American Kennel Club within ninety days of date of show, a complete financial statement and receipt from the organization for which the show was held.

SECTION 21. The duration of a dog show will not exceed two days, unless permission be granted by The American Kennel Club for a longer period.

CHAPTER 6
DOG SHOW CLASSIFICATIONS

SECTION 1. The following breeds and/or varieties of breeds, divided by groups, shall be all the breeds and/or varieties of breeds for which regular classes of The American Kennel Club may be provided at any show held under American Kennel Club rules. The Board of Directors may either add to, transfer from one group to another, or delete from said list of breeds and/or varieties of breeds, whenever in its opinion registrations of such breed and/or variety of breed in the Stud Book justify such action.

GROUP 1—SPORTING DOGS
GRIFFONS (WIREHAIRED POINTING)
POINTERS
POINTERS (GERMAN SHORTHAIRED)
POINTERS (GERMAN WIREHAIRED)
RETRIEVERS (CHESAPEAKE BAY)
RETRIEVERS (CURLY-COATED)

Initial training in learning how to show your own dog need not be undertaken with champion quality animals. These German Shepherds are very poor specimens and could never win their championships, but they are excellent for practicing and they are probably equally as good as housepets or working dogs.

RETRIEVERS (FLAT-COATED)
RETRIEVERS (GOLDEN)
RETRIEVERS (LABRADOR)
SETTERS (ENGLISH)
SETTERS (GORDON)
SETTERS (IRISH)
SPANIELS (AMERICAN WATER)
SPANIELS (BRITTANY)
SPANIELS (CLUMBER)
SPANIELS (COCKER)
    Three varieties: Solid Color, Black.
                  Solid Color Other Than Black including Black and Tan.
                  Parti-color.
SPANIELS (ENGLISH COCKER)
SPANIELS (ENGLISH SPRINGER)
SPANIELS (FIELD)
SPANIELS (IRISH WATER)
SPANIELS (SUSSEX)
SPANIELS (WELSH SPRINGER)
VIZSLAS
WEIMARANERS

GROUP 2—HOUNDS

AFGHAN HOUNDS
BASENJIS
BASSET HOUNDS
BEAGLES
    Two varieties: Not exceeding 13 inches in height.
               Over 13 inches but not exceeding 15 inches in height.
BLOODHOUNDS
BORZOIS
COONHOUNDS (BLACK AND TAN)
DACHSHUNDS
    Three varieties: Longhaired.
              Smooth.
              Wirehaired.
DEERHOUNDS (SCOTTISH)
FOXHOUNDS (AMERICAN)
FOXHOUNDS (ENGLISH)
GREYHOUNDS
HARRIERS
IRISH WOLFHOUNDS
NORWEGIAN ELKHOUNDS
OTTER HOUNDS
RHODESIAN RIDGEBACKS
SALUKIS
WHIPPETS

GROUP 3—WORKING DOGS

ALASKAN MALAMUTES
BELGIAN MALINOIS
BELGIAN SHEEPDOGS

BELGIAN TERVUREN

BERNESE MOUNTAIN DOGS

BOUVIERS DES FLANDRES

BOXERS

BRIARDS

BULLMASTIFFS

COLLIES
Two varieties: Rough.
                Smooth.

DOBERMAN PINSCHERS

GERMAN SHEPHERD DOGS

GIANT SCHNAUZERS

GREAT DANES

GREAT PYRENEES

KOMONDOROK

KUVASZOK

MASTIFFS

NEWFOUNDLANDS

OLD ENGLISH SHEEPDOGS

PULIK

ROTTWEILERS

SAMOYEDS

SCHNAUZERS (STANDARD)

SHETLAND SHEEPDOGS

SIBERIAN HUSKIES

ST. BERNARDS

WELSH CORGIS (CARDIGAN)

WELSH CORGIS (PEMBROKE)

GROUP 4—TERRIERS

AIREDALE TERRIERS

AUSTRALIAN TERRIERS

BEDLINGTON TERRIERS

BORDER TERRIERS

BULL TERRIERS
Two varieties: White.
                Colored.

CAIRN TERRIERS

DANDIE DINMONT TERRIERS

FOX TERRIERS
Two varieties: Smooth.
                Wire.

IRISH TERRIERS

KERRY BLUE TERRIERS

LAKELAND TERRIERS

MANCHESTER TERRIERS
Two varieties: Standard, over 12 pounds and not exceeding 22 pounds.
                Toy (in Toy Group).

NORWICH TERRIERS

SCHNAUZERS (MINIATURE)

SCOTTISH TERRIERS

Miniature Schnauzers are very popular dogs. This champion is owned by Ledahof Kennels, New Brunswick, New Jersey. Photo by Three Lions, Inc.

This champion German Short-haired Pointer is being posed by his handler inside his home. Posing and handling routines must be familiar to both the dog and the handler. Photo by Louise Van der Meid.

SEALYHAM TERRIERS
SKYE TERRIERS
STAFFORDSHIRE TERRIERS
WELSH TERRIERS
WEST HIGHLAND WHITE TERRIERS

GROUP 5—TOYS

AFFENPINSCHERS
CHIHUAHUAS
Two varieties: Smooth Coat.
Long Coat.
ENGLISH TOY SPANIELS
Two varieties: King Charles and Ruby.
Blenheim and Prince Charles.
GRIFFONS (BRUSSELS)
ITALIAN GREYHOUNDS
JAPANESE SPANIELS
MALTESE
MANCHESTER TERRIERS
Two varieties: Toy, not exceeding 12 pounds.
Standard (in Terrier Group).
PAPILLONS
PEKINGESE
PINSCHERS (MINIATURE)
POMERANIANS
POODLES
Three varieties: Toy, not exceeding 10 inches.
Miniature (in Non-Sporting Group).
Standard (in Non-Sporting Group).
PUGS
SILKY TERRIERS
YORKSHIRE TERRIERS

GROUP 6—NON-SPORTING DOGS

BOSTON TERRIERS
BULLDOGS
CHOW CHOWS
DALMATIANS
FRENCH BULLDOGS
KEESHONDEN
LHASA APSOS
POODLES
Three varieties: Miniature, over 10 inches and not exceeding 15 inches.
Standard, over 15 inches.
Toy (in Toy Group).
SCHIPPERKES

SECTION 2. No class shall be provided for any dog under six months of age except at sanctioned matches when approved by The American Kennel Club.

SECTION 3. The regular classes of The American Kennel Club shall be as follows:

Puppy
Novice

Bred-by-Exhibitor
American-bred
Open
Winners

SECTION 4. The Puppy Class shall be for dogs that are six months of age and over, but under twelve months, that were whelped in the United States of America or Canada, and that are not champions. The age of a dog shall be calculated up to and inclusive of the first day of a show. For example, a dog whelped on January 1st is eligible to compete in a puppy class at a show the first day of which is July 1st of the same year and may continue to compete in puppy classes at shows up to and including a show the first day of which is the 31st day of December of the same year, but is not eligible to compete in a puppy class at a show the first day of which is January 1st of the following year.

SECTION 5. The Novice Class shall be for dogs six months of age and over, whelped in the United States of America or Canada, which have not, prior to the date of closing of entries, won three first prizes in the Novice Class, a first prize in Bred-by-Exhibitor, American-bred, or Open Classes, nor one or more points toward their championships.

SECTION 6. The Bred-by-Exhibitor Class shall be for dogs whelped in the United States of America, that are six months of age and over, that are not champions, and that are owned wholly or in part by the person or by the spouse of the person who was the breeder or one of the breeders of record.

Dogs entered in this class must be handled in the class by an owner, or by a member of the immediate family of an owner.

For purposes of this section, the members of an immediate family are: husband, wife, father, mother, son, daughter, brother, sister.

SECTION 7. The American-bred Class shall be for all dogs (except champions) six months of age and over, whelped in the United States of America, by reason of a mating which took place in the United States of America.

SECTION 8. The Open Class shall be for any dog six months of age or over except in a member specialty club show held only for American-bred dogs, in which case the Open Class shall be only for American-bred dogs.

SECTION 9. The Winners Class, at shows in which the American-bred and Open Classes are divided by sex, also shall be divided by sex and each division shall be open only to undefeated dogs of the same sex which have won first prizes in either the Puppy, Novice, Bred-by-Exhibitor, American-bred or Open Classes, excepting only in the event that where either the Puppy, Novice or Bred-by-Exhibitor Class shall not have been divided by sex, dogs of the same sex, winning second or third prizes but not having been defeated by a dog of the same sex may compete in the Winners Class provided for their sex. At shows where the American-bred and Open Classes are not divided by sex there shall be but one Winners Class which shall be open only to undefeated dogs of either sex which have won first prizes in

A Saint Bernard champion and well-known Specialty winner Traci La Mardoug, from the famous Mardoug line of Beau Cheval Saints. Traci has won under specialists from the USA and Europe.

American and Canadian Ch. Baron von Shagg-Bark, owned by Ann and Tom Renner of Wells, Maine. This excellent St. Bernard is shown here winning Best of Breed at the 1971 Brookhaven Kennel Club show under judge Earl Adair.

A lineup of St. Bernard bitches being judged at an outdoor show.

either the Puppy, Novice, Bred-by-Exhibitor, American-bred or Open Classes. There shall be no entry fee for competition in the Winners Class.

After the Winners prize has been awarded in one of the sex divisions, where the Winners Class has been divided by sex, any second or third prize winning dog otherwise undefeated in its sex which, however, has been beaten in its class by the dog awarded Winners, shall compete with the other eligible dogs for Reserve Winners. After the Winners prize has been awarded, where the Winners Class is not divided by sex, any otherwise undefeated dog which has been placed second in any previous class to the dog awarded Winners shall compete with the remaining first prize-winners, for Reserve Winners. No eligible dog may be withheld from competition.

Winners Classes shall be allowed only at shows where American-bred and Open Classes shall be given.

A member specialty club holding a show for American-bred dogs only may include Winners Classes, provided the necessary regular classes are included in the classification.

A member club holding a show with restricted entries may include Winners Classes, provided the necessary regular classes are included in the classification.

SECTION 10. No Winners Class, or any class resembling it, shall be given at sanctioned matches.

SECTION 11. Bench show committees may provide such other classes of recognized breeds or recognized varieties of breeds as they may choose, provided they do not conflict with the conditions of the above mentioned classes and are judged before Best of Breed competition.

Local classes, however, may not be divided by sex in shows at which local group classes are provided.

No class may be given in which more than one breed or recognized variety of breed may be entered, except as provided in these rules and regulations.

SECTION 12. A club that provides Winners Classes shall also provide competition for Best of Breed or for Best of Variety in those breeds for which varieties are provided in this chapter. The awards in this competition shall be Best of Breed or Best of Variety of Breed.

The following categories of dogs may be entered and shown in this competition:

Dogs that are Champions of Record.

Dogs which according to their owners' records have completed the requirements for a championship but whose championships are unconfirmed. The entry and showing of dogs whose championships are unconfirmed is limited to a period of 90 days from the date of the show where a dog completed the requirements for a championship according to the owners' records. If, at the end of the 90 day period, the championship of a dog has not been confirmed by The American Kennel Club, no further entries of the dog for Best of Breed competition are to be made until its championship has been confirmed by the AKC.

In addition, the Winners Dog and Winners Bitch (or the dog awarded

Winners, if only one winners prize has been awarded), together with any undefeated dogs that have competed at the show only in additional non-regular classes shall compete for Best of Breed or Best of Variety of Breed.

If the Winners Dog or Winners Bitch is awarded Best of Breed or Best of Variety of Breed, it shall be automatically awarded Best of Winners; otherwise, the Winners Dog and Winners Bitch shall be judged together for Best of Winners following the judging of Best of Breed or Best of Variety of Breed. The dog designated Best of Winners shall be entitled to the number of points based on the number of dogs or bitches competing in the regular classes, whichever is greater. In the event that Winners is awarded in only one sex, there shall be no Best of Winners award.

After Best of Breed or Best of Variety of Breed and Best of Winners have been awarded, the judge shall select Best of Opposite Sex to Best of Breed or Best of Variety of Breed. Eligible for this award are:

Dogs of the opposite sex to Best of Breed or Best of Variety of Breed that have been entered for Best of Breed competition.

The dog awarded Winners of the opposite sex to the Best of Breed or Best of Variety of Breed.

Any undefeated dogs of the opposite sex to Best of Breed or Best of Variety of Breed which have competed at the show only in additional non-regular classes.

SECTION 13. At specialty shows for breeds in which there are varieties as specified in Chapter 6, Section 1, and which are held apart from all-breed shows, Best of Breed shall be judged following the judging of Best of each variety and best of opposite sex to best of each variety. Best of Opposite Sex to Best of Breed shall also be judged. Dogs eligible for Best of Opposite Sex to Best of Breed competition will be found among the best of variety or the bests of opposite sex to bests of variety, according to the sex of the dog placed Best of Breed.

At an all-breed show (even if a specialty club shall designate classes as its specialty show), the judge of a breed in which there are show varieties shall make no placings beyond Best of Variety and Best of Opposite Sex to Best of Variety.

SECTION 14. A club or association holding a show may give six group classes not divided by sex, such groups to be arranged in same order and to comprise the same breeds and recognized varieties of breeds as hereinbefore set forth in Chapter 2, and Section 1 of Chapter 6. All dogs designated by their respective breed judges Best of Breed at the show at which these group classes shall be given shall be eligible to compete in the group classes to which they belong according to this grouping, and all dogs designated Best of Variety in those breeds with more than one recognized variety, shall be eligible to compete in the group classes to which they belong according to this grouping. All entries for these group classes shall be made after judging of the regular classes of The American Kennel Club has been finished and no entry fee shall be charged. In the event that the owner of a dog designated Best of Breed or Best of Variety shall not exhibit the dog in the group

A lovely Maltese, not in the best of condition, but willing to pose at the spur of the moment for a portrait surrounded by a few ribbons. The dog is owned by Mr. and Mrs. Andrew Stodel; photo by Louise Van der Meid.

English Champion Studbriar Chieftain, owned by the Derek Kings, Burghfield, Bucks, England. A magnificent Doberman.

The 1975 W.E.L.K.S. show in England with Mrs. Julia Curnow of Tavey fame judging Doberman Pinschers in the Puppy Bitch Class. First in line is the winner, Ariki Arataki, handled by Derek King. "Sammy" is one of the Dobes owned and shown by Margaret and Derek King, Burghfield, Bucks, England.

class to which it is eligible, no other dog of the same breed or variety of breed shall be allowed to compete.

SECTION 15. A club giving group classes must also give a Best in Show, the winner to be entitled "Best Dog in Show." No entry fee shall be charged but the six group winners must compete.

SECTION 16. A club or association holding a show, if it gives brace classes in the several breeds and recognized varieties of breeds, may also give six brace group classes, not divided by sex; such groups to be arranged in the same order and to comprise the same breeds and recognized varieties of breeds as hereinbefore set forth in Chapter 2 and Section 1 of Chapter 6. All braces of dogs designated by their respective breed judges as Best of Breed or Best of Variety as the case may be at shows at which these brace group classes shall be given, shall be eligible to compete in the brace group classes to which they belong according to this grouping. All entries for these brace group classes shall be made after the judging of the regular classes of The American Kennel Club has been finished and no entry fee shall be charged. In the event that the owner of a brace of dogs designated Best of Breed or Best of Variety shall not exhibit the brace of dogs in the group class to which it is eligible, no other brace of dogs of the same breed or variety of breed shall be allowed to compete.

SECTION 17. If a club or association holding a show shall give these six group classes, it must also give a "Best Brace in Show" in which the six braces of dogs winning the first prizes in the six group classes must compete, but for which no entry fee shall be charged. The winner shall be entitled "The Best Brace in Show."

SECTION 18. A club or association holding a show, if it gives team classes in the several breeds and recognized varieties of breeds, may also give six team group classes not divided by sex, such groups to be arranged in the same order and to comprise the same breeds and recognized varieties of breeds as hereinbefore set forth in Chapter 2 and Section 1 of Chapter 6. All teams of dogs designated by their respective breed judges as Best of Breed or Best of Variety as the case may be at shows at which these team group classes shall be given, shall be eligible to compete in the team group classes to which they belong according to this grouping. All entries for these team group classes shall be made after the judging of the regular classes of The American Kennel Club has been finished and no entry fee shall be charged. In the event that the owner of a team of dogs designated Best of Breed or Best of Variety shall not exhibit the team of dogs in the group class to which it is eligible, no other team of dogs of the same breed or variety of breed shall be allowed to compete.

SECTION 19. If a club or association holding a show shall give these six group classes it must also give a "Best Team in Show" in which the six teams of dogs winning the first prizes in the six group classes must compete, but for which no entry fee shall be charged. The winner shall be entitled "The Best Team in Show."

SECTION 20. A club or association holding a show may give six group classes not divided by sex, open only to local dogs (as designated in its premium list), such groups to be arranged in the same order and to comprise the same breeds and recognized varieties of breeds as hereinbefore set forth in Chapter 2 and Section 1 of Chapter 6. All dogs designated by their respective breed judges "Best in Local Class of the Breed" or "Best in Local Class of the Variety of Breed" at the show at which these group classes shall be given shall be eligible to compete in the group classes to which they belong according to this grouping. No entry fee shall be charged. In the event that the owner of the dog designated "Best in Local Class" shall not exhibit the dog in the group class to which it is eligible, no other dog of the same breed or variety of breed shall be allowed to compete.

SECTION 21. A club giving local group classes may also give a "Best Local Dog in Show." No entry fee shall be charged but the local group winners must compete.

SECTION 22. The Miscellaneous Class shall be for pure-bred dogs of such breeds as may be designated by the Board of Directors of The American Kennel Club. No dog shall be eligible for entry in the Miscellaneous Class unless the owner has been granted an Indefinite Listing Privilege, and unless the ILP number is given on the entry form. Application for an Indefinite Listing Privilege shall be made on a form provided by the AKC and when submitted must be accompanied by a fee set by the Board of Directors.

All Miscellaneous Breeds shall be shown together in a single class except that the class may be divided by sex if so specified in the premium list. There shall be no further competition for dogs entered in this class.

The ribbons for First, Second, Third and Fourth prizes in this class shall be Rose, Brown, Light Green, and Gray, respectively.

At present the Miscellaneous Class is open to the following breeds:
> *Akitas*
> *Australian Cattle Dogs*
> *Australian Kelpies*
> *Border Collies*
> *Cavalier King Charles Spaniels*
> *Ibizan Hounds*
> *Miniature Bull Terriers*
> *Shih Tzus*
> *Soft-Coated Wheaten Terriers*
> *Spinoni Italiani*
> *Tibetan Terriers*

SECTION 23. A registered dog that is six months of age or over and of a breed for which a classification is offered in the premium list may be entered in a show for Exhibition Only at the regular entry fee provided the dog has been awarded first prize in one of the regular classes at a licensed or member show held prior to the closing of entries of the show in which the Exhibition Only entry is made, and provided further that the premium list has not specified that entries for Exhibition Only will not be accepted. The name and

A magnificent face on a
grand champion Shih
Tzu.

Norwegian Elkhound International Champion Trygvie Vikingson, bred and owned by Glenna and Bob Crafts. Photo courtesy of the *Cleveland Plain Dealer*.

date of the show at which the dog was awarded the first prize must be stated on the entry form.

A dog entered for Exhibition Only shall not be shown in any class or competition at that show.

CHAPTER 7
APPROVAL OF JUDGES LISTS AND
PREMIUM LIST PROOFS

SECTION 1. After a club or association has been granted permission by The American Kennel Club to hold a show, it must send for approval by and in time to reach The American Kennel Club at least EIGHT WEEKS before the show date, a list of the names and addresses of the judges whom it has selected to judge its show, giving in each instance the particular breed or breeds of dogs and group classes, if any, which it is desired that each judge shall pass upon, and the name and address of the judge selected to pass upon Best in Show.

The show-giving club must not advertise or publish the name or names of any of the judges which it has selected until the complete list has been approved by The American Kennel Club.

SECTION 2. Each club or association which has been granted permission by The American Kennel Club to hold a dog show or obedience trial must submit in time to reach The American Kennel Club at least EIGHT WEEKS before its date, two printers' proof copies of its proposed premium list. The Show Plans Department of The American Kennel Club will return, not later than six weeks before the show or trial date, one copy of the proof indicating thereon all necessary corrections, deletions and revisions. Attached to the returned proof will be a conditional authorization of The American Kennel Club to print and distribute the premium list. This authorization will list the conditions to be observed or carried out by the show or trial-giving club and its superintendent or show or trial secretary, before printing the premium list.

SECTION 3. Premium lists and entry forms must be printed and sent to prospective exhibitors at least FOUR WEEKS prior to the first day of the show. Two copies of the premium list must be sent to The American Kennel Club at time of distribution.

SECTION 4. Premium lists and entry forms, in order to insure uniformity, must conform to The American Kennel Club official size of 6 x 9 inches and the entry form must conform in every respect with the official form, a sample of which may be had without charge by application to the Secretary of The American Kennel Club.

CHAPTER 8
RIBBONS, PRIZES AND TROPHIES

SECTION 1. All clubs or associations holding dog shows under the rules of The American Kennel Club, except sanctioned matches, shall use the following colors for their prize ribbons or rosettes, in the regular classes of The American Kennel Club and the regular group classes.

First prize —Blue.

Second prize—Red.

Third prize—Yellow.

Fourth prize—White.

Winners—Purple.

Reserve Winners—Purple and White.

Best of Winners—Blue and White.

Special prize—Dark Green.

Best of Breed and Best of Variety of Breed—Purple and Gold.

Best of Opposite Sex to Best of Breed and Best of Opposite Sex to Best of Variety of Breed—Red and White.

and shall use the following colors for their prize ribbons in all additional classes:

First prize—Rose.

Second prize—Brown.

Third prize—Light Green.

Fourth prize—Gray.

SECTION 2. The prize ribbon for Best Local Dog in Show shall be Blue and Gold, and the prize ribbons in local classes and local groups shall be:

First prize—Rose.

Second prize—Brown.

Third prize—Light Green.

Fourth prize—Gray.

SECTION 3. Each ribbon or rosette, except those used at sanctioned matches, shall be at least 2 inches wide, and approximately 8 inches long; and bear on its face a facsimile of the seal of The American Kennel Club, the name of the prize, and the name of the show-giving club with numerals of year, date of show, and name of city or town where show is given.

SECTION 4. If ribbons are given at sanctioned matches, they shall be of the following colors, but may be of any design or size:

First prize—Rose.

Second prize—Brown.

Third prize—Light Green.

Fourth prize—Gray.

Special prize—Green with pink edges.

Best of Breed—Orange.

Best of Match—Pink and Green.

Best of Opposite Sex to Best in Match—Lavender.

SECTION 5. If money prizes are offered in a premium list of a show, a fixed amount for each prize must be stated. All other prizes offered in a premium list of a show must be accurately described or their monetary value must be stated. Alcoholic beverages will not be acceptable as prizes.

SECTION 6. A show-giving club shall not accept the donation of a prize for a competition not provided for at its show.

SECTION 7. All prizes offered in a premium list of a show must be offered to be awarded in the regular procedure of judging, with the exception of those prizes provided for in Sections 9 and 13 of this Chapter.

A champion Shetland Sheepdog with its honors. The honors are attached to the hurdle barrier used in training working dogs.

Opposite:

This beautiful Shetland Sheepdog just relaxed after taking a drink at the Westminster Dog Show in New York (1974).

SECTION 8. Prizes may be offered for outright award at a show for the following placings:

First, Second, Third, Fourth in the Puppy, Novice, Bred-by-Exhibitor, American-bred or Open Classes, or in any division of these designated in the Classification.

First, Second, Third, Fourth in any additional class which the show-giving club may offer in accord with the provisions of Chapter 6, Section 11, and in the Miscellaneous Class (at all-breed shows only).

Winners, Reserve Winners, Best of Winners, Best of Breed or Variety, Best of Opposite Sex to Best of Breed or Variety. At all-breed shows only; First, Second, Third, Fourth in a Group Class and for Best in Show, Best Local in Show, Best Brace in Show and Best Team in Show.

SECTION 9. At specialty shows held apart from all-breed shows, prizes, for outright award, may also be offered for:

Best in Puppy Classes, Best in Novice Classes, Best in Bred-by-Exhibitor Classes, Best in American-bred Classes, Best in Open Classes, Best in any additional classes which the show-giving club may offer in accord with the provisions of Chapter 6, Section 11, in which the sexes are divided.

(In breeds in which there are varieties, a prize may be offered for Best in any of the above classes within the variety.)

SECTION 10. At all-breed shows, prizes may be offered on a three-time win basis for the following awards, provided permanent possession goes to an exhibitor winning the award three times not necessarily with the same dog, and further provided such prizes are offered by the show-giving club itself or through it for competition at its shows only:

Best in Show, Best Local in Show, Best in any one group class.

SECTION 11. At specialty shows, prizes may be offered on a three-time win basis for the following awards, provided permanent possession goes to an exhibitor winning the award three times not necessarily with the same dog and further provided such prizes are offered by the specialty club itself or through it for competition at its specialty shows only:

Best of Breed or Best of Opposite Sex to Best of Breed (where a specialty club considers the classes at an all-breed show as its specialty show, there can be no award for Best of Breed in those breeds in which there are varieties), Best of Variety of Breed or Best of Opposite Sex to Best of Variety, Best of Winners, Winners Dog and Winners Bitch.

SECTION 12. Perpetual prizes and such three-time win prizes as have been in competition prior to September 9, 1952 and which would not be allowed under the terms of the sections in this Chapter will continue to be permitted to be offered under the terms of their original provisions until won outright or otherwise retired. Should premium list copy submitted to the AKC for approval contain such non-allowable prizes, a certification by the Club Secretary stating that the prizes have been in competition prior to September 9, 1952 must be included.

SECTION 13. Annual Specials are prizes offered by member or non-member specialty clubs for outright award at the end of a twelve-month period, the award to be based on the most number of wins at shows, in a designated competition, throughout the period.

Only those clubs which have held specialty shows can offer annual specials.

Specialty clubs must submit two lists of their proposed prizes to The American Kennel Club for its approval. When approval has been obtained, the specialty club shall send copies of the list to its members, with one such copy to The American Kennel Club.

No annual specials may be put into competition until these procedures have been followed and approval obtained.

The terms of such prizes are not to be printed in full in any premium list, but reference may be made to the prizes by listing the name of the specialty club under an appropriate heading. It shall be the obligation of the specialty club to contact superintendents, show secretaries and show-giving clubs, notifying them that their list of annual specials has been approved and that the offer may be published in premium lists by giving the name of the club under an appropriate heading. However, it shall be understood that competition for the various prizes is to count at all licensed or member club dog shows held in the designated period, whether the specialty club's name has been listed in a premium list or not.

If a specialty club wishes to confine competition for its annual specials to certain shows, it may do so, but such restriction must be specified in the terms of its proposed prizes submitted to the AKC and, if approved, the copies of the list sent to members must include the restrictive provision.

SECTION 14. Regular Specials are prizes offered by show-giving member or non-member specialty clubs for outright and automatic award at any show where the terms have been published in full in the premium list and catalog of the show. No prize may be offered for an award higher than Best of Breed or Best of Variety of Breed. It shall be the obligation of specialty clubs offering such regular specials to notify superintendents, show secretaries and show-giving clubs that said prizes may be offered provided the terms are set forth in full in the premium list and catalog of the show. The specialty club will be solely responsible for the distribution of such prizes within 60 days after the completion of a show when it has been determined that all the terms of the awards have been met. No show-giving club is obligated to accept an offering of regular specials.

CHAPTER 9
PREMIUM LISTS AND CLOSING OF ENTRIES

SECTION 1. The awards at a dog show, or the scores made at an obedience trial, will be officially recorded by The American Kennel Club only if the certification of the Secretary of The American Kennel Club is published on the first, second or third page of the premium list stating that permission has been granted by The American Kennel Club for the dog show or obedience trial to be held under American Kennel Club rules and regulations.

If the show shall be given by a club or association not a member of The

Ch. Damae's Caesar, a Silky Terrier (by Ch. Sarszegi Buttons ex Ch. Queen's Own Blue Coral) is shown winning the Toy Group under Judge Langdon Skarda, handled by Michele Leathers. He has a number of Group placings, including two firsts, and is owned by his breeder, Earl D Edge. This Silky has excellent rich silver blue, clear and even through his body coat; he also excels in movement.

Mavrob Fair Jo-Dee, C.D. (by Ch. Fair Dinkum Maverik, C.D., ex Koola-
mina Kristabel). Owner Miss Dee Bierer of Los Angeles wanted a small
Silky, and Jo-Dee weighs only 6½ pounds, but she is a big winner in
Obedience Trials. She is pictured with the F.G. Franciscus Award for the
dog making the highest average score for five times shown with no fail-
ures, presented to her by the Hollywood Dog Obedience Club for her
score average of 191. This mighty mite and her owner are now working
toward advanced Obedience degrees. Miss Bierer also owns a full sister
of Jo-Dee with a conformation title, Ch. Mavrob Rosalie. Jo-Dee and
Rosalie were bred by Ruth and Dick LaBarre. (Note: Jo-Dee's very rich tan
did not reproduce well for the picture).

233

American Kennel Club the words "Licensed Show" must be plainly printed on the title page of the premium list.

SECTION 2. The premium list shall contain a list of the officers of the show-giving club, the address of the secretary, the names of all members of the bench show committee, together with the designation of "Chairman" (and "Obedience Trial Chairman" if an obedience trial is being held by a club in connection with its dog show), the names of the Veterinarians (or name of the local Veterinary Association), the names and addresses of the judges, together with their assignments, and the name and address of the superintendent or show secretary who has been approved by The American Kennel Club. The premium list shall also specify whether the show is Benched or Unbenched, and shall give the exact location of the show, the date or dates on which it is to be held, and the times of opening and closing of the show.

SECTION 2A. An all-breed show-giving club may, at its option, use a condensed form of premium list which shall be identical with the content and format of a regular premium list, and comply with all the pertinent rules except that the listing of breed prizes and trophies offered is omitted as well as the listing of all prizes and trophies offered for an obedience trial if held by the show-giving club with its show. Such prizes and trophies as are offered for best in show and group placements are to be included in a condensed premium list as well as any schedule of class cash prizes that a club proposes to offer.

Two copies of the proposed list of breed and obedience prizes and trophies are to be submitted to AKC for approval at the same time that printers' proof copies of the condensed premium list are submitted. The conditions of all prizes and trophies offered must conform to the provisions of Chapter 8 of these rules and Chapter 1, Section 32 of the Obedience Regulations. A club using a condensed form of premium list is obligated to prepare lists of the breed and obedience prizes and trophies for distribution to prospective entrants and exhibitors on request. Such lists can be printed, multilithed, multigraphed, mimeographed or typed (and photostated) on paper of any suitable size with both sides of the paper being used if the club wishes. In each condensed form of premium list there must be the notation, "A list of breed and obedience prizes and trophies offered can be obtained by writing to (name and address of club secretary and/or superintendent and address)".

A club which chooses to use a condensed form of premium list may also prepare for printing a regular premium list for other than mail distribution. The regular premium list can then be used to fill requests for a listing of breed and obedience prizes and trophies offered and no separate list of breed and obedience prizes and trophies need be prepared.

However, if a regular premium list is used in addition to the condensed premium list, two copies of the printers' proofs of the full premium list must be submitted to the AKC for approval with the notation that it is the club's intention to print a condensed premium list for mailing purposes.

An all-breed obedience trial-giving club may, at its option, use a condensed form of premium list which shall be identical with the content and format of a regular premium list, and comply with all the pertinent rules and regulations except that the listing of prizes and trophies offered is omitted. When a condensed form of premium list is used, the same procedure is to be followed with respect to the prize and trophy list as is required of show-giving clubs and as is set forth in this section.

SECTION 3. Except at specialty club shows, the general classification of recognized breeds divided into six groups and in the same order as set forth in Chapter 2, with the varieties of distinct breeds as described in Section 1 of Chapter 6 added thereto, in their proper groups and alphabetical position, shall be published in the premium list.

SECTION 4. If an all-breed club or association permits a specialty club to consider the classes at its show as their specialty show, the winner of Best of Breed or Best of Variety of Breed if no Best of Breed is awarded, may compete in the group classes of the all-breed show.

SECTION 5. If more than one judge has been approved to judge a specialty show held apart from an all-breed show, the premium list must designate the particular assignments of each judge as approved by The American Kennel Club, except when the specialty club has requested and received approval for the drawing of assignments at the show, in which case a statement to this effect shall appear in the premium list in place of designated assignments.

SECTION 6. A show-giving club shall assume the responsibility of collecting all recording fees for The American Kennel Club, which fact shall be stated in the premium list.

SECTION 7. Bench show committees may make such regulations or additional rules for the government of their shows as shall be considered necessary, provided such regulations or additional rules do not conflict with any rule of The American Kennel Club, and provided they do not discriminate between breeds or between dogs entered in show classes and those entered in obedience classes in the required hour of arrival and the hour of removal. If permission is granted to a club other than the show-giving club for the holding of an obedience trial in connection with a dog show, the obedience club so authorized, must comply with the show-giving club's rules adopted hereunder.

Such regulations or additional rules shall be printed in the premium list and violations thereof shall be considered the same as violations of the rules and regulations of The American Kennel Club.

SECTION 8. No prizes may be accepted or offered by a show-giving club unless they are published in the premium list of the show or in the separate list of prizes if the condensed form of premium list is used; nor may any be withdrawn or the conditions thereof changed after they have been published in the premium list or in the separate list of prizes.

If the donor of a prize that has been published in the premium list of a show or in the separate list of prizes shall fail to furnish the prize, the show-

Ch. Chotovotka's Nota Yankidrink wins Best of Breed and Group First under judge Lorna Demidoff at the Steel City Kennel Club Show in Indiana. Nota is owned by Bob and Dorothy Page of the Chotovotka Kennels. Photo by Robert Holiday.

American, Bermudian and Canadian Ch. Fra-Mar's Soan Diavol pictured winning a Working Group at the Dan Emmett Kennel Club Show with his handler George Heitzman. Judge was Nelson Groh. Photo by Norton of Kent. Owner Marie Wamser of Cleveland, Ohio. Soan was handled and finished to his championship in 29 days at 14 months of age by his owner and was top Husky in the Phillips System in 1966, 1968 and 1969. He was top Siberian Husky in Canada in 1970. Soan and his father, Ch. Frosty Aire's Alcan King, are the first father and son combination to each win a Best in Show award. His record is one Best in Show, 37 Group placings in the U.S.A., five Group placings in Bermuda, and six Group placings in Canada.

giving club shall promptly supply a prize of the same description and of no less value.

The show-giving club shall be responsible for all errors made in publishing offers of prizes and shall, in the event of error, award prizes of equal value; except that if an error has been made in the premium list or in the separate list of prizes in publishing the conditions of a specialty club's Regular Specials (as described in Chapter 8, Section 14) prizes shall be awarded according to the current terms of the specialty club's Regular Specials.

SECTION 9. Every premium list shall specify the date and time at which entries for a show shall close. The premium list shall also specify the name and address of the Superintendent or Show Secretary who is to receive the entries. For all shows other than specialty shows, the specified closing date and time must be no later than as outlined in the following schedule:

For a show which opens on Saturday, Sunday, or Monday, entries not accepted later than noon the Tuesday prior to the Tuesday immediately preceding the show.

For a show which opens on Tuesday, entries accepted not later than noon the Wednesday prior to the Wednesday of the week preceding the show.

For a show which opens on Wednesday, entries accepted not later than noon the Thursday prior to the Thursday of the week preceding the show.

For a show which opens on Thursday, entries accepted not later than noon the Friday prior to the Friday of the week preceding the show.

For a show which opens on Friday, entries accepted not later than noon the Saturday prior to the Saturday of the week preceding the show.

Whenever the closing day noted above falls on a postal holiday, entries received in the first mail only on the following day may be accepted.

CHAPTER 10
JUDGES

SECTION 1. Any reputable person who is in good standing with The American Kennel Club may apply for leave to judge any breed or breeds of pure-bred dogs which in his or her opinion he or she is qualified by training and experience to pass upon, with the exception of persons connected with any publication in the capacity of solicitor for kennel advertisements, persons connected with dog food, dog remedy or kennel supply companies in the capacity of solicitor or salesman, persons employed in and about kennels, persons who buy, sell and in any way trade or traffic in dogs as a means of livelihood in whole or in part, whether or not they be known as dealers (excepting in this instance recognized private and professional handlers to a limited extent as will later appear) and professional show superintendents.

No Judge shall be granted a license to be an annual superintendent.

SECTION 2. Licensed handlers are eligible to judge Specialty Shows which are held apart from All-Breed shows.

Handlers invited by clubs to judge Specialty Shows must apply to The American Kennel Club for approval of each assignment.

Only licensed handlers will be considered for approval to judge Junior Show-manship Classes.

SECTION 3. The application for license to judge must be made on a form which will be supplied by The American Kennel Club upon request and when received by said club will be placed before the Board of Directors of The American Kennel Club who shall determine in each instance whether a license shall be issued.

SECTION 4. The American Kennel Club will not approve as judge for any given show the superintendent, show secretary, or show veterinarians, or club officials of said show acting in any one of these three capacities, and such person cannot officiate or judge at such show under any circumstances.

SECTION 5. Only those persons whose names are on The American Kennel Club's list of eligible judges may, in the discretion of The American Kennel Club, be approved to judge at any member or licensed show, except that if it becomes necessary to replace an advertised judge after the opening of the show and no person on the eligible judges list is available to take his place, the Bench Show Committee may select as a substitute for the advertised judge a person whose name is not on the eligible judges list provided such person is not currently suspended from the privileges of The American Kennel Club, is not currently suspended as a judge and is not ineligible to judge under the provisions of Sections 1, 2 and 4 of this Chapter.

SECTION 6. The American Kennel Club may in its discretion approve as a judge of any sanctioned match, futurity or sweepstake a person who is not currently suspended from the privileges of The American Kennel Club or whose judging privileges are not currently suspended.

SECTION 7. Bench show committees or superintendents shall, in every instance, notify appointed judges of the breeds and group classes upon which they are to pass and such notifications shall be given before the publication of the premium lists.

SECTION 8. Bench show committees or superintendents shall not add to or subtract from the number of breeds or variety groups which a selected judge has agreed to pass upon without first notifying said judge of and obtaining his consent to the contemplated change in his assigned breeds or variety groups, and the judge when so notified may refuse to judge any breeds or variety groups added to his original assignment.

SECTION 9. A bench show committee which shall be informed at any time prior to A WEEK before the opening day of its show that an advertised judge will not fulfil his or her engagement to judge shall substitute a judge in his or her place, which substitute judge must be approved by The American Kennel Club, and shall give notice of the name of the substitute judge to all those who have entered dogs in the classes allotted to be judged by the advertised judge. All those who have entered dogs to be shown under the advertised judge shall be permitted to withdraw their entries at any time prior to the opening day of the show and the entry fees paid for entering such dogs shall be refunded.

Vincent Buoniello's team ready to race at Gardner, Maine, in 1972 in the Open C Class. The Buoniellos, Phyllis and Vincent, of Northport, New York, own the Fortsalong Kennels and have been in Huskies since 1963. Mr. Buoniello is also a judge of Siberian Huskies at the bench shows.

A Miniature Pinscher shows his glory! Photo by Louise Van der Meid.

A Welsh Terrier Champion with some of his honors. Photo by Louise Van der Meid.

Since an entry can be made only under a breed judge, changes in Group or Best in Show assignments do not entitle an exhibitor to a refund.

SECTION 10. Should a Bench Show Committee be informed at any time within a week before the opening of its show, or after its show has opened, that an advertised judge will not fulfil his or her engagement to judge, it shall substitute a qualified judge in his or her place, and shall obtain approval of the change from The American Kennel Club if time allows.

No notice need be sent to those exhibitors who have entered dogs under the advertised judge.

The Bench Show Committee will be responsible for having a notice posted in a prominent place within the show precincts as soon after the show opens as is practical informing exhibitors of the change in judges. An exhibitor who has entered a dog under an advertised judge who is being replaced may withdraw such entry and shall have the entry fee refunded, provided notice of such withdrawal is given to the Superintendent or Show Secretary prior to the start of the judging of the breed which is to be passed upon by a substitute judge.

SECTION 11. In case an advertised judge shall have judged part of the classes of a breed and then finds it impossible to finish, a substitute judge shall be selected by the bench show committee, and in that event the awards made by the regular judge shall stand, and his or her substitute shall judge only the remaining entries in the breed. No dogs entered under the regularly selected judge shall be withheld from competition.

SECTION 12. A substitute judge shall finish the judging of the breed class or group he or she is adjudicating upon if he or she has begun to judge before the advertised judge arrives at the show.

SECTION 13. Any club or association that holds a dog show must prepare, after the entries have closed and not before, a judging program showing the time scheduled for the judging of each breed and each variety for which entries have been accepted. The judging program shall also state the time for the start of group judging, if any. The program shall be based on the judging of about 25 dogs per hour by each judge. Each judge's breed and variety assignments shall be divided into periods of about one hour, except in those cases where the entry in a breed or variety exceeds 30. A copy of the program shall be mailed to the owner of each entered dog and shall be printed in the catalog.

No judging shall occur at any show prior to the time specified for the judging program.

SECTION 14. The maximum number of dogs assigned to any judge in one day, exclusive of groups and best in show, shall never exceed 200; nor shall it exceed the number of advertised hours of the show's duration multiplied by 20, less one hour if the advertised hours exceed six. The advertised hours of a show's duration shall be the hours from the scheduled start of judging to the time shown in the premium list for the closing of the show.

When the entries have closed, if the entry under any judge exceeds the lower of these limits, the Bench Show Committee must select some other judge or judges to whom sufficient breeds or varieties (or at a specialty show, one of the sexes or varieties) can be assigned to bring the total assignment of every judge within the limits, Approval must be obtained from The American Kennel Club for each such reassignment.

Notice must be sent to the owner of each dog affected by such a change in judges at least five days before the opening of the show, and the owner has the right to withdraw his entry and have his entry fee refunded provided notification of his withdrawal is received before the opening of the show by the Superintendent or Show Secretary named in the premium list to receive entries.

SECTION 15. A judge shall not exhibit his dogs or take any dog belonging to another person into the ring at any show at which he is officiating, nor shall he pass judgment in his official capacity upon any dog which he or any member of his immediate household or immediate family (as defined in Chapter 6, Section 6) has handled in the ring more than twice during the preceding twelve months.

SECTION 16. A judge's decision shall be final in all cases affecting the merits of the dogs. Full discretionary power is given to the judge to withhold any, or all, prizes for want of merit. After a class has once been judged in accordance with these rules and regulations, it shall not be rejudged. A class is considered judged when the judge has marked his book which must be done before the following class is examined. If any errors have been made by the judge in marking the awards as made, he may correct the same but must initial any such corrections.

SECTION 17. A judge may order any person or dog from the ring. For the purpose of facilitating the judging, judges are required to exclude from the rings in which they are judging all persons except the steward or stewards and the show attendants assigned to the ring and those actually engaged in exhibiting.

SECTION 18. A judge shall be supplied with a book called the judge's book in which he shall mark all awards and all absent dogs. The original judges' books at shows shall be in the custody of the judge, steward, superintendent, or superintendent's assistant. None other shall be allowed access to them. At the conclusion of the judging, the book must be signed by the judge and any changes which may have been made therein initialed by him.

SECTION 19. A judge's decision, as marked in the judge's book, cannot be changed by him after filing, but an error appearing in the judge's book may be corrected by The American Kennel Club after consultation with the judge.

SECTION 20. Only one judge shall officiate in each Group Class and only one judge shall select the Best in Show.

The Board of Directors suggests that whenever possible the Best in Show be determined by one who has not already judged any breed or group class of said show.

SECTION 21. If a judge disqualifies a dog at any show, he shall make a note in the judge's book giving his reasons for such disqualification. In

Upper photo:
Pekingese Canadian Ch. Toccata's Shadow of Geodan, Winners Bitch and Best of Opposite Sex at the Sandusky Kennel Club show under Judge Ruth Turner. Owner-handled by Jean Carrol of Euclid, Ohio.

Lower photo:
Pekingese American and Canadian Ch. Half Note's Toccata of Su-Con, Best of Breed at a recent Sandusky Kennel Club show under Virginia Keckler. Toccata won the Canadian title at 10 months of age and the American championship under two years of age. Breeder-owned and handled by Jean Carroll, Su-Con Pekingese, Euclid, Ohio.

Upper photo:
Ch. June Valentin, bred and owned by the late Zara Smith of the State of Washington. This fine Pekingese's sire was Alderbourne Chuty Tuo of Kam-Tin, and the dam was Jalna's Star-Ling.

Lower photo:
Swallowdale Bumblebee, a gorgeous red Pekingese sitting pretty at a recent dog show waiting for owner Mrs. E.H. Gatewood of Burlington, New Jersey. Bred by Lt. Col. and Mrs. D.L. Swallow. The sire is Dawoo Prince Orsil ex Swallowdale Mittens. Stephen Klein photograph.

computing the championship points for a breed, said dog shall not be considered as having been present at the show.

CHAPTER 11
HANDLERS

SECTION 1. Any person handling dogs for pay or acting as agent for another for pay at any show held under the rules of The American Kennel Club must hold a license from The American Kennel Club.

Any reputable person who is in good standing with The American Kennel Club may apply to said Club for license to act as a handler or as an agent, which application must be made on a form which will be supplied by said Club upon request. When the application is received by The American Kennel Club the Board of Directors shall determine whether a license shall be issued to the applicant.

SECTION 2. The fee for being granted a license to be a handler or an agent, or an assistant to a handler or an agent, shall be determined by the Board of Directors of The American Kennel Club from time to time in its discretion. Any such license may be granted for any such period of time that the Board of Directors deems appropriate in its discretion. All granted licenses shall expire December 31 of the year in which they are granted.

Effective January 1, 1954, no fee is required with applications for Handler's or Assistant Handler's licenses.

No handler's license will be granted to a person residing in the same household with a licensed judge.

CHAPTER 12
SELECTION OF SUPERINTENDENT, SHOW SECRETARY
AND VETERINARIANS

When a club or association, which has been granted permission to hold a show, sends to The American Kennel Club its list of judges to be approved, it must enclose with that list the names and addresses of its proposed Superintendent or Show Secretary, and Veterinarian or Veterinarians, all of whom must be approved by the Board of Directors of The American Kennel Club before the premium list of the show can be printed.

CHAPTER 13
SUPERINTENDENTS AND SHOW SECRETARIES

SECTION 1. The Superintendent of a Dog Show held under the rules of The American Kennel Club must hold a license from The American Kennel Club.

SECTION 2. Any qualified person may make application to The American Kennel Club for approval to act as Show Secretary of a dog show.

SECTION 3. Superintendents and Show Secretaries will be responsible along with bench show committees for making complete arrangements for attendance at a show with each one of the veterinarians selected to service a show. In the event that a recognized Veterinary Association is to furnish the veterinarians, the complete arrangements shall be made with the secretary of the Association.

SECTION 4. Superintendents and Show Secretaries shall have on hand at every show the various official American Kennel Club forms for the use of veterinarians.

SECTION 5. Superintendents and Show Secretaries shall be prepared, at any show, to furnish the forms to be used by any exhibitor or handler who seeks a health examination of a dog. Upon the filing of the completed form by an exhibitor or handler, it shall be the superintendent's and show secretary's duty to see that the owner or agent of the dog takes his dog to the "Veterinarian Headquarters" for the examination.

SECTION 6. Superintendents and Show Secretaries will be responsible for providing at every show a suitable space which will serve as the headquarters of the show veterinarians. At an indoor show this space will be marked off in some adequate way and a sign "Veterinarian Headquarters" must be prominently displayed. At an outdoor show, where canvas is available, the veterinarians' office shall be set up under its own individual tent. Where no tenting is used the Headquarters must be arranged so that the veterinarians are afforded protection from the weather.

SECTION 7. Superintendents and Show Secretaries are required, with their report of a show, to list the names of all veterinarians who served at a show and give the hours that each veterinarian was present.

SECTION 8. Superintendents and Show Secretaries shall have the sole authority to enforce the rules having to do with the benching of dogs.

SECTION 9. Superintendents and Show Secretaries shall have the sole authority to excuse a dog from being shown on the recommendation of the veterinarian under Chapter 15, Section 4 (c) and to release dogs from a show prior to the published time for the releasing of dogs, except in the event that a dog has been dismissed from a show by a veterinarian under Chapter 15, Section 4 (b).

SECTION 10. Bench show committees and superintendents of dog shows shall be held responsible for the enforcement of all rules and regulations relating to shows and must provide themselves with a copy of The American Kennel Club rules and regulations for reference.

SECTION 11. The Superintendent or Show Secretary will be held accountable for the maintenance of clean and orderly conditions throughout the precincts of the show during all hours when dogs are permitted to be present.

SECTION 12. Any reputable person who is in good standing with The American Kennel Club may apply to said Club for license to act as Superintendent of a Dog Show, which application must be made on a form which will be supplied by said Club upon request. When the application is received by The American Kennel Club its Board of Directors shall determine whether the applicant is reasonably qualified from training and experience to act as Superintendent of a Dog Show and whether a license shall be issued to said applicant.

The fee for being granted a yearly license to be a Superintendent and the fee for renewal of said license each year shall be determined by the Board

A champion Briard at a dog show. Briards, long used as hunting and guard dogs in rural sections of continental Europe, are becoming more popular in the United States, Canada and Great Britain.

Regardless of the breed of dog you choose to meet your own particular circumstances, the sport of showing dogs offers much room for personal satisfaction in learning how to do a job well. Whether your breed is Bulldog (right) or Golden Retriever (below), showing your dog opens up new avenues of learning and fulfillment.

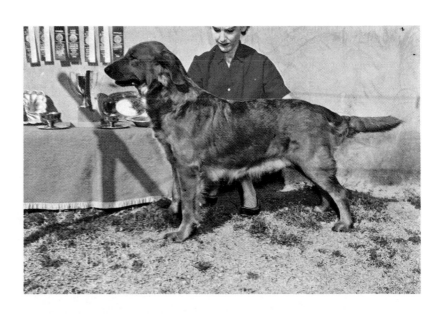

of Directors of The American Kennel Club. The fee for being granted a license to superintend one show and/or one field trial only shall be determined in like manner.

No yearly license will be issued to any person until he or she has superintended at least three dogs shows or field trials.

No annual superintendent shall be granted a license to be a judge.

CHAPTER 14
ADMISSION AND EXAMINATION OF DOGS
ENTERED IN A SHOW

SECTION 1. The bench show committee of an all-breed club or a specialty club holding a dog show must elect whether all dogs are to be inspected in respect to their apparent health before being admitted to the show or whether dogs will be allowed to enter a show's premises without such inspection. If the bench show committee decides that all dogs are to be inspected, the designation "Examined Show" shall be printed on the title page of the premium list and catalog.

SECTION 2. An "Examined Show" is one at which each dog is subject to a health inspection by one of the show's veterinarians before being allowed to enter a show's premises.

SECTION 3. For an "Examined Show" a club must employ a sufficient number of qualified veterinarians to insure the inspection and admission of dogs without undue delay, and shall arrange to have its full complement of veterinarians present during the hours of the show when dogs will be admitted. If dogs are to be admitted to a show's premises before the published opening hour, then the bench show committee of a club must arrange to have one or more of its veterinarians on duty during such time.

SECTION 4. For an "Examined Show" a club or its superintendent shall provide a "Veterinarian Enclosure" into which and through which every dog must pass before it is admitted to a show's premises. The "Enclosure" is to be set up between an entrance to a show's building or grounds and the premises of a show and shall be of sufficient size to meet the needs of the veterinarians and allow for the orderly and prompt passage of exhibitors and dogs. Clubs and superintendents will be responsible for providing safeguards against the possibility of a dog getting into a show's premises without first having passed through the "Enclosure."

There shall also be provided within the "Enclosure" a quarantine area in which there will be benches for dogs that the show veterinarians may wish to hold for an examination.

SECTION 5. For an "Examined Show" a club or its superintendent shall provide in the enclosure for the use of its veterinarians the following items:

Examination tables (with non-slip footing surface and large enough to hold the largest dogs);

Tables for the use of the Veterinarians;

Rubber gloves;

250

Disinfectant (either zepheran chloride or roccal);
Wash bowls and paper towels;
Waste disposal cans;
"Passed" rubber stamps and stamp pads;
Forms to be completed by Veterinarians for all dogs not passed.

In addition a club or its superintendent shall appoint persons to serve in the Enclosure whose duty it will be to provide such help for the veterinarians as they may require and to direct the orderly passage of exhibitors and dogs through the Enclosure.

SECTION 6. If the bench show committee of a club chooses to hold an "Examined Show" the chairman shall complete a form that shall be supplied by The American Kennel Club which is to be attached to the club's application for a date. This form will include a representation that the club is prepared to provide an adequate number of veterinarians, that the layout of the club's proposed building or grounds is such that an adequate "Veterinarians Enclosure" (and benches) can be set up as described in these rules and that the club and its superintendent will properly administer the admission of dogs to the show premises in accordance with these rules.

SECTION 7. When a club is holding an "Examined Show" of more than one day's duration, all of the requirements set forth in this chapter shall be applicable to all dogs that have been temporarily removed from the show premises at the close of the first day and are required to be returned to the show premises on the second day.

CHAPTER 15
DUTIES AND RESPONSIBILITIES OF
SHOW VETERINARIANS

SECTION 1. Any reputable person who is in good standing with The American Kennel Club and who has been duly qualified to practice his profession by law may act as veterinarian of a dog show.

SECTION 2. Every club that holds a licensed or member show shall employ one or more veterinarians who are qualified as described in Section 1, to serve in an official capacity. At least one of these veterinarians shall be in attendance during the entire progress of the show. The duties of the veterinarians shall be to give advisory opinions to Judges and to Bench Show Committees on the physical conditions of dogs, when requested by such officials as provided for in these rules to examine the health of dogs at the request of exhibitors and handlers; and to render first aid to dogs in cases of sickness or injury occurring at the show. Show veterinarians are not required to be familiar with the Dog Show Rules or breed standards affecting the disqualification or eligibility of dogs, and should not attempt to interpret the effect of their advisory opinions on the status of dogs under the rules or standards. They should not discuss with exhibitors or handlers the advisory opinions given to Judges and Bench Show Committees. Show

Ch. Starheir's Aaron Ardee, the #1 winning Irish Setter in the history of the breed! Aaron has won more Bests in Show, Groups and Bests of the Breed than any other Irish Setter. Over 380 judges awarded him more than 465 top placement ribbons during his show career, which also established a record with his defeating over 68,000 other dogs of all breeds to win his top position in the Phillips System. He is pictured above winning a February, 1974 Best in Show at Louisville under judge Vincent Perry. Handled by Dick Cooper for owners Hugh and Virginia Rumbaugh, Fleetwood Farms, Akron, Ohio.

Opposite:
Irish Setter Dual Champion Duffin Miss Duffy, C.D., owned by Emily Schweitzer, Verbu Kennels in Dundee, Illinois, and trained in the field by Jake Huizenga of Oxton Kennels in Salinas, California. Miss Duffy is pictured here being awarded a prize by Louis Iacobucci, President of the Irish Setter Club of America.

veterinarians are not to be called on to treat dogs for physical conditions that existed before they were brought to the show. In addition, at an Examined Show it will be the duty of the veterinarian to pass or reject all dogs coming into the Veterinarians Enclosure.

SECTION 3. At an "Examined Show," it will also be the duty of the show veterinarians to make a visual inspection of every dog that comes into the "Veterinarians Enclosure." Dogs with outward symptoms of illness or disease are to be held within the Enclosure for examination to determine whether they are to be admitted. The identification cards of admitted dogs shall be stamped "passed" by the examining veterinarian.

SECTION 4. Veterinarians serving a show will have complete authority to:

(a) Reject any dog at the entrance to a show's premises which he considers may endanger the health of any other dogs;

(b) Dismiss any dog that has been admitted to a show which he considers may endanger the health of other dogs;

(c) Recommend to the superintendent or show secretary the excusing of any dog from being shown or from the show premises provided he considers that the showing of the dog in the ring or its remaining within the show premises would impair the dog's health.

In all cases where a dog is rejected, dismissed or recommended for excusing from judging or the show premises, the veterinarian shall complete a form, which will be provided giving the basis for his decision, or opinion, and shall file the form with the superintendent or show secretary.

SECTION 5. Veterinarians may request exhibitors and handlers to open dogs' mouths, but when they consider it necessary may do so themselves, provided however that in the latter instance they wear rubber gloves and take proper sanitary precautions.

SECTION 6. Upon the presentation at the "Veterinarians Headquarters" of a dog whose health has been questioned by an exhibitor or handler, it shall be the duty of one of the show veterinarians, as soon as practical, to make an examination of the dog. If he considers that the dog should be dismissed from the show, he will ask the superintendent or show secretary to see that the dog is removed.

SECTION 7. Veterinarians serving a show will be expected to make full use of the area provided for them as a headquarters. Where practical, at least one veterinarian should be in attendance at the headquarters during the entire time that a show is in progress. At an "Examined Show" the "Veterinarians Enclosure" is to be used as a headquarters until such time as the entrance to the enclosure has been closed and no more dogs are to be admitted to it.

CHAPTER 16
DOG SHOW ENTRIES
CONDITIONS OF DOGS AFFECTING ELIGIBILITY

SECTION 1. No dog shall be eligible to be entered in a licensed or member dog show, except for dogs entered in the Miscellaneous Class, unless it is either individually registered in the AKC Stud Book or part of an AKC registered litter, or otherwise, if whelped outside the United States of America and owned by a resident of the U.S.A. or Canada, unless it has been registered in its country of birth with a foreign registry organization whose pedigrees are acceptable for AKC registration.

An unregistered dog that is part of an AKC registered litter or an unregistered dog with an acceptable foreign registration that was whelped outside the U.S.A. and that is owned by a resident of the U.S.A. or Canada may, without special AKC approval, be entered in licensed or member dog shows that are held not later than 30 days after the date of the first licensed or member dog show in which the dog was entered, but only provided that the AKC litter registration number or the individual foreign registration number and the name of the country of birth, are shown on the entry form, and provided further that the same name, which in the case of an imported or Canadian owned dog must be the name on the foreign registration, is used for the dog each time.

No dog that has not been individually registered with The American Kennel Club when first entered in a licensed or member dog show shall be eligible to be entered in any licensed or member dog show that is held more than 30 days after the date of the first licensed or member dog show in which it was entered, unless the dog's individual AKC registration number is shown on the entry form, or unless the owner has received from The American Kennel Club an extension notice in writing authorizing further entries of the dog for a specified time with its AKC litter number or individual foreign registration number. No such extension will be granted unless the owner can clearly demonstrate, in a letter addressed to the Show Records Department of The American Kennel Club requesting such extension, that the delay in registration is due to circumstances for which he is not responsible.

Such extension notice will be void upon registration of the dog or upon expiration of the period for which the extension has been granted if that occurs earlier, but upon application further extensions may be granted.

If a dog is later individually registered with a name that is not identical to the name under which it has been entered in dog shows prior to individual registration, each entry form entering the dog in a licensed or member dog show after the owner has received the individual registration certificate must show the registered name followed by "formerly shown as" and the name under which the dog was previously shown, until the dog has been awarded one of the four places in a regular class at a licensed or member show.

SECTION 2. At every show held under the rules of The American Kennel Club, a recording fee not to exceed 25 cents may be required for every dog entered. This recording fee is to help defray expenses involved in keeping show records, and applies to all dogs entered. If a dog is entered in more than one class at a show, the recording fee applies only to first entry.

Suffolk Nicholas Nikita, owned by Mrs. Claire Wolff of Sayville, New York; this Samoyed won his first points toward championship at seven months of age.

The Board of Directors shall determine, from time to time, whether a recording fee shall be required, and the amount of it.

Effective June 1, 1954 *recording fees are not required.*

SECTION 3. Every dog must be entered in the name of the person who actually owned the dog at the time entries closed. The right to exhibit a dog cannot be transferred. A registered dog which has been acquired by some person other than the owner as recorded with The American Kennel Club must be entered in the name of its new owner at any show for which entries close after the date upon which the dog was acquired, and application for transfer of ownership must be sent to The American Kennel Club by the new owner within seven days after the last day of the show. The new owner should state on the entry form that transfer application has been mailed to The American Kennel Club or will be mailed shortly. If there is any unavoidable delay in obtaining the completed application required to record the transfer, The American Kennel Club may grant a reasonable extension of time, provided the new owner notifies the show records department of The American Kennel Club by mail within seven days after the show, of the reason for the delay. If an entry is made by a duly authorized agent of the owner, the name of the actual owner must be shown on the entry form. If a dog is owned by an association, the name of the association and a list of its officers must be shown on the entry form.

SECTION 4. To be acceptable, an entry must be submitted with required entry fee, on an official American Kennel Club entry form, signed by the owner or his duly authorized agent, and must include all of the following information: Name of the club holding the show; date of the show; breed; variety, if any; sex; full description of the class or classes in which entered; full name of dog; individual registration number or AKC litter number or, for a dog entered in the Miscellaneous Class, ILP number; name and address of the actual owner or owners. For a dog whelped outside the U.S.A. that is not AKC registered, the entry form must show the individual foreign registration number and country of birth. In addition, an entry in the Puppy, Novice, Bred-by-Exhibitor, or American-bred class must include the place of birth; an entry in the Puppy Class must include the date of birth; and an entry in the Bred-by-Exhibitor class must include the name or names of the breeder or breeders.

No entry may be accepted unless it is received by the Superintendent or Show Secretary named in the premium list to receive entries prior to the closing date and hour as published in the premium list, and unless it meets all the requirements of the foregoing paragraph and all other specific requirements printed in the premium list.

SECTION 5. No entry shall be made and no entry shall be accepted by a Superintendent or Show Secretary which specifies any condition as to its acceptance.

SECTION 6. No change may be made in any otherwise acceptable entry form unless the change is received in writing or by telegraph, by the Superintendent or Show Secretary named in the premium list to receive entries, prior to the published closing date and hour for entries, except that a correction may be made in the sex of a dog at a show prior to the judging. No dog wrongly entered in a class may otherwise be transferred to another class. Owners are responsible for errors in entry forms, regardless of who may make such errors.

SECTION 7. No entry shall be received from any person who is not in good standing with The American Kennel Club on the day of the closing of the entries. Before accepting entries, a list of persons not in good standing must be obtained by the Show Superintendent or Show Secretary from The American Kennel Club.

SECTION 8. No entry shall be made under a kennel name unless that name has been registered with The American Kennel Club. All entries made under a kennel name must be signed with the kennel name followed by the word "registered." An "exhibitor" or "entrant" is the individual or, if a partnership, all the members of the partnership exhibiting or entering in a dog show. In the case of such an entry by a partnership every member of the partnership shall be in good standing with The American Kennel Club before the entry will be accepted; and in case of any infraction of these rules, all the partners shall be held equally responsible.

SECTION 9. A dog which is blind, deaf, castrated, spayed, or which has been changed in appearance by artificial means except as specified in the standard for its breed, or a male which does not have two normal testicles normally located in the scrotum, may not compete at any show and will be disqualified. A dog will not be considered to have been changed by artificial means because of removal of dew claws or docking of tail if it is of a breed in which such removal or docking is a regularly approved practice which is not contrary to the standard.

A dog which is lame may not compete at any show and will be disqualified unless an official show veterinarian, after examining the dog at the judge's request, certifies that the lameness is due to a temporary condition.

When a judge finds evidence of any of these conditions in any dog he is judging he must, before proceeding with the judging, notify the Superintendent or Show Secretary and must call an official show veterinarian to examine the dog in the ring and to give the judge an advisory opinion in writing on the condition of the dog. Only after he has seen the veterinarian's opinion in writing shall the judge render his own decision and record it in the judge's book, marking the dog "disqualified" and stating the reason if he determines that disqualification is required under this rule. The judge's decision is final and need not necessarily agree with the veterinarian's opinion except in the case of lameness to the extent specified in the second paragraph of this Section. The written opinion of the veterinarian shall in all cases be forwarded to The American Kennel Club by the Superintendent or Show Secretary.

When a dog has been disqualified under this rule or under the standard for its breed, either by a judge or by decision of a Bench Show Committee, any awards at that show shall be cancelled by The American Kennel Club

Here is a wonderful example of a good handler. These photographs were taken during the judging of a Junior Showmanship Class. Note how well set up the dog is in both pictures; note the child is paying attention at all times to the dog, not the ringside; note when the judge is in the rear how she is holding the dog's head to keep him calm and also from turning around; note that she has even removed the lead which would be done with this breed in breed competition.

and the dog may not again be shown unless and until, following application by the owner to The American Kennel Club, the owner has received official notification from The American Kennel Club that the dog's show eligibility has been reinstated. The American Kennel Club will not entertain any application for reinstatement of a male which has been disqualified as not having two normal testicles normally located in the scrotum until the dog is twelve (12) months old.

SECTION 9-A. Any dog whose ears have been cropped or cut in any way shall be ineligible to compete at any show in any state where the laws prohibit the same except subject to the provisions of such laws.

SECTION 9-B. No dog shall be eligible to compete at any show and no dog shall receive any award at any show in the event the natural color or shade of natural color or the natural markings of the dog have been altered or changed by the use of any substance whether such substance may have been used for cleaning purposes or for any other reason. Such cleaning substances are to be removed before the dog enters the ring.

If in the judge's opinion any substance has been used to alter or change the natural color or shade of natural color or natural markings of a dog, then in such event the judge shall withhold any and all awards from such dog, and the judge shall make a note in the judge's book giving his reason for withholding such award. The handler or the owner, or both, of any dog or dogs from which any award has been withheld for violation of this section of the rules, or any judge who shall fail to perform his duties under this section shall be subject to disciplinary action.

SECTION 10. No dog shall be eligible to compete at any show, no dog shall be brought into the grounds or premises of any dog show, and any dog which may have been brought into the grounds or premises of a dog show shall immediately be removed, if it

(a) shows clinical symptoms of distemper, infectious hepatitis, leptospirosis or other communicable disease, or ·

(b) is known to have been in contact with distemper, infectious hepatitis, leptospirosis or other communicable disease within thirty days prior to the opening of the show, or

(c) has been kenneled within thirty days prior to the opening of the show on premises on which there existed distemper, infectious hepatitis, leptospirosis or other communicable disease.

SECTION 11. A club may engage dogs not entered in its show as a special attraction provided the written approval of The American Kennel Club is first obtained.

SECTION 12. No dog not regularly entered in a show, other than one engaged as a special attraction, shall be allowed within the show precincts, except when the club has stated in its premium list that space will be provided for dogs not entered in the show. The club must then provide an area, clearly identified by an appropriate sign. This area shall be exclusively for dogs which are either en route to or from other shows in which entered, or which are being delivered to new owners or custodians, or being returned to their owners. No dog may be placed in this area if it is entered in the show, nor unless it is registered or registrable and eligible to be shown under American Kennel Club rules and the standard for its breed.

An owner or agent who wishes to use this facility shall, upon entering the show, file with the Superintendent or Show Secretary a form giving the dog's registration data and the reason for its presence. The Superintendent or Show Secretary will then issue a tag identifying the dog. This tag is to be attached to the crate or container which the owner or agent must supply.

No one except owners or agents in charge of these dogs and show officials shall be admitted to the area, and there shall be no benching, nor any offering for sale, breeding, nor displaying of these dogs. Such dogs will not be permitted in any other part of the show precincts except for minimum periods when necessary for exercising, and then only when accompanied by the owners or their agents.

Dogs in this area shall be subject to all the rules relating to health and veterinarians. The Superintendent or Show Secretary shall be responsible for compliance with this rule.

SECTION 13. Any person acting in the capacity of Superintendent (or Show Secretary where there is no Superintendent), official veterinarian, or judge at a show, or any member of his immediate household or immediate family (as defined in Chapter 6, Section 6) shall not exhibit, act as agent or handler at the show, and dogs owned wholly or in part by him or by any member of his immediate household or immediate family shall be ineligible to be entered at that show.

SECTION 14. No entry shall be made at any show under a judge of any dog which said judge or any member of his immediate household or immediate family (as defined in Chapter 6, Section 6) has been known to have owned, handled in the ring more than twice, sold, held under lease or boarded within one year prior to the date of the show.

SECTION 15. Any show-giving club which accepts an entry fee other than that published in its premium list, or in any way discriminates between exhibitors or entrants, shall be disciplined. No show-giving club shall offer to any one owner or handler any special inducement, such as trophies, reduced entry fees, rebates, additional prize money, or any other concession, for entering more than one dog in the show.

SECTION 16. A Bench Show Committee may decline any entries or may remove any dog from its show for cause, but in each such instance shall file good and sufficient reasons for so doing with The American Kennel Club.

CHAPTER 17
THE CATALOG

SECTION 1. Every Bench Show Committee shall provide a printed catalog which shall contain all particulars required of exhibitors entering dogs as hereinafter provided. It shall also contain the exact location of the show, the date or dates on which it is to be held, the times of opening and closing of the show, a list of all officers and members of the Bench Show Committee, names and complete addresses of all judges and of the Superintendent or Show Secretary, the names of the veterinarians or local veterinary association providing veterinary service at the show, and an alphabetical list of the names and addresses of all exhibitors.

SECTION 2. Every catalog must bear on its cover or title page: "This show is held under American Kennel Club rules."

SECTION 3. If the show shall be given by a club or association not a member of The American Kennel Club the words "Licensed Show" must be plainly printed on the title page of the catalog.

SECTION 4. The catalog shall be in book form 6 x 9 inches in size. It shall contain the names and particulars of all dogs entered in the show, arranged as follows: catalog number; name of owner; name of dog; AKC registration number, or litter number or "ILP" number for an unregistered dog, or foreign registration number and country for an unregistered imported dog; date of birth; name of breeder; names of sire and dam. The entries shall be catalogued by groups, breeds, varieties, and regular classes, in the order given in Chapter 6. The information on dogs entered in any additional classes shall appear following the space provided for recording Winners Bitch and Reserve Winners Bitch followed by the particulars of those dogs entered for Best of Breed except that the entries in Brace, Team, Stud Dog, Brood Bitch, or any other classes in which the judge's decision is based on the merits of more than one dog shall appear following the list of dogs entered for Best of Breed and the space provided for Best of Breed, Best of Winners and Best of Opposite Sex awards. The particulars of those dogs entered for Exhibition Only shall appear following all other entries in the breed or variety.

Additional requirements for format and contents of the catalog may be prescribed by the Board of Directors.

SECTION 5. The schedule of points toward championship governing each breed in the show shall be published in the catalog.

SECTION 6. All prizes offered in the premium list of a show or in the separate list of prizes if the condensed form of premium list is used, shall be printed in the catalog, and no change shall be made in the descriptions or conditions of these prizes, nor shall any prize or trophy be added that was not offered in the premium list or in the separate list of prizes.

CHAPTER 18

BENCHING OF DOGS

SECTION 1. At a Benched Show to which admission is charged, every dog twelve months old and over that is entered and present must be on its bench throughout the advertised hours of the show's duration, except for the necessary periods when it is actually being prepared for showing at its crate, or is being shown, or is in the exercise ring, or is being taken to or from these places. The advertised hours of the show's duration shall be the hours from the scheduled start of judging to the time shown in the premium list for the closing of the show.

No such dog shall be in its crate during the advertised hours of the show's duration except by written permission of the Superintendent or Show Secretary, and except for a period of one hour before the time printed in the program for the judging of its breed or variety and, if it becomes eligible for its Group or for Best in Show, for a period of one hour before the time printed in the program for the judging of such competition.

SECTION 2. The provisions of Section 1 also apply to a dog under 12 months of age except that it need not be benched until after the judging of the breed classes for which it is entered or becomes eligible and it may be in its crate until the judging of those classes. At a two day show it is required to be present only on the day it is to be judged.

SECTION 3. Failure to comply with these rules may cause cancellation of the dog's winnings, and subject the owner, handler, and Superintendent or Show Secretary to a fine and suspension of license and privileges.

SECTION 4. No signs shall be displayed on a bench except the plaque or emblem of a show-giving specialty club to which the dog's owner belongs, and signs not over 11 x 14 inches offering dogs or puppies for sale, or giving the kennel name and address of the owner, or the dog's name and a list of awards won by it at that show, or the name of a show-giving specialty club of which the dog's owner is a member. No prizes or ribbons shall be displayed on the bench except those won by the dog at that show.

SECTION 5. At an Unbenched Show, a sign stating that the show is unbenched shall be prominently displayed wherever admission tickets are sold.

CHAPTER 19
MEASURING, WEIGHING AND COLOR DETERMINATIONS WHEN FACTORS OF DISQUALIFICATION IN BREED STANDARDS OR ELIGIBILITY UNDER THE CONDITIONS OF A CLASS OR DIVISION OF A CLASS.
CANCELLATION OF AWARDS

SECTION 1. Every dog entered and present at a show must compete in all competitions in its breed or variety for which it is entered or becomes eligible, unless it has been excused, dismissed, disqualified or found to be ineligible, under the rules.

SECTION 2. Any club or association giving a dog show must provide arm cards and shall see that every person exhibiting a dog wears, when in the ring, an arm card containing thereon the catalog number of the dog being exhibited; but no badges, coats with kennel names thereon or ribbon prizes shall be worn or displayed, nor other visible means of identification used, by an individual when exhibiting a dog in the ring.

SECTION 3. Any club or association giving a dog show must provide in every ring a board upon which the awards must be written after each class is judged.

SECTION 4. The owner of a dog that is entered in a show, or the owner's agent, may request a determination of a dog's height or a dog's weight, if these factors are breed standard disqualifications, conditions of a class or conditions of a division of a class in which the dog is entered. Such requests may be made at any time after the opening of a show, but must be made before the scheduled time of the judging of the breed or variety. The determination, as made, shall be recorded on an American Kennel Club measuring and weighing form, and note of the height or weight of the dog, as the case may be, must promptly be made in the judge's book, by the superintendent or show secretary.

If the height or weight of the dog as determined under this Section is in accord with the breed standard or the conditions of the class or division thereof in which it is entered, the determination shall hold good for the duration of that show, and that show only and the dog cannot be in any way challenged or protested as to height or weight at that show, except that a judge may request a reweighing of the dog when it comes under judgment, and a determination made at that time shall supersede the previous determination.

If the height or weight of the dog as determined under this Section is not in accord with the breed standard or the conditions of the class or division thereof in which it is entered, the dog shall immediately be declared ineligible to compete by the Superintendent or Show Secretary and shall be marked absent in the Judge's Book. Such a dog shall not be brought into the judging ring and may be excused from the show immediately. The eligibility of such a dog to compete at subsequent shows shall not be affected.

SECTION 5. In those breeds where certain heights or weights are specified in the standard as disqualifications, or in any class or division of a class the conditions of which include a height or weight specification, it shall be the judge's responsibility to initiate a determination as to whether a dog is to be disqualified or declared to be ineligible for the class.

If, in the judge's opinion, the height or weight of a dog under judgment appears not to be in accord with the breed standard or the conditions of a class or division thereof, the judge, before proceeding with the judging, must notify the superintendent or show secretary and request that the dog's height or weight be determined by persons appointed by the bench show committee for that purpose, unless the dog's height has previously been determined at the show, or unless the dog's weight has previously been determined at the show other than under the provisions of Chapter 19, Section 4. When a completed AKC measuring and weighing form has been submitted to the judge by such persons, giving the height or weight of the dog, the judge shall then disqualify the dog if its height or weight is such as to require disqualification under the standard of the breed, or shall declare the dog to be ineligible if its height or weight is such as to not conform with the conditions of the class or division in which it is competing, in either case making note of the fact in the judge's book.

If, in the opinion of any competing exhibitor or handler then in the ring, the height or weight of a dog under judgment (not previously determined at the show) appears not to be in accord with the breed standard or the conditions of a class or division thereof, such exhibitor or handler may, prior to the time the judge has marked his book, request the judge to proceed as above in obtaining a determination of the dog's height or weight. After the judge has obtained the completed AKC measuring and weighing form giving the height or weight of the dog, he shall then disqualify the dog if its height or weight is such as to require disqualification under the standard of the breed, or shall declare the dog to be ineligible if its height or weight is such as to not conform with the conditions of the class or division in which it is competing, in either case making note of the fact in the judge's book.

Any dog thus disqualified by the judge may not again be shown unless and until, following application by the owner to The American Kennel Club the owner has received official notification from The American Kennel Club that the dog's show eligibility has been reinstated.

Any dog thus declared ineligible by the judge for a class or division thereof shall be considered to have been wrongly entered in the class and cannot be transferred to any other class or division at the show.

Any dog that has been found to be ineligible as to height under the conditions of a class may not again be shown in that class unless and until, following application by the owner to The American Kennel Club, the owner has received official notification from The American Kennel Club that the dog's show eligibility has been reinstated. However, without making such application to The American Kennel Club, the owner of such a dog may enter the dog in a different class, provided the measurement made at the show is within the specified height limits of such class.

SECTION 6. Bench Show Committees shall be responsible for providing a suitable measuring stand and accurate scales at every show. Bench Show Committees must appoint three persons whose duty it will be, when called upon, to determine a dog's height or weight.

SECTION 7. In those breeds where certain colors or markings are specified in the standard as disqualifications, or in any class or division of a class where a certain color, or colors or combinations of colors are required by the conditions of the class or division thereof, it shall be the judge's responsibility to determine whether a dog is to be disqualified or declared to be ineligible for the class.

If, in the opinion of the judge, the dog's color or markings are such as to require disqualification, the judge shall disqualify the dog, making note of the fact in the judge's book.

If, in the opinion of the judge, the dog's color markings do not meet the requirements of the class or division of a class in which the dog is competing, the judge shall declare the dog ineligible to compete in that class or division of class, making note of the fact in the judge's book.

If, in the opinion of any competing exhibitor or handler then in the ring, the color or markings or combination of colors of a dog under judgment are such as to disqualify under the standard or are such as not to meet the requirements of the class or division thereof, such exhibitor or handler may, prior to the time the judge has marked his book, request the judge to render an opinion of the dog's color(s) and markings. Before proceeding with the judging, the judge must write his opinion on an AKC form that will be supplied by the superintendent or show secretary for that purpose, and shall disqualify the dog if its color or markings are such as to require disqualification under the breed standard or shall declare the dog ineligible if the color or markings do not meet the requirements of the class or division thereof in which the dog is competing, in either case making note of the fact in the judge's book.

Any dog thus disqualified by the judge under the standard may not again be shown unless and until, following application by the owner to The American Kennel Club, the owner has received official notification from The American Kennel Club that the dog's show eligibility has been reinstated.

Any dog thus declared by the judge to be ineligible for a class or division thereof shall be considered to have been wrongly entered in the class and cannot be transferred to any other class or division at that show.

SECTION 8. If an ineligible dog has been entered in any licensed or member dog show, or if the name of the owner given on the entry form is not that of the person or persons who actually owned the dog at the time entries closed, or if shown in a class for which it has not been entered, or if its entry form is deemed invalid or unacceptable by The American Kennel Club under these rules, all resulting awards shall be cancelled by The American Kennel Club. In computing the championship points the dog shall not be counted as having competed.

SECTION 9. If the catalog and/or the judge's book of any show shall by error or mistake set forth any information contrary to the information which appears on the entry form of the dog for that show, the Bench Show Committee and/or the Superintendent of the show, upon request of the owner or handler of said dog prior to the judging, shall correct the entry in the judge's book and in the marked catalog to be sent to The American Kennel Club and said dog properly may compete in all classes and for all prizes for which its entry form discloses it was properly entered.

SECTION 10. If an award in any of the regular classes is cancelled, the dog judged next in order of merit shall be moved up and the award to the dog moved up shall be counted the same as if it had been the original award. If there is no dog of record to move up, the award shall be void.

SECTION 11. If the win of a dog shall be cancelled by The American Kennel Club the owner of the dog shall return all ribbons and prizes to the show-giving club within ten days of receipt of the notice of the cancellation from The American Kennel Club. The show-giving club shall in each instance of failure to comply with this rule notify The American Kennel Club of such failure and The American Kennel Club upon receipt of such notice forthwith shall suspend the exhibitor so in default from all privileges of The American Kennel Club and notify the exhibitor so in default that it has done so, and said suspension shall continue until The American Kennel Club is notified that restitution has been made.

CHAPTER 20
PROTESTS AGAINST DOGS

SECTION 1. Every exhibitor and handler shall have the right to request through the superintendent or show secretary the examination, by one of a show's veterinarians, of any dog within a show's premises which is considered to endanger the health of other dogs in a show. The request is to be in writing and on a form obtainable from a superintendent or show secretary, whose duty it will be to see that the subject dog is promptly taken to the "Veterinarian Headquarters" by its owner or the owner's agent.

SECTION 2. A protest against a dog may be made by any exhibitor, entrant or any member of a member club of The American Kennel Club. It shall be in writing, and be lodged with the secretary of the show-giving club within seven (7) days of the last day of the show unless the same be made by The American Kennel Club, provided, however, that a protest calling for a decision as to the physical condition of a dog which can be determined only with the advice of a veterinarian or at the time of showing shall be made before the closing of the show.

No protest will be entertained unless accompanied by a deposit of five ($5.00) dollars, which will be returned if the protest is sustained. This does not apply to protests by The American Kennel Club, nor to a protest made in the ring previous to the rendering of his decision by the judge.

SECTION 3. If a protest shall be made during the holding of a show the bench show committee shall hold a meeting as soon as possible and give all parties concerned an opportunity to be heard and shall at once render its decision. If a protest shall be made subsequent to the show it shall be decided by the show-giving club within thirty (30) days of its receipt. Five days' notice of the date and place of hearing shall be given to all parties concerned. Written copies of all decisions on protests shall be forwarded immediately to The American Kennel Club.

SECTION 4. An appeal to The American Kennel Club from a decision of a bench show committee where a dog has been protested may be taken and shall be forwarded to The American Kennel Club within seven (7) days of the date on which the decision was rendered together with a deposit of ten ($10.00) dollars. If the decision be sustained the deposit shall be forfeited, but if reversed, the deposit shall be returned.

SECTION 5. Any person who is handling a competing dog in the ring in any breed competition may then verbally protest to the judge before the judge has marked any award in his book, alleging that a dog being shown in the competition has a condition which makes it ineligible to compete under Chapter 16, Section 9, or Chapter 16, Section 9-B, of these rules, or a condition requiring disqualification under the standard for the breed; except that a verbal protest alleging that the height or weight or natural color and markings of a dog requiring its disqualification under the breed standard or a determination of its ineligibility under the conditions of its class must be made under Chapter 19, Sections 5 or 7.

When such a protest is made, the judge, before proceeding with the judging, must notify the superintendent or show secretary and must call an official show veterinarian to examine the dog in the ring and give the judge an advisory opinion, in writing, on the condition of the dog. Only after he has seen the veterinarian's opinion in writing shall the judge render his own decision and record it in the judge's book, marking the dog "Disqualified" and stating the reason if he determines that disqualification is required under Chapter 16, Section 9, or under the breed standard.

If the judge, after seeing the veterinarian's written opinion, determines that the dog is ineligible to compete because of violation of Chapter 16, Section 9-B, he shall withhold any award to the dog and mark the judge's book "Ineligible to compete, award withheld," stating the reason for his decision.

A dog determined by a judge to be ineligible to compete under Chapter 16, Section 9-B, unless such determination is based on the use of a substance only for cleaning purposes, may not again be shown until an official record has been made by The American Kennel Club of its true color or markings. If the color and markings of the dog as recorded are such as not to be a disqualification under the standard of its breed, the dog's show eligibility will be reinstated.

The written opinion of the veterinarian shall in all cases be forwarded to The American Kennel Club by the Superintendent or Show Secretary.

CHAPTER 21
CHAMPIONSHIPS

SECTION 1. Championship points will be recorded for Winners Dog and Winners Bitch, when Winners Classes are divided by sex, for each breed or variety listed in Chapter 6, Section 1, at licensed or member dog shows approved by The American Kennel Club, provided the certification of the Secretary as described in Chapter 9, Section 1, has been printed in the premium list for the show.

Championship points will be recorded according to the number of eligible dogs competing in the regular classes of each sex in each breed or variety, and according to the Schedule of Points established by the Board of Directors. In counting the number of eligible dogs in competition, a dog that is disqualified, or that is dismissed, excused or ordered from the ring by the Judge, or from which all awards are withheld, or for which all awards are cancelled by The American Kennel Club, shall not be included.

If the Winners Class is not divided by sex, championship points will be recorded for the dog or bitch awarded Winners, based on the schedule of points for the sex of the breed or variety for which the greater number in competition is required.

SECTION 2. A dog which in its breed competition at a show shall have been placed Winners and which also shall have won its group class at the same show shall be awarded championship points figured at the highest point rating of any breed or recognized variety or height of any breed entered in the show and entitled to winners points in its group, or if it also shall have been designated Best in Show, shall be awarded championship points figured at the highest point rating of any breed or recognized variety or height of any breed entered and entitled to winners points in the show. The final points to be awarded under this section shall not be in addition to but inclusive of any points previously awarded the dog in its breed competition or under the provisions of this section.

SECTION 3. At shows in which the winners' classes of certain breeds are divided into recognized varieties of those breeds as specified in Section 1 of Chapter 6 of these Rules and Regulations, the procedure for computing championship points shall be the same as if each recognized variety were a separate breed.

SECTION 4. Any dog which shall have won fifteen points shall become a Champion of Record, if six or more of said points shall have been won at two shows with a rating of three or more championship points each and under two different judges, and some one or more of the balance of said points shall have been won under some other judge or judges than the two judges referred to above. A dog becomes a champion when it is so officially recorded by The American Kennel Club and when registered in the Stud Book shall be entitled to a championship certificate.

SECTION 5. Any dog which has been awarded the title of Champion of Record may be designated as a "Dual Champion" after it also has been awarded the title of Field Champion, but no certificate will be awarded for a Dual Championship.

CHAPTER 22
SUBMISSION OF A SHOW'S RECORDS TO AKC

SECTION 1. A show-giving club shall pay or distribute all prizes offered at its show within thirty (30) days after The American Kennel Club has checked the awards of said show.

SECTION 2. After each licensed or member club dog show a catalog marked with all awards and absent dogs, certified to by the superintendent or show secretary of the show, together with all judges' books, all original entry forms and a report of the show must be sent to The American Kennel Club so as to reach its office within seven (7) days after the close of the show. Penalty for noncompliance, one ($1.00) dollar for each day's delay and such other penalties as may be imposed by the Board of Directors of The American Kennel Club. All recording fees shall be paid to The American Kennel Club within seven (7) days after the close of the show.

CHAPTER 23
STEWARDS

The following policy has been adopted by the Board of Directors regarding stewarding at dog shows:

Clubs should appoint a chief steward well in advance of the date of their show whose duty it will be to invite a sufficient number of experienced persons to act as stewards in the judging rings on the day of the show. No person should be asked to serve as a steward whose judging or handling privileges are suspended or whose superintending privileges have been revoked. The chief steward should, as soon as practicable, confirm in writing, to each person who accepts an invitation to steward, the date and location of the show, the time at which they are to report for duty, and their particular ring assignment.

In preparing the schedule of ring assignments, the chief steward and other club officials should keep in mind that no person should serve as a steward with a judge under whom he has an entry, or under whom, in the course of the day's judging, such entry may become eligible to compete. If it becomes necessary during the show to reshuffle stewarding assignments, care should be taken to see that a person is not assigned to serve as steward with a judge if there is any possibility that the judge, later in the show, will be passing upon an entry of the steward.

Persons should be selected who are familiar with judging procedure, breed classifications and rules. It should be borne in mind that a good steward makes the work of judging easier by relieving the judge of necessary detail; by assembling classes promptly, he will be able to keep the judging program on schedule and eliminate to a large extent delays between classes.

The chief steward should use his discretion in the assigning of more than one steward to a ring, but it is advisable that two stewards be asked to serve in those rings where judges have heavy assignments.

Stewards will notify the judge when all the dogs are in the ring for each class and call his attention to known absentees. Under no circumstances should a steward make any notation in the judge's book or erase or strike out any notation made by the judge.

Stewards should mark the blackboard or awards board promptly after each class has been judged and will be responsible for returning to the chief steward or superintendent upon the completion of the judging all prize money, trophies and ribbons not awarded.

Stewards should have in mind that they have been selected to help the judge and not to advise him. They should carefully refrain from discussing or seeming to discuss the dogs or the exhibitors with the judge and should not, under any circumstances, show or give the appearance of showing the catalog to a judge. Stewards should not take or seem to take any part in judging. When they are not actively engaged in their duties, they should place themselves in such part of the rings as will not interfere with the view of those watching the judging, and should not permit persons to crowd about the ring entrance and interfere with access to the ring.

The foregoing policy should be observed by clubs holding member and licensed obedience trials, in addition to the applicable obedience regulations and the practices established for persons stewarding in obedience rings.

EXTRACTS FROM BY-LAWS
CHAPTER 24
DISCIPLINE

Article XII of the Constitution and By-Laws of The American Kennel Club provides:

SECTION 1. Any club or association or person or persons interested in pure-bred dogs may prefer charges against any other club or association, or person or persons, for conduct alleged to have been prejudicial to the best interests of pure-bred dogs, dog shows, obedience trials or field trials, or prejudicial to the best interests of The American Kennel Club, which charges shall be made in writing in duplicate setting forth in detail the nature thereof, shall be signed and sworn to by an officer of the club or association or by the person or persons making the same before some person qualified to administer oaths and shall be sent to The American Kennel Club together with a deposit of ten ($10.00) dollars, which sum shall become the property of The American Kennel Club if said charges shall not be sustained, or shall be returned if said charges are sustained, or if The American Kennel Club shall refuse to entertain jurisdiction thereof.

SECTION 2. The bench show, obedience trial or field trial committee of a club or association shall have the right to suspend any person from the privileges of The American Kennel Club for conduct prejudicial to the best interests of pure-bred dogs, dog shows, obedience trials, field trials or The American Kennel Club, alleged to have occurred in connection with or during the progress of its show, obedience trial or field trial, after the alleged offender has been given an opportunity to be heard.

Notice in writing must be sent promptly by registered mail by the bench show, obedience trial or field trial committee to the person suspended and a duplicate notice giving the name and address of the person suspended and full details as to the reasons for the suspension must be forwarded to The American Kennel Club within seven days.

An appeal may be taken from a decision of a bench show, obedience trial or field trial committee. Notice in writing claiming such appeal together with a deposit of five ($5.00) dollars must be sent to The American Kennel Club within thirty days after the date of suspension. The Board of Directors may itself hear said appeal or may refer it to a committee of the Board, or to a Trial Board to be heard. The deposit shall become the property of The American Kennel Club if the decision is confirmed, or shall be returned to the appellant if the decision is not confirmed.

SECTION 3. Upon receipt of duly preferred charges the Board of Directors of The American Kennel Club at its election either may itself consider the same or send the same to a Trial Board for hearing.

In either case a notice which shall state that said charges have been filed and shall set forth a copy of the same shall be sent to the club or association, or person or persons against which or whom said charges have been preferred, which club or association, or person or persons herein shall be known as and called the defendant. The club or association or person or persons which or who shall have preferred said charges herein shall be known as and called the complainant.

Said notice also shall set forth a time and place at which the defendant may attend and present any defense or answer which the defendant may wish to make.

If the complainant shall fail or refuse to appear and prosecute said charges or if the defendant shall fail or refuse to appear and present a defense at the time and place designated for the hearing of said charges, without giving a reasonable excuse for such failure or refusal, the Board of Directors or the Trial Board to which said charges have been referred may suspend whichever party shall be so in default from the privileges of The American Kennel Club for a period of six months or until such time as the party so in default shall be prepared to appear ready and willing to prosecute or defend said charge, as the case may be.

SECTION 4. The Board of Directors shall have the power to investigate any matters which may be brought to its attention in connection with the objects for which this Club was founded, or it may appoint a committee or Trial Board to investigate, in which event the same procedure shall be followed and the same rules shall apply as in a trial before a Trial Board.

If after such investigation the Board of Directors believes that sufficient evidence exists to warrant the filing of charges, it may file or direct the filing of such charges. The Board of Directors acting in accordance with the provisions of this Article may prefer charges for conduct prejudicial to the best interests of The American Kennel Club against persons who shall bring to its attention any matter which upon investigation shall be found to have been reported to it from malicious or untruthful motives or to have been based upon suspicion without foundation of fact or knowledge.

SECTION 5. The Board of Directors of The American Kennel Club shall have power to prefer charges against any association or other club, or person or persons, for conduct alleged to be prejudicial to pure-bred dogs, dog shows, obedience trials or field trials or to the best interests of The American Kennel Club, and pending the final determination of any such charges, may withhold the privileges of The American Kennel Club from any such other person or body against whom charges are pending.

SECTION 6. The Board of Directors shall have the power to suspend from the privileges of The American Kennel Club any member or delegate pending final action by the delegates in accordance with the provisions of this section, for conduct alleged to have been prejudicial to the best interest of The American Kennel Club or for violation of its constitution, by-laws or rules.

The Board of Directors shall then file charges and promptly set a date for a hearing and send to such suspended member or delegate by registered mail at least ten days prior to the date so fixed, notice of the time when and the place where the suspended member or delegate may be heard in its or his defense. Said notice shall also set forth a copy of the charges.

The Board of Directors may itself hear the evidence of the suspended member or delegate and any witnesses or may refer the charges to a committee of the Board or to a Trial Board to take the testimony and to report its findings or recommendations to the Board of Directors.

The Board of Directors, after hearing or reviewing the evidence, shall report its findings to The American Kennel Club at the next regular meeting of the Club, whereupon the delegates shall take action upon said findings and by a majority vote of the delegates present may reinstate, continue the suspension for a stated time or expel such member or delegate from The American Kennel Club.

SECTION 7. The American Kennel Club shall have the power by a two-thirds vote of the Delegates present and voting at any regular meeting to suspend from the privileges of The American Kennel Club any member or delegate for conduct alleged to have been prejudicial to the best interests of The American Kennel Club or for violation of its constitution, by-laws or rules.

The order of suspension thus made shall then be referred to the Board of Directors for hearing and report under the procedure as set forth in Paragraphs 2, 3 and 4 of Section 6 of this article.

SECTION 8. The Board of Directors of The American Kennel Club shall have power to hear as an original matter any charges preferred and to review and finally determine any appeal which may be made to the Board of Directors from the decision of a Trial Board or Bench Show, Obedience Trial or Field Trial Committee, and in each instance in which it shall find the charges to have been sustained, it shall impose such penalty as said Board of Directors may decide to be just and proper.

SECTION 9. The Board of Directors of The American Kennel Club and any Trial Board of The American Kennel Club with the permission of the Board of Directors of The American Kennel Club first obtained in writing, may in the discretion of said Board of Directors, and if necessary at the Club's expense, summon witnesses or a member of any Trial Board, Bench Show Committee, Obedience Trial Committee or Field Trial Committee to attend any and all hearings held under the provisions of Articles XII and XIII of the Constitution and By-Laws of The American Kennel Club. Said Board of Directors may suspend from the privileges of The American Kennel Club for a period of six months or until such time as he or she shall appear and be prepared and willing to testify any person so summoned who without reasonable excuse shall fail to appear and testify.

SECTION 10. The Board of Directors of The American Kennel Club shall, at the next meeting of the Board after an appeal is made from the decision of a Trial Board or Bench Show, Obedience Trial or Field Trial Committee, name a date for the hearing of such appeal and shall cause notice of the time when and place where said hearing is to be held to be sent to all parties in interest by registered mail at least fourteen (14) days prior to the date named.

SECTION 11. Penalties may range from a reprimand or fine to suspension for life from all privileges of The American Kennel Club.

SECTION 12. The Treasurer of The American Kennel Club shall enforce all monetary penalties.

SECTION 13. The suspension or disqualification of a person shall date from the day of the perpetration of the act or from any date subsequent thereto which shall be fixed after hearing by a Trial Board or by the Board of Directors of The American Kennel Club and shall apply to all dogs owned or subsequently acquired by the person so suspended or disqualified.

SECTION 14. All privileges of The American Kennel Club shall be withheld from any person suspended or disqualified.

SECTION 15. Any club, association or organization which shall hold a dog show, obedience trial, field trial or dog exhibition of any kind not in accordance with the rules of The American Kennel Club which apply to such show, obedience trial, field trial or exhibition may be disciplined even to the extent of being deprived of all privileges of The American Kennel Club for a stated period of time or indefinitely, and if such club, association or organization shall be a member of The American Kennel Club, it may be expelled from membership therein.

SECTION 16. No Club or association licensed by The American Kennel Club to give a show, obedience trial, hold a field trial or give a dog exhibition of any kind shall employ in any capacity, accept the donation of a prize or money from, or permit to be within the walls or boundaries of its building or grounds, if a dog show or obedience trial, or its grounds, if a field trial, save only as a spectator, any person known to be under suspension or disqualification from the privileges of The American Kennel Club or any employee or member of a corporation which shall be under suspension or disqualification from the privileges of The American Kennel Club. And any contract for floor space at a show, or contract for advertising space in a catalog, premium list or other printed matter, in connection with the giving of said show, shall bear upon it the following condition: "This space is sold with the understanding that should the privileges of The American Kennel Club be withdrawn from the purchaser of this space prior to the carrying out of this contract, this contract is thereby automatically cancelled, and any money paid by the purchaser for such space shall be refunded."

SECTION 17. No member club or association under suspension shall be represented by its delegate and no delegate under suspension shall act for a member or in any official capacity for The American Kennel Club during the period of suspension.

SECTION 18. Any association, club, person or persons suspended or disqualified by The American Kennel Club or from whom the privileges of The American Kennel Club have been withheld, may apply for reinstatement or restoration of privileges upon paying a fee, the amount of which may be fixed and determined by the Board of Directors of The American Kennel Club. Until said fee has been paid the application shall not be acted upon.

SECTION 19. As much of Article XII of these By-Laws as the Board of Directors of The American Kennel Club shall indicate shall be printed in any book or pamphlet which The American Kennel Club shall cause to be published containing the Rules of said Club.

CHAPTER 25

TRIAL BOARDS

Article XIII of the Constitution and By-Laws of The American Kennel Club provides:

SECTION 1. Trial Boards shall be appointed from time to time by the Board of Directors of The American Kennel Club and shall consist of three members for each Board, one of whom, if practicable, should be an attorney-at-law, and no one of whom shall be a director of The American Kennel Club. In case one or more members of a Trial Board shall be unable to sit in any given case, the President, or in his absence, the Executive Vice-President of The American Kennel Club, may appoint a substitute or substitutes for such case. In case of the absence of one or more members of said Board, the remaining member or members may hear and determine a case if the parties being heard shall consent thereto.

SECTION 2. Trial Boards shall hear and decide by a majority vote matters submitted to them by the Board of Directors and shall have power to impose a fine not to exceed twenty-five ($25.00) dollars and/or withhold the privileges of the Club for a period of not more than six months, or may recommend to said Board of Directors the withholding of privileges for a longer period or may recommend disqualification or the imposition of fines exceeding twenty-five ($25.00) dollars.

If a Trial Board recommends the withholding of privileges or disqualification to the Board of Directors, the privileges of the Club shall be automatically withheld until the Board of Directors has adopted or refused to adopt such recommendation.

SECTION 3. Trial Boards shall have power to disqualify any person or withhold from any person all the privileges of The American Kennel Club for a period of not more than six months or to recommend to said Board of Directors the penalty of disqualification or the withholding of privileges for a longer period for improper or disorderly conduct during a hearing or a trial.

SECTION 4. Trial Boards shall keep minutes of their sittings.

SECTION 5. The decisions of Trial Boards shall be in writing signed by all members attending, and have annexed thereto all exhibits and papers offered before them. Each decision, together with complete copies of the minutes and testimony taken, shall be filed with the Secretary of The American Kennel Club within ten days of the date of the rendering of the decision. It shall be the duty of the Secretary of The American Kennel Club, when received, at once to notify in writing all parties in interest of the decision of a Trial Board.

SECTION 6. An appeal may be taken to the Board of Directors from any decision of a Trial Board, whether it be a decision in which the Trial

Board itself imposes a certain penalty and/or fine, or one in which the Trial Board recommends that the Board of Directors shall impose a certain penalty and/or fine. Notice in writing claiming such appeal together with a deposit of twenty-five ($25.00) dollars must be sent to The American Kennel Club within thirty days after the receipt of the notice of the decision or recommendation of the Trial Board. The Board of Directors may itself hear said appeal or may refer it to a committee of the Board to be heard. The deposit of twenty-five ($25.00) dollars shall become the property of The American Kennel Club if the decision or recommendation of the Trial Board shall be confirmed, or shall be returned to the appellant if it shall not be confirmed. If the aggrieved party shall fail to take such appeal to the Board of Directors, there shall be no further right of appeal of any kind.

SECTION 7. Article XIII of these By-Laws shall be printed in any book or pamphlet which The American Kennel Club shall cause to be published containing the Rules of said club.

GENERAL INDEX OF SUBJECT MATTER

A

Absentees, 127
Advertising, 86
Advice, 180
Afghan Hounds, 44, 53, 96
All-Breed Club, 57
All-Breed Show, 57, 58, 59
All-Round Judge, 35
Amateur Dog Judges Association, 164
American-Bred Class, 51, 67
American Field, 77
American Field, The (Newspaper), 77
American Kennel Club, 25, 26, 27, 42, 44, 46, 52, 57, 58, 69–74, 77, 78, 82, 84, 89
Applause, 166
Apple-Headed, 71
Application for Registration of Dog of Registered Litter, 78
Apron, 71
Arched Neck, 148
Arm Bands, 24, 124, 125, 166
Ashtabula Kennel Club, 116
Attire, 163
Attitude, 105

B

Back Legs, 145
Bad Losers, 163
Bad Manners, 163
Baiting, 138, 148
Baltimore County Kennel Club, 116
Basset Hound, 141, 192
Bath, 112
Bathing, 106
Beagle, 53, 59, 65, 80, 175, 192
Behrendt, Mrs. Bernice, 88
Bench, 12, 69, 74, 106, 118–121, 123
Bench Chain, 106, 113, 118, 119, 122, 123

Bench, Relaxing on, 121, 122
Bench Show, 19, 26, 69, 112, 118
Bench Shows, U.K.C., 75
Benching, 19, 24
Benching Tents, 12
Best in Show, 26, 52, 53, 172
Best of Breed, 26, 51, 52, 53, 59, 162, 170, 178
Best of Breed Class, 51
Best of Breed Competition, 68, 69
Best of Opposite Sex, 51, 52, 170
Best of Variety, 59, 61
Best of Winners, 51–53, 69, 170
Bitch, Brood, 65
Bitch, Definition of, 54, 56
Bite, 138
Bloodlines Journal, 75
Book, Judge's, 166, 168
Border Collies, 21
Boxer, 53, 175
Boxer, Miniature, 75
Bradshaw, Mrs. Jack, 88
Bred By Exhibitor Class, 51, 66
Breed Popularity, 175
Breed Representative, 170
Breeder, 30, 32, 38, 39, 62, 63, 82
Brood Bitch, 65
Brood Bitch Class, 63, 65
Brown, William, 172, 173
Brush, 113
Brushing, 96, 102, 124
Bucket, 113
Bull Terrier, American, 75
Bulldog, 141
Burket, Mrs. Helen Rosemont, 88

C

Call Name, 78, 186
Car, 97, 112
Car Breaking, 97, 114
Carpeting, 136
Carsickness, 106

Photo Index